# MAD MIKE

## BY THE SAME AUTHOR

*Sir Charles Arden-Clarke*
Rex Collins, 1982

*Kwame Nkrumah*
IB Tauris, 1988

*Burma Victory*
Arms and Armour Press, 1992

*Wingate and the Chindits*
Arms and Armour Press, 1994

# MAD MIKE

A Life of Michael Calvert

by

DAVID ROONEY

LEO COOPER
LONDON

First published in Great Britain in 1997 by
LEO COOPER
an imprint of Pen & Sword Books Ltd
47 Church Street
Barnsley
South Yorkshire
S70 2AS

ISBN 0 85052 543.8

A catalogue record for this book is
available from the British Library

Printed in England by Redwood Books, Trowbridge, Wiltshire

# CONTENTS

# INTRODUCTION

Having spent some years studying and writing on the Burma campaign, I was delighted when, in 1995, Leo Cooper invited me to write the biography of Brigadier Michael Calvert. I was already familiar with his outstanding bravery and intrepid leadership in the Chindit campaigns, and I deemed it a privilege to write at greater length about his whole career.

The research for this led me into the lesser known aspects of his life, including his brief but dramatic service in Norway in 1940, his rôle in the foundation of the Commandos, and, after the Chindit campaigns, his command of the SAS in the dying months of the war in Europe.

His court martial in Germany in the early 1950s was fairly well known, and its verdict clouded his later years. Further research has now, to my great satisfaction, uncovered new evidence which should overturn the court-martial verdict, and which has now been submitted to the military authorities in the hope that he may yet achieve a pardon.

I am particularly grateful to the following people for the assistance I received: Firstly to Michael Calvert himself with whom I spent many hours in discussion and who placed at my disposal his voluminous but chaotic papers which are now in the Imperial War Museum; to General Sir Michael Rose who wrote the foreword to Calvert's recently re-published *Prisoners of Hope*, and to General Sir Patrick Howard-Dobson, both of whom revere Michael Calvert as a brave fighting soldier; to Colonel John Woodhouse, SAS, together with Hugh Bailey, Bill Hillier and Dr John Pirrie who advised on the Malayan campaign; to Colonel Alan Wells in Melbourne who helped with enquiries into the two periods Calvert spent in Australia; to Colonel Hugh Patterson who was one of Calvert's outstanding officers in 77 Brigade; to Dr Hansjurgen Schuppe and Herr Fritz Voss who greatly helped in the inquiries in Germany; to Dr Desmond Whyte the medical officer of 111 Brigade; to Professor M R D Foot; to Randall Gray; to Philip Chinnery; to Michael Elliott-Bateman; and to Tony Harris who has so generously devoted his time to caring for Michael Calvert. Finally, to Carol Cooper for her technical assistance, to our daughter Kathy Rooney for professional advice, and to my wife Muriel, not only for her support, but for her fortitude in putting the entire book on the computer despite a horrendous house move in the last few months.

David Rooney
Cambridge,
December, 1996.

# CHAPTER ONE

# EARLY YEARS

In August, 1995, the Government and people of Britain, in celebrating the fiftieth anniversary of the end of the Second World War, paid generous, if belated, tribute to the men of the 14th Army and all those who had fought against the Japanese in the Far East. Fittingly, for he was ever one to lead from the front, Brigadier Michael Calvert DSO, pushed in his wheelchair by his friend Tony Harris, led the contingent of the Chindit Old Comrades Association when on Saturday, 19 August more than two hundred contingents marched from Buckingham Palace and down the Mall to salute the Queen. This was the climax and finale of celebrations which had stretched over months, as had the television and radio programmes about the Burma War. One feature in the majority of these was the presence of Michael Calvert.

His outstanding bravery as a Chindit leader in the Burma campaign more than justified his inclusion, but it did in some ways surprise him. From the peak of his wartime fame, when he was a Brigadier with two DSOs by the time he was thirty, and had been recommended by his three battalion commanders for the VC, his post-war career had met with tragedy and disaster. Invalided home from Burma in 1944, he swiftly recovered and was given overall command of the Special Air Service (SAS), including French and Belgian contingents, for operations in Belgium, Holland and Germany. He retained this command until the SAS were disbanded in October, 1945.

Soon afterwards, the post-war crises proved the need for the SAS, and Calvert was sent to Malaya to form the Malayan Scouts (SAS Regiment). From here he was again invalided home with a full gamut of tropical diseases, and then posted to Germany as a colonel. There in 1952 he was court-martialled for an offence of which he still claims he was completely innocent. He was dismissed the service, and this led him into a period of near despair. From being a heavy drinker, he became an alcoholic and spent nearly ten years in Australia almost as a down and out. Through this time of trouble he retained the respect and affection of people in many parts of the world, and with their help he was eventually able to return to England where he began a long, hard struggle towards rehabilitation. In the early 1960s he conquered his alcoholism, itself a test of real character, and gradually restored his self-respect. He obtained several posts as an engineer and then launched himself into a career as a military historian where his encyclopaedic knowledge of military and strategic affairs carried great weight. He discovered too late the pitfalls of making an adequate living by writing and faced a prolonged period of financial difficulty. Finally, in 1995 he was rescued from this rather gloomy twilight and at last received flattering recognition.

His celebrations started in May with an invitation from the Corporation of London to a banquet, in the presence of the Queen and the Duke of Edinburgh, to celebrate the end of the war in Europe. During that summer he was guest of honour at commemorative functions in St Paul's Cathedral, in Brussels with the Belgian SAS, in Paris with the French SAS, both of which he had commanded at the end of the War, and finally, as a guest of the Army Board and Her Majesty's Government at Lancaster House on 17 August to commemorate the final victory over Japan. Here among Field Marshals and Generals, many of whom had served in the Special Air Service Regiment, he felt that he had once again been fully accepted. One of many indications of Calvert's reputation as an outstanding wartime leader is shown by a letter in the *Cambridge Evening News* on 5 September, 1995, from a former private soldier who had served in the Chindits, G. Hatchman of Royston:-

"Before the events of VJ Day disappear into the distant past, there is an observation I wish to make regarding the BBC programmes on the Burma Campaign in which viewers saw clips of Brigadier Mike Calvert being interviewed.

"I was a member of the 77th Chindit Brigade which he commanded in 1944 and what the TV presenters didn't disclose was that this quietly-spoken man was an inspiration to everyone in the Brigade.

"His bravery was outstanding and – unlike most other brigadiers in the British Army – he did his business from the end of a rifle and bayonet in the same way as we ordinary rank and file.

"Brigadier Calvert would always be found directing operations from the most exposed positions and, in spite of the added stress of command, he treated the welfare of his men as a top priority.

"Our four months continuous operations culminated in the battle for Mogaung, which he had been ordered to capture at all costs, although brigade strength had dwindled from 4,000 to just under 2,000 men through battle casualties and sickness. More than 1,200 dead and wounded.

"Through all the bitteriness of the fighting in atrocious conditions, our Brigadier stood head and shoulders above the rest.

"It was a tribute to his leadership that, in the history of infantry fighting, the feat of 77th Brigade is seen as unsurpassed as a tactical model and an example of the real face of infantry combat.

"Had it been any other theatre of the war, in Europe or Africa, he would have been awarded the highest honour for his actions, which in fact his fellow officers recommended to GHQ Delhi.

"But the small-minded staff, who had taken such a dislike to the Chindits' commander Orde Wingate, also chose to carry on a vendetta with anyone associated with him. Consequently, Brigadier Calvert's leadership and bravery did not receive the full recognition it deserved.

"The war in Europe was still raging when he returned to England and it is a measure of his dedication that he took command of the SAS and was involved in several vital operations before the final German capitulation.

"In closing this letter I would like to wish him well and to say, 'Thank you, sir. It was a privilege.'
G. Hatchman."

On 6 March, 1913, Oclanis Calvert gave birth to a sturdy boy at Rohtak near Delhi. He was the youngest of a large family, with three elder brothers – Brian, Denis and Wilkie – and two sisters, Kathleen and Eileen, who were considerably older. Their father, Hubert Calvert, a Cambridge graduate in Classics, had joined the Indian Civil Service, become a financial expert and been acting governor of the Punjab. His very senior position in the Indian Civil Service brought him some interesting tasks. He was once sent by Curzon to

Tibet to see if the goldfields were worth annexing. Despite his seniority and financial expertise, the family were far from wealthy and, although he and his wife wanted public school and university education for their children, it was made plain that this would have to be achieved by scholarships. Educational demands meant that the family were frequently divided, with the children at home in England, while one or both parents remained in India. Partly because of this, his father appeared a rather remote figure, and it was his mother, a warmer character, who provided the love and affection a growing family needed.

At the age of six in 1920 Michael was brought back to England and then enrolled at a preparatory school in Eastbourne. The school was run by an eccentric headmaster and the boys were subjected to a spartan regime, including cross-country running, cold baths and nude swimming. On one occasion the boys were taken to France and left to their own devices to return to school – sound basic training for Michael's future life. When he was eight his mother went back to India to join her husband, and the family who were left in England centred on Aunt Eileen, their mother's sister, who lived in Cheltenham. A widow who had lost her husband in Allenby's campaign in 1918, she was remembered by her nephews and nieces with great affection for providing a warm, cheerful home while their parents were in India. Her kindness was particularly appreciated because the alternative was the cold and lonely prospect of staying in a boarding school during the holidays.

When Michael was thirteen the family had to consider his future schooling. Brian and Denis had won scholarships to Clifton, and Wilkie to Bradfield. Michael failed in his first attempt at a scholarship, but, aged nearly fourteen, he was offered scholarships at both Radley and Bradfield. His father, showing remarkable detachment, said, "Choose which you like". Rather to Wilkie's embarrassment, he chose Bradfield.

He achieved remarkable success at Bradfield proving himself quite able academically, excelling at maths and science, but making his mark more particularly at swimming, boxing and cross-country running. He was a bit of a rebel and received his fair share of beatings.

The Calvert parents made clear to the girls that they ought to get married and achieve financial independence, equally, the four boys

4

understood that their father could not support them financially through university. The three eldest brothers had all been commissioned into the Royal Engineers under a scheme which virtually assured them a place at Cambridge to read for the Mechanical Sciences Tripos. In 1931, as he reached the end of his time at Bradfield, Michael, like many young brothers, began to feel that he did not wish merely to follow in the footsteps of his elder brothers. To show his independence he therefore applied for a commission in the Royal Navy, a decision which led to one of the many amusing incidents in his career. He was called for a medical and was interviewed by a red-bearded Naval doctor. Trying to illustrate his enthusiasm and military precision Michael executed every instruction with brisk vigour. While he stood naked, the doctor, bending down behind him, told him to bend his right leg back. This he did and he felt his heel make sharp contact with something. He looked round, and to his horror he saw the doctor clutching his nose while a torrent of blood spattered all over his red whiskers. To make matters worse, being both naked and embarrassed, Michael started to giggle and could not stop. Shortly afterwards he learned he had failed his medical because of defective arches.

The failure of the Navy to recognize his qualities forced him to follow in his brothers' footsteps. He applied for a commission in the Royal Engineers and was accepted. He joined the RMA Woolwich as a Gentleman Cadet in 1931. Here he really flourished and received consistently good reports. One said that it was a pleasure to have so keen and bright a youngster, while another referred to his very good all-round achievements and added that he had imagination and wrote intelligently and forcefully. He approached everything enthusiastically, except for horse-riding. He really disliked this because at Woolwich riding seemed to centre on "silly drills, spit and polish, and bullshit.".

After a highly successful career at Woolwich, he was commissioned into the Royal Engineers in February 1933, and posted to the RE depot at Chatham. Here he took a very positive interest in every aspect of the training and then, in October, 1933, he went up to St John's College, Cambridge, to read for the Mechanical Sciences Tripos. He was already beginning to succeed in the athletic world and he won a Blue for swimming. At the same time his boxing skills had been noted in the Army. He boxed at the Albert Hall for the Army against the RAF and subsequently became army middleweight champion. In one memorable bout he turned up in the ring only to find he had no seconds. The crowd took his side, yelling that three against one was not a fair contest. The Minister of War, presenting the medals, commiserated with him for losing, but said it was probably a useful experience, for if war came that would probably be the odds he would face. In addition to his boxing and cross-country running, he captained the Army Water Polo Team. He successfully completed his Honours Degree course at Cambridge in July, 1935, and then his brothers once again influenced his decision. He was offered postings in the Royal Engineers in various parts of the world – Egypt, Singapore and India – but since his brothers were already serving there, and in order to be different, he chose Hong Kong. Here he was soon to gain valuable experience of war at first hand.

While Michael was still at Cambridge, his father retired from the Indian Civil Service. During their home leaves the family often spent summer holidays at Salcombe, South Devon, where they would rent a large house and spend most of August in family activities, especially swimming, which became a lifelong passion for Michael. When serving abroad during the war his notion of home was always Salcombe. When his parents started to think of a retirement home their first choice was Salcombe, but Oclanis Calvert was seriously overweight and they felt that the hills of Salcombe would be too much for her health, so they compromised and bought a family home at Seaton in South Devon. Their dream during their long stay in the Punjab had been for a house in an attractive part of southern England, with ample rainfall and a large garden where they could grow fruit and vegetables, with enough space for their robust family. The house at Seaton certainly met these criteria, and during Michael's service in Burma his father's regular letters frequently regaled him with news of the fruit and vegetable crop.

His father had a slight drink problem, but he controlled it, helped by the strict rule of the Indian Civil Service that under no circumstances should you drink before 6 pm. He also bought the exact number of bottles of beer for the month and rationed himself strictly. In his wartime letters to his sons, who were serving all over the world, he would report when the local pub had run out of beer, or when due to some favourable chance he had obtained an extra bottle of whisky.

Though fairly typical of his class and generation, Michael took his training for war more seriously than most. By 1935, when he left Cambridge, Mussolini's threats to Ethopia were already causing concern. An old school friend who had been on holiday in Italy wrote in September, 1935, fairly light-heartedly, suggesting that Michael should lead a British Expeditionary Force "to land secretly from dinghies on the Italian coast, and then march on Rome, hang the Duce (Mussolini) and annex Italy as a Crown Colony". At the same time Michael received a letter from his elder brother Brian who was serving with the Madras Sappers and Miners in Bangalore in southern India. He recommended the easy life, "with no work on Thursday because it had been Queen Victoria's birthday, nor on Sundays". He also referred to Churchill's well-known distrust of the Indians, something that later was to play an important part in Michael's future.

Calvert arrived in Hong Kong in 1936 to join the Hong Kong Royal Engineers and was delighted to be given the responsibility of increasing the strength of his unit from 70 to 250 and to be responsible for their training. At that time the prospect of war seemed distant, although Japan, largely unnoticed by the West, had been for several years waging war against China. As early as 1931 Japan fabricated the Mukden incident and had used this as an excuse to invade Manchuria and set up the puppet state of Manchukuo. Like any subaltern, Calvert was less concerned with the international situation than with making a success of his immediate task. In order to be able to communicate with his recruits, he learned Cantonese and this produced an admirable response from his men. For young Chinese the prospect of joining the army and receiving regular food, regular wages and decent living conditions was most attractive, and it was easy to obtain fit, intelligent and enthusiastic recruits.

While they responded eagerly to Calvert's imaginative training, he fought many battles on their behalf. With his acute observation he quickly summed up the different types of regular officer. One with whom he had an early clash was a peppery apoplectic major not far from retirement, who was the unit paymaster. Calvert approached him to ask if one of his men who had two wives could have two marriage allowances. Before telling him to get out and reporting him to the CO, the major added "If you think that I have nothing better

7

to do than worry about your over-sexed coolies, then you must be more stupid than you look, which is difficult to believe."

In contrast to this, Calvert realized that there were some first-rate officers and he was eager to learn from them. "They were firm disciplinarians but they were fair and even kindly when kindness was needed, and the troops would have followed them anywhere." He had considerable contact with the Royal Scots battalion in the garrison and learnt a lot from their CO. Calvert described how much he learnt from the CO taking "Orders" – i.e. punishing men for serious breaches of discipline. A young Scot on guard at the Governor's palace had relieved the monotony by firing occasionally at passing cars. This could have resulted in a court martial and several years in jail, but the CO mixed severity with avuncular advice and punished the lad within the Unit. Calvert was full of admiration for the way the case was handled.

He learned too from an interesting case in the Royal Welch Fusiliers. They had a man who, while being a good soldier, a fine boxer, and a good rugby player, frequently got into drunken brawls and landed in serious trouble. The CO pointed out that he was a persistent trouble-maker and could therefore be court-martialled, but he would give him one more chance. He appointed the man as his batman and in future only confined him to barracks when he needed to be fit for a boxing or rugby match. After deep consideration of these issues, Calvert commented, "An officer gets a tremendous feeling of satisfaction and pride in knowing that he has the confidence and loyalty of the men serving under him." In a little over a year he had had valuable experience in implementing his own ideas on training, in man-management and in organizing an enthusiastic and loyal unit. With his positive leadership, his small unit had beaten much larger units at soccer and water polo, and it was given pride of place in a march past of all Royal Engineer units in the Colony, a satisfying achievement which was to stand him in good stead when he was posted to Shanghai in 1937.

In the nineteenth century China agreed to allow several major powers to establish international settlements along its coastline. These so-called "Treaty Ports", including Hong Kong till 1997, were the centres of most of the trade between China and the outside world, and Shanghai was the largest and most valuable. A further concession allowed the settlements to be protected by the armed

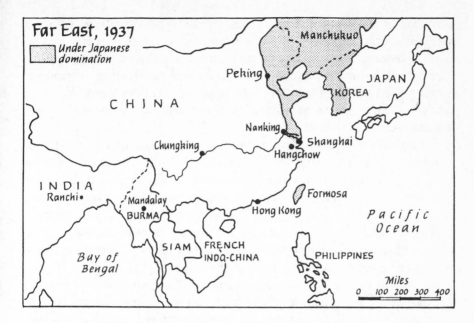

**Far East, 1937**

Under Japanese domination

Manchukuo

Peking

CHINA

JAPAN

KOREA

Nanking

Chungking

Shanghai

Hangchow

INDIA

Ranchi

Mandalay

BURMA

Formosa

Hong Kong

Pacific Ocean

Bay of Bengal

SIAM

FRENCH INDO-CHINA

PHILIPPINES

Miles

0   100   200   300   400

forces of the treaty power, hence the need for a substantial British garrison in 1937. By then the continued Japanese aggression against China had flared into open warfare and it became increasingly obvious that the wealth of Shanghai was under serious threat.

In his short time in Shanghai, Calvert reckoned he witnessed as much fighting and bloodshed as he did in the whole of the Second World War. In the fighting around Shanghai, which did not exactly threaten the treaty port itself, the Japanese and the Chinese are each estimated to have lost over 200,000 men. Calvert saw this as an ideal opportunity to study war at close quarters and, instead of joining the cocktail and tennis circuit, he would hide in bullock carts going into the fighting areas. In this way, hidden among sacks of potatoes, he actually witnessed the Japanese attack on Hangchow Bay just outside Shanghai. He watched with amazement as hundreds of soldiers were brought ashore in flat-bottomed boats with protected sides and, as they reached the shore, the prow opened up for the troops to pour out. These were landing craft in action, something that the British army had never thought of. He continued to watch the assault, and with his engineer's training he made detailed notes. His report went at once to the Area Commander who was impressed and sent it to the War Office. They awaited a response, but there was none.

9

Many other reports about the Japanese armies were sent to London, but completely ignored, just adding to the frustration of keen observers on the spot who wished to help their country prepare for war. From this experience Calvert gained one further advantage. Having seen the Japanese soldier in action – brave, tenacious and ready to die – he never underestimated him, as so many British leaders were later to do.

Family letters at this time paint a fascinating picture of a service family. In October, 1937, his father thanked him for his interesting letter from Shanghai, and passed on news that Wilkie was in Palestine, cousin Dick at Rawalpindi, Molly in Singapore and Brian at Mandalay. Apart from gardening, his father had become a governor of Colyton Grammar School, adding ruefully, "I would have preferred to be governor of the Punjab." An even more interesting letter reached Shanghai from Brian who had been posted to Mandalay to set up a Sappers and Miners Unit similar to the Madras Sappers and Miners Unit at Bangalore. He gave an excellent description of peacetime service life in the very area where a few years later Michael was to be involved in some of the most desperate fighting of the war. After setting up his unit, Brian had had ten days leave at Maymyo for Maymyo Week, which was "the best party of the year". During that time he took part in tennis singles, four-ball golf, squash and the mixed doubles tennis final. He won the open swimming, judged classes of polo ponies, won a cup for the best horse, and reached the final of the pig-sticking competition. His unit also won the hockey cup and the athletic sports. An even greater achievement for his company was to have been three months in Burma without getting one case of venereal disease. This was the envy of many units whose VD rates were notorious. Mandalay was reckoned to have the worst VD record in India and Burma combined. Brian added that Maymyo had the usual flock of flighty girls looking for husbands among the subalterns of the KOYLI (King's Own Yorkshire Light Infantry) while the Sappers hardly got a look in.

In Shanghai, Calvert's escapades took place against an increasingly dangerous military threat from Japan across the whole Pacific. Japan had left the League of Nations in 1933 after the League disapproved of the invasion of Manchuria. Japan rejected the Naval Treaty which limited her warship construction and in 1936 made a treaty with Hitler, sinister events which Britain chose to ignore.

By this time Calvert was becoming well known in the Shanghai garrison as a tough character. He had continued his boxing career and in 1937 in a highly publicized fight was matched against an American marine who was called champion of the Pacific. This man normally knocked out his opponent in the first or second round but Calvert, a tough and experienced boxer, was much fitter and, after surviving an initial onslaught, wore down the American and eventually knocked him out.

In 1937 serious incidents took place, including attacks on British ships in the Shanghai area. Then, in December, 1937, the Japanese army conquered Nanking and this was followed by weeks of massacre, slaughter, rape and pillage. This appalling incident, much worse than the obliteration of Guernica by the Fascists in Spain, shocked the world and is still, in the 1990s, one of the great blots on the reputation of Japan. The capture of Nanking shortly impinged more directly on Calvert's life. He had been in the battle area around Shanghai with a civilian engineer called Whitehouse, who spoke Japanese, when they were captured. They were taken away and slung into the Japanese unit guardroom. Calvert was alarmed because it was understood that the Japanese normally made you strip down to your underpants, and he was wearing underpants with the Rising Sun on the bottom. From the guard room they heard increasing noise and singing and noticed the guards getting more and more drunk. Whitehouse shouted in Japanese until a young officer came. He was told there would be a serious complaint at the highest level about the disgusting way senior British officers had been treated by drunken Japanese troops. This bluff worked and they were escorted home, to discover that the drunken orgy had been to celebrate the capture of Nanking.

Through this time the main role of the Royal Engineers had been to dispose of the various bombs and shells which accidently landed in the International Settlement, but in 1938 the Japanese had driven the Chinese out of Shanghai and they continued to respect the borders of the International Settlement. Shortly afterwards Calvert had a well-earned leave in England and a new posting.

# CHAPTER TWO

# THE PHONEY WAR

After two years in Hong Kong during which he had had a remarkable range of experience and had proved himself to be a serious-minded and enthusiastic young officer, in 1938 Calvert, after leave in Devon, became Adjutant of the London Divisional Engineers as a temporary Captain. By this time, after years of neglect and the policy of appeasement towards the Fascist powers, Britain was trying desperately to make good serious deficiencies, both in war materials and trained manpower. Once again Calvert was involved in recruiting young soldiers, but under much greater pressure than the leisurely days of Hong Kong. The training post which he held from 1938 through to the early years of the war kept him fully occupied and stretched to the limit. Although he found the office work uncongenial, he nonetheless received a glowing report from his CO, who said that Calvert faced a task which would have daunted many an older and more senior officer. He had shown a strong and resolute character and his personality had won respect and admiration through the unit. He showed determination and judgement beyond his years and had proved to be a natural leader and an instructor of exceptional merit, with rare qualities of tact and loyalty.

Early in 1940, despite the success of his work at the Royal Engineers depot, Calvert felt dissatisfied with his rôle. He was soon to prove his real mettle and to show that he was different from the average officer. As he said, "I wanted to fight". From September, 1939, to March, 1940, during the so-called Phoney War, apart from the initial rape of Poland, no major attacks took place, except for the Russian assault on Finland. This was soon to give Calvert his chance.

In November, 1939, Russia demanded the use of the Finnish ports, and then, after creating a spurious incident, used this as an excuse for invading Finland. Russia attacked with twenty-six divisions, but to the surprise of the world, the Finns, although desperately short of aircraft, artillery, ammunition and equipment, fought heroically and inflicted huge losses on their Russian attackers. In December the League of Nations, whose failure Calvert had witnessed in the Far East, demanded an end to hostilities, but was again ignored. At this stage, and really too late in the day, the British government called for volunteers to go and fight for the Finns. Among the mountains of paper which landed on his desk, it was this announcement which caught Calvert's attention, but it presented him with a dilemma.

Since 1933 he had devoted his life to training as an officer, and he saw in the announcement that all volunteers would revert to private, with no guarantee of future re-instatement. He did not hesitate for long, and within a few weeks he had enlisted as a Private in what was called the 5th Ski Battalion of the Scots Guards, based at Borden in Hampshire. Most of the volunteers were men of similar mettle, and Calvert thought they were "the grandest bunch of men he had ever served with". The group included many who later served in the Commandos, the Long Range Desert Group, the Chindits and the SAS. The volunteers came from many different units or straight from civvy street, but after a couple of weeks of initial training were sent off to Chamonix in the Alps for ski training. After six weeks of hectic training they were considered ready to fight and travelled to Glasgow to embark on the Polish ship *Batory*, but by this time, in spite of their brave fight, the Finns had been forced to surrender. The initial inept performance of the Russians was partly attributed to the savage purge of senior officers carried out by Stalin in the 1930s, and it was also significant in influencing Hitler's decision to attack Russia in 1941, but for the 5th Scots Guards it came as a bitter disappointment. For Calvert the anticlimax was complete, for he was taken off the *Batory* with pneumonia and sent to a hospital in Glasgow.

As soon as he was able to walk, he discharged himself from the hospital and travelled to London. He felt some mental confusion. Was he Private Calvert, temporary Sergeant Calvert Scots Guards, or Captain Calvert RE? When he reached Wellington Barracks a suspicious Guards Sergeant Major added to his misery, advising him to go back to the London Engineers. Far from well, and totally depressed, he walked off, but cheered up after a boisterous party in Piccadilly. The next morning he decided, as Captain Calvert, to sign a leave certificate and railway warrant for Sergeant Calvert to go to

Seaton to his parents' home. Here warm hospitality soon restored him, and after a couple of weeks and fully recovered, he returned to London and was welcomed back into the Royal Engineers. The military authorities agreed to forget that the 5th Scots Guards had ever existed.

Within a few weeks of the abortive Finland operation Calvert, now qualified to fight in the snow – though he confessed he never got on well with skis – volunteered to join an expeditionary force going to Norway. This expedition, like the Finland one before it, centred on the German need to safeguard the crucial supplies of iron ore from Scandinavia. One route crossed the Baltic from southern Sweden, but the main supply route, which was kept open all the year round, ran from the port of Narvik in northern Norway, from where iron ore carriers tried to slink down the coast in neutral Norway's territorial waters. The Finnish campaign prompted both Hitler and the Allies to realize the significance of Narvik and to plan an invasion.

## Norway

The unfortunate Allied troops who took part in the Norwegian campaign were victims of the ill-fated peacetime policies of both the British and Norwegian governments. The Norwegian socialist administration had gravely neglected all its armed forces. The Army, badly trained and poorly led, had no tanks, no anti-aircraft guns, and only obsolete weapons. The Navy had seventy old ships and only a few of these escaped the German attack. The Air Force had just a few obsolete Italian aircraft obtained in return for dried fish. Norwegian mobilization became a shambles and took place on 9 April, the day the Germans attacked. The British forces in Norway suffered from frequent changes of plan and had little hope of effectively defeating the enemy. Intelligence reports had given ample warning of German preparations, but they had been ignored, and when the Germans made the sea-borne landings in six different places including Narvik and Trondheim they achieved almost complete surprise. Their forces numbered 8,500 men with tanks, artillery and massive air support, including Stuka dive-bombers which ranged almost unhindered over the battlefields. There were some severe naval clashes with heavy losses on both sides, but the whole German

operation, better planned and more efficiently executed, was never seriously challenged. On the ground there was heavy fighting around Narvik where British, French, Polish and Norwegian troops temporarily outnumbered the Germans who had landed. Fighting continued here until early June but in the south the Germans overran the resistance more swiftly. It was here in the area of Aandalsnes that Calvert's group had their first taste of battle.

The British plan had been to land forces at Namsos north of Trondheim, and at Aandalsnes to the south, and from those two points to cut off Trondheim. Almost as soon as they had landed it was realized that this was impossible and the brief campaign quickly developed into an attempt to extricate their beaten forces in face of the rapid German advance.

After embarking at Rosyth Calvert and his small group of sappers on the cruiser HMS *Calcutta* landed at Aandalsnes on 16 April, one week after the German invasion. The plan to encircle Trondheim had already been abandoned and Calvert, after he had grabbed an empty house for his men, was given the task of carrying out a detailed recce of the Romsdal Fjord. His object, as soon as the British troops had withdrawn, was to demolish the road and railway which led up the fjord to the village of Dombaas. He had had little experience of

*15*

demolitions since his training at Chatham four years before, and his task was now made more complicated when he discovered that the only explosives available to him were naval depth charges and mines. There was also a serious shortage of timed fuses.

While still at the little port, his ingenuity and his knowledge of engineering proved useful. A large crane had been damaged by bombing and had fouled the superstructure of a ship tied up at the wharf. As a result valuable stores could not be unloaded and no one could move the crane. Calvert took charge and asked for 300 men. He carefully instructed them that each one must get a direct hold on the crane, and at his signal to heave they did so. To everyone's amazement the crane was lifted free, the ship was released and the stores came ashore. He set off his recce with a resourceful sergeant, Jerry Humphreys, whom Calvert described as "a wonderful chap". After three days working slowly up the valley and marking positions on bridges, tunnels and viaducts where the explosives should be placed, the pair reached the village of Dombaas.

Here Calvert witnessed for the first time the fear and anguish of a unit whose leaders had failed them, and who were paralysed with fear. The remnants of a TA brigade were cowering in the village, many too frightened to fight on effectively. By contrast, his feelings were greatly improved by the example of an elderly Colonel who always kept a rifle at the ready and whenever a Stuka appeared would fire at it. He never hit one but it was good for morale. At Dombaas, where there was a hotch-potch of units, the remaining task was to carry out a withdrawal back down the fjord to Aandalsnes, while holding off the German advance. This meant that the demolitions had often to be delayed as long as possible so that the frequently demoralized troops could get through a tunnel or across a bridge before Calvert blew it up.

From then onwards Calvert and Humphreys worked night and day to achieve their objective. They used an old Velocette motor bicycle, which Humphreys drove, with Calvert on the pillion seat. They had to traverse icy snow-covered roads at great speed, sometimes pursued by German Stukas or fighters. Often they skidded off and landed in banks of snow. Frequently, because they were the only sign of life, and as the Germans had been alerted to what they were doing, they seemed to have the undivided attention of the Stukas.

As most of their demolitions were under culverts or bridges, when they were actually working on a demolition they were relatively safe, but they still had some narrow escapes. Their task was made much more difficult because they had to manhandle the depth charges into position, and these could weigh up to 250 lbs. At each site, having put the explosives in place, Calvert lit the final fuse while Humphreys sat ready on the motor bike with the engine running. Calvert then rushed away, jumped on the pillion, and they sped off hoping to get clear before all the debris landed on them, or, as sometimes happened, they were engulfed by an avalanche of snow caused by the explosion.

The constant harassment by German Stukas infuriated Calvert because he felt he had no way of really hitting back. Then, on one occasion, some Stukas attacked just when a depth charge was put in place. He had a clever idea. He had noticed how high the depth charge sent debris into the air, so he tried to judge the timing of the explosion for the exact moment when the Stuka was at its lowest point. He lit the fuse, dived for cover and thought for a glorious moment that he had succeeded, but the Stuka flew off and with it his hopes of being the only person to bring down a Stuka with a depth charge.

During the retreat General Paget tried to co-ordinate the movements of the motley collection of units, some of which were just a liability. One marine unit gave way in face of the enemy, until they were rallied by a young subaltern who saved the day and, by doing so, won the MC on Calvert's recommendation.

The defeated troops pouring back towards Aandalsnes were a major problem and often forced Calvert to delay his demolitions until the advancing Germans were dangerously close. Once he and Humphreys, in total darkness, had fixed explosives at the entrance to a tunnel and were ready to detonate when they peered further into the tunnel. To their horror they saw hundreds of exhausted British troops whose discipline had collapsed so completely that they had not even posted a sentry!

One of his most difficult operations took place at a bridge which crossed a swiftly flowing torrent. Calvert had to spend three hours in the icy water fixing the depth charges and the fuses. When it was ready he was so cold that Humphreys had to carry him to a cottage to thaw out. They were both close to starving and in the deserted cottage they found some raspberry cordial which helped to bring Calvert round. Punctilious as ever, he insisted on leaving behind some money to cover the cost.

He was always eager to make himself a more effective leader and to learn the lessons of war. He had noticed that the Germans often bombed the railway yards at Aandalsnes which were an easy target, but the attacks caused little serious damage. In contrast, further along the single-track railway one well-placed bomb had brought the whole military operation to a halt. He learnt this lesson well and later used this knowledge in Burma in countless attacks on the railways behind the Japanese lines.

With Humphreys coaxing the Velocette on the last drops of petrol, they got nearly back to the coast and then joined the few crowded carriages of Paget's final train returning to the port. There they were taken on to a British destroyer and later transferred to HMS *Calcutta* which eventually landed them at Scapa Flow on 30 April, 1940.

Calvert had taken part in what was a small and unsuccessful sideshow to the main Norway campaign. Further north, in the area of Narvik and the Lofoten Islands, there had been heavier land fighting, and serious naval engagements centred on the approaches to Narvik harbour. These battles resulted in the loss to Britain of an aircraft carrier (HMS *Glorious* – sunk by the *Gneisenau* and *Scharnhorst*), three cruisers, seven destroyers and four submarines. Germany lost seven crusiers, sixteen destroyers and six submarines which were sunk or seriously damaged. The most important result was that the Germans could reopen the coastal sea route for its iron ore ships as soon as the port of Narvik was repaired. Many Norwegian fishing boats escaped and received a warm welcome in the fishing ports of north-east Scotland, from where later the Navy was able to mount raids on the Norwegian coast. This convinced Hitler that another attack was likely and he therefore kept a fairly substantial number of troops in Norway who could have been used elsewhere; but his main plan had succeeded – to safeguard his supply of iron ore.

## Defending England

During the first week of May, 1940, the remnants of General Paget's troops, code-named Sickleforce, were evacuated from southern

Norway and, although the forces around Narvik in the north hung on grimly until the beginning of June, it was already realized that the whole operation would end in failure. This disaster precipitated a political crisis in London which was raging even as the ships approached Scapa Flow. In one of the most dramatic debates in the House of Commons, in which the Norway defeat had been made a motion of confidence, the opposition demanded Chamberlain's resignation. Amid fierce tension, with the future of the country at stake, the climax came when Leo Amery, quoting Cromwell, shouted to Chamberlain, "In the name of God, go".

Chamberlain resigned, and thus Churchill became Prime Minister. He did not deny that he had had some responsibility for the fiasco in Norway, but, despite this, the country rallied to his leadership.

As Churchill took over the reins of government, the Nazis launched their blitzkrieg against the west, and on 10 May, 1940, they invaded Holland and Belgium. Rotterdam became the first modern city to suffer full-scale aerial bombardment, even though it had already surrendered. By 15 May the Netherlands had surrendered, followed shortly by Belgium and France. As German armour, having divided the French and British forces, drove towards the channel ports the British people made a supreme effort, and from 26 May to 3 June over 200,000 British and 100,000 French and Belgian troops were brought back from Dunkirk. After Dunkirk Britain stood alone, an island fortress, and faced a European coastline dominated by the Nazis from Narvik to the coast of Spain.

This situation prompted one of Churchill's earliest interventions in military strategy. It has been said that for much of the war he caused severe problems to his Chiefs of Staff by interfering in military decisions, by backing maverick leaders whom they regarded as charlatans, and by supporting many schemes which they considered crack-brained, but in this early crisis situation he acted decisively. As Britain faced an unbroken hostile European coast, he at once saw the value of setting up a new strike force which could attack specific targets anywhere along the coast. By doing this they would tie down vast numbers of German troops and give a valuable fillip both to home morale and to the resistance fighters. Thus, with Churchill's backing, pioneers like Robert Laycock were given their head, and the Commandos were formed. They soon went into action. On 24 June and 14 July the first Commando raids were made on the

French coast and on Guernsey. These achieved little and were military failures, but they gave a great boost to morale and encouraged the more adventurous characters in the services to volunteer for this tough and aggressive force.

Calvert was among the first volunteers. He had already been thinking deeply about the role irregular forces could play in war. He realized that such forces could not win the war, but he believed that they would be invaluable in throwing the enemy off balance by a sudden attack, by disrupting their communications behind the lines and by destroying crucial installations. The idea of darting in quickly by sea, land or air and carrying out swift demolitions appealed enormously to Calvert. Before the end of May he was posted as a demolition instructor to the Special Training Centre at Lochailort, situated on an inlet of the sea some thirty miles west of Fort William in Scotland.

Here he met several old friends from the 5th Scots Guards, including Bill and David Stirling and many other outstanding characters who became leading figures in the Commandos, the Long Range Desert Group, the Chindits and the SAS. This outstanding group were eager to fight and responded positively to a forward-looking challenge. Many had volunteered in order to get away from training units and what they considered out-of-date and irrelevant First World War thinking, and bloody-minded, mind-numbing restrictions. Some, including David Stirling, arrived at Lochailort with a reputation for being wild, arrogant and insubordinate, but they reacted enthusiastically to the tough training régime, including frequent gruelling exercises, survival techniques, field craft, unarmed combat and demolitions. Calvert again proved himself an outstanding instructor and was pleased with his growing reputation as a demolitions expert in the field of irregular warfare. This soon cut short his stay at Lochailort and he was called urgently to the War Office. Furious at being taken away from such an excellent unit where he felt that he was doing a really vital job, and where he had made many good friends, he was nonetheless intrigued by his new posting to the Military Intelligence Directorate at the War Office, and he wondered what new challenge he might face.

In spite of the urgent summons to leave Lochailort, he was left for some time hanging about at the War Office, and while he was waiting he wrote an interesting and significant pamphlet entitled "The

Operations of Small Forces Behind the Enemy Lines". In this he began to assemble his thoughts about an aspect of war in which he was later to excel. At the War Office he met Peter Fleming, the writer and traveller, with whom he was to work for the next few months. They were to meet again in desperate circumstances in Burma, and they became lifelong friends.

The Intelligence Directorate gave them the task of preparing booby traps and demolitions at strategic sites across Kent and Sussex on the assumption that the area had been occupied by the Germans. The view of the authorities that this could actually happen vividly brought home to them the gravity of the military situation and they tackled their task with determination. Now the lessons Calvert had learned in the Romsdal Fjord and at Lochailort could be put into practice. Although the background was grim and sinister, these two bright young officers enjoyed the imaginative challenge which faced them and which they could tackle untrammelled by bureaucracy or regimental bullshit. They travelled over the two counties looking carefully at buildings and bridges, weighing up whether an occupying enemy force would be likely to use them. They concentrated first on railways and bridges, then on large houses which might be taken over as headquarters of German units. In the basements of those houses they placed explosives which were safe until they were properly fused.

Their next task was to choose the people to carry out these demolitions if or when the Germans occupied the country. In a predominantly rural area they naturally chose farming types who would be unlikely to panic in a war situation, and who, because of their work, would not be posted away into the forces. Many had sons or brothers in the forces and all were eager to help. Calvert described one farmer in Romney Marsh who said, "If any of them Huns try to settle round here they'll soon wish they were somewhere else." This enthusiasm to take part in the fight reassured Calvert and Fleming that the demolitions would be effectively carried out if the Germans arrived. In the face of imminent invasion, the Government formed the Local Defence Volunteers, an uninspiring title which Churchill soon changed to Home Guard. This force, brilliantly guyed in the TV series "Dad's Army", would nonetheless have given a good account of itself, as Calvert realized.

Hitler had no firm advanced plans for invasion and his military and naval advisers disagreed with each other. The army proposed an attack on a wide front from Dover to Dorset, while Admiral Raeder, fearing the power of the Royal Navy, suggested a much narrower front. After bitter arguments, in the middle of July, 1940, Hitler gave directions for Operation Sea Lion, in which twenty divisions would invade southern England as soon as the Luftwaffe had achieved air supremacy. One major thrust by the German 7th Corps would have taken in Calvert's farmer on Romney Marsh.

Barbed wire and mines had already been laid along south coast beaches, but it fell to Calvert to deal with the south coast piers. At Brighton, Eastbourne and Worthing he blew up the middle section of the piers and booby trapped the remainder. He had one narrow escape when he had just completed the booby traps on Brighton pier and a seagull set one off. This set off another and explosions leap-frogged all the way along the pier. Another useful lesson for his later operations, that booby traps should not be placed too close together! After the war, when he was on Montgomery's staff, he had to go back to Brighton and the Mayor berated him for the damage he had done to the pier. Similarly, the Burma Oil Company tried to sue Field Marshal Slim for the damage he caused when, during the Burma retreat, he blew up the oil wells at Yenangyaung.

By the middle of August, 1940, Goering was masterminding the German aerial attack, using 2,500 aircraft against an estimated 600 British fighters, but under the stimulus of all-out war, the production of Spitfires and Hurricanes increased to 500 per month, a major factor in the Battle of Britain. While the battle raged over Kent and Sussex, Calvert and Fleming continued with their preparations. Supplies of medical equipment and explosives were located at stra-tegic points, with the details of all these and all the planned demolitions carefully recorded. They were then given the task of testing the security at the divisional headquarters of the up and coming young General Bernard Montgomery, already recognized for his fierce efficiency. His headquarters were in a large country house set in substantial grounds, and it was well known to Montgomery's staff that Calvert and Fleming had been given the task of testing the security. The two realized that HQ would be on full alert and Calvert therefore devised a double-bluff. They went into the mess and the local pub and in a loud-mouthed way managed to be overheard saying that they would approach from the front of the house and put the explosives into the flower pots along the terrace. The defenders clearly thought that this was just a bluff and tried to work out what was the real plan. Then, on a moonless night, Calvert and Fleming carefully crept through the shadows at the edge of the lawn and, without being discovered, put explosives with a long time-fuse into the flower pots. Fleming even went into the house and attached a booby trap to the leg of the sleeping duty officer. The next morning they reported to Montgomery in his room facing over the terrace. In a jocular mood he said they had clearly failed, when, to their great delight, all the explosives in the flowerpots started to go off. Montgomery took it in good part and offered them a drink. The duty officer did not report anything.

The country remained tense and alert as the RAF gradually won the Battle of Britain. The invasion never came, and in October, 1940, Calvert once more returned to the East. He had already impressed the authorities at Lochailort, and he was posted to Australia to set up a Commando Training School.

# CHAPTER THREE

# AUSTRALIAN INTERLUDE

At Lochailort Calvert had established a close friendship with Freddie Spencer Chapman, who had been in charge of the fieldcraft training, while he supervised training in explosives and demolitions. The great success of the commando courses in which they had played a conspicuous role, convinced the Chiefs of Staff that it should be adapted to different theatres and different terrain, and consequently in October, 1940, Calvert and Spencer Chapman embarked on the SS *Rimutaka* bound for Australia, to set up a Commando school. To avoid U-boat attacks, the ship crossed the North Atlantic, then veered south to Bermuda, through the Panama Canal, across the Pacific to New Zealand and finally reached Melbourne.

The decision to set up a Commando school had been made, but the strategic use of the Independent Companies, as they were to be called, had not been fully thought through. Thus a certain amount of time was spent while this issue was discussed. Spencer Chapman (*The Jungle is Neutral*, p. 19) wrote, "We talked of guerrilla and irregular warfare, of special and para-military operations, stay-behind parties, resistance movements, sabotage and incendiarism, and still more vaguely of 'agents', but the exact role of the Commandos and Independent Companies had never been made quite clear."

As the threat from Japan became more obvious, attention focused on the role Independent Companies could play if the Japanese attacked and overran the Pacific Islands. The Companies could stay behind in the jungle, supplied by air, and could come out of the jungle to strike at installations. Alternatively, small groups by good fieldcraft could effect long-range penetration in order to keep contact with native peoples and encourage their resistance.

The British Military Mission, which included Calvert and Spencer Chapman, arrived in Melbourne in November, 1940, and went to the newly established Infantry Training Centre at Wilson's Promontory south of Melbourne, the southern tip of Australia. This site had many advantages. As a National Park it had an abundance of wild life, including kangaroos and wallabies, but very few inhabitants, and strict security was easy to enforce. It was approached by a 20-mile shingle bank and it contained a great variety of terrain from low-lying swamps to Mount Latrobe, over 2400 feet. The natural vegetation, too, varied from thick eucalyptus forest to mountain scree and, as no one at that time could tell where the Independent Companies would have to fight, this was very valuable.

When Calvert and Spencer Chapman arrived at the new Training Centre they resumed their Lochailort rôles, with responsibility for demolitions and fieldcraft respectively. Later, Calvert believed that the fieldcraft Spencer Chapman taught him both at Lochailort and at Wilson's Promontory frequently saved his life in Burma. He cited, in particular, training his eye to recognize a good spot for an ambush – whether to set one up or to avoid an enemy ambush – and, equally important, to listen and understand the noises of the jungle, especially the sign of danger when all animal noises fall silent. Spencer Chapman, for his part, wrote, "Calvert, with his infectious enthusiasm, taught them how to blow up everything from battleships to brigadiers, and I can still see the gleam that used to come into his eye as he looked at a bridge and worked out exactly how much explosive to use and where to place it." Describing their training exercises, he continued, "I shall never forget the extraordinary enthusiasm and ingenuity shown on these schemes – and not only because, as umpires, Calvert and I were dragged through the deepest swamps and the most impenetrable thickets."

Calvert and Spencer Chapman, together with Colonel Mawhood who commanded the Mission, rapidly evolved a training programme for the volunteer officers and NCOs who came on the courses. Each course lasted six weeks and consisted of extremely severe fitness training, fieldcraft and endurance, comprehensive weapon training, including enemy weapons where possible, and the handling of explosives and booby-trap schemes. These fairly brief courses nonetheless established a camaraderie between Calvert and the Independent Company members, and in the 1950s, in what was for him a less happy time, they gave him terrific support and loyalty, and this affection and caring has lasted throughout his life.

At the end of each course those who had passed were posted away to form new Independent Companies, a title later changed to "Commando Squadrons". Each unit was commanded by a major, with 273 members including seventeen officers, an unusually high ratio of officers to men. The company was divided into three platoons under a captain, and each platoon into three sections under a lieutenant. Officers also commanded the two specialist groups: the signals section, and engineering section, which was responsible for explosives and demolitions. The shape and structure of these units, each with its medical officer and with specialist signals and engineer sections, are mirrored fairly closely by the Chindit columns which Calvert was soon to set up.

The Training Centre at Wilson's Promontory, based on Darby River and Tidal River, started its training courses early in 1941 with the nucleus of one Australian company and one New Zealand company. A second New Zealand company followed, but the New Zealand Command did not use them in an independent rôle. The Australian companies continued to train and by October three Independent Companies had been formed and had left for active service. No 1 Company left for the New Ireland and Bougainville Islands lying to the east of Papua New Guinea; No 2 to Timor, the nearest Pacific island to Darwin; and No 3 to New Caledonia, north east of Brisbane. During 1941 a hectic training schedule was kept up, shaped largely by Calvert's methods and enthusiasm. Then the Centre was temporarily run down, but the Japanese attack on Pearl Harbor on Sunday 7 December, 1941, quickly changed the situation, and Wilson's Promontory again became the centre for the active training of Command units.

The rapid Japanese advance after Pearl Harbor gave little opportunity for the Allied forces to use their limited resources to the best advantage. Most of No 1 Company was caught by the Japanese offensive in the Bougainville area, while No 2 fought prolonged guerrilla actions against the Japanese in Timor, and subsequently re-established a radio link with Australia long after it had been assumed that all was lost. For the remainder of the war the Independent Companies served successfully in the Northern Territory and in the Pacific Islands along Australia's northern coast, including New Guinea, Timor and Bougainville, a tribute to the sound foundations laid by Calvert and Spencer Chapman.

As it became clear that most of the action for the Independent Companies would take place in the tropical islands of the Pacific, the Australian army decided to move the Training Centre from Wilson's Promontory to a new base at Canungra in Queensland. When the Jungle Training Centre was set up at Canungra, the Independent Companies returned there after their operations to be re-trained and re-equipped, but, despite the success of this work, the veterans of the Independent Companies felt a greater loyalty to Wilson's Promontory. Years later, in November, 1964, at Tidal River, General Sir Edward Herring KCMG, KBE, DSO, MC, the Lieutenant-Governor of Victoria, unveiled a memorial to the men of the Australian and New Zealand Independent Companies, Commando Units and Special Units.

In August, 1941, when the training of only the first few companies had been completed, Calvert had to hand over his duties because he had been posted to an interesting assignment at the Bush Warfare School in Burma. He served for less than a year at Wilson's Promontory, but he always felt a strong loyalty to the Independent Companies which he had helped to found. Throughout his service in many parts of the world, he retained strong links with the members of The Commando Association (Victoria). This connection was facilitated by the admirable magazine of the Association entitled *Double Diamond*, the logo of which was based on the proud wartime badge of the Independent Companies.

CHAPTER FOUR

# THE BURMA RETREAT

During 1941, when Calvert was training the Independent Companies and preparing Australian instructors to take over his post at Wilson's Promontory, he had once again started to hanker after a rôle in an active fighting unit rather than a training school. Then, in August, 1941, came news of his posting to Maymyo in Burma, about which he had mixed feelings. Since his experiences in Shanghai in 1938, he had had no illusions about the Japanese or their ruthless determination, and having a positive interest in Japanese strategy he was better informed than most young officers about what might happen. On the other hand there was no sign of war in Burma, his posting was to yet another training school and he remembered the vivid description of his brother Brian, who had been in the idyllic hill station of Maymyo in 1938.

Calvert arrived in Maymyo in October, 1941, and found a more interesting situation than he had inticipated. The purpose of the Bush Warfare School, of which he was to be Chief Instructor was not to train British commandos, but to train small cadres of experts to go up the Burma Road and to pass on their expertise to Chiang Kai-shek's army based in Chungking in Southern China. In this way they tried to help the Chinese forces continue their fight against the Japanese invaders. Its top-secret role appealed to Calvert's outlook, and as Chief Instructor of the school he had considerable scope to implement his ideas. Within the school the sub-divisions were called "Commandos" – a title intended to confuse enemy intelligence – but as Calvert found to his cost, it also confused Burma headquarters, and, later, General Alexander blamed him for not training more commando units to fight the Japanese.

Japanese plans for conquest in the Pacific did not initially include the capture of the whole of Burma. They set out to take Malaya, but only intended to take the southern part of Burma and the capital, Rangoon. After some initial skirmishes in the extreme south during December, 1941, they stepped up air attacks on Rangoon, and then on 20 January, 1942, the advanced divisions of the Japanese 15th Army attacked Moulmein and advanced rapidly towards Rangoon. At this stage they changed their plans, because they realized the very substantial volume of war materials and supplies that were being transported through Rangoon, past Mandalay and Lashio, up the Burma Road to Kunming, and to Chiang Kai-shek's headquarters in Chungking.

The clarity, confidence and flexibility of Japanese operations contrast starkly with the bumbling unpreparedness on the British side. During the 1930s some progress had been made in response to Burmese claims to political independence from Britain, but little thought had been given to defence, and the Burma Division was designed for little more than internal security. During 1941 responsibility for the defence of Burma was undertaken by Far Eastern Command in Singapore, but in the middle of December, 1941, the responsibility was handed back to India Command, and on 30 December transferred yet again to the newly formed American British Australian Command (ABDA). No wonder the Burma defences were ill-prepared. The débâcle of the Burma retreat is well known, but the blame which has been accorded to the unfortunate British, Indian and Burmese troops is misplaced, and belongs properly to the almost complete lack of defensive preparedness. To face the Japanese threat, the 17th Indian Light Division, which had been trained for rapid motorized movement in the western desert, was rushed to Burma, and during January took up positions east of Rangoon to counter the Japanese attack. Under General Smyth, a First World War VC who proved unable to cope with a new form of warfare, the Division suffered a series of defeats, including the disaster of Sittang Bridge when a substantial body of troops were left behind after the bridge was blown. The Japanese advance continued relentlessly and on 8 March, 1942, they captured Rangoon.

After the fall of Rangoon the demoralized British troops conducted a series of hurried withdrawals north. On 19 March General Slim flew in to take command of the so-called Burma Corps (Burcorps). His forces included the Burma Division, the 17th Division, already sorely battered, and the 7th Armoured Brigade which had just arrived

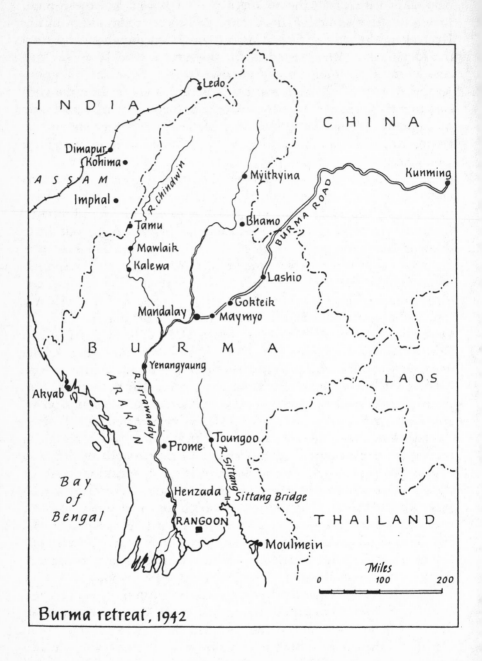

Ledo

INDIA

CHINA

Dimapur
Kohima
ASSAM
Imphal

Myitkyina

R. Chindwin

Kunming

Bhamo

BURMA ROAD

Tamu
Mawlaik
Kalewa

Lashio

Mandalay

Gokteik
Maymyo

B U R M A

Yenangyaung

ARAKAN

R. Irrawaddy

LAOS

Akyab

Prome

Toungoo

R. Sittang

Bay
of
Bengal

Henzada

Sittang Bridge

THAILAND

RANGOON

Moulmein

Miles
0    100    200

Burma retreat, 1942

30

from the Middle East. On the eastern flank lay the relatively untried forces of the 5th Chinese Army under the American General Stilwell, which was operating in the area between Toungoo and Mandalay. The lives and destiny of Slim, Stilwell and Calvert were to be entwined throughout the rest of the Burma campaign, but in March, 1942, they were all overwhelmed by the speed of the Japanese advance. Stilwell and the 38th Chinese Division suffered a serious setback when they failed to hold the town of Toungoo on the upper Sittang River (30 March). This allowed the Japanese to advance rapidly northward and, on 29 April to capture Lashio, the real base of the Burma Road, and to capture Mandalay on 1 May. Thus their initial objective of closing the Burma Road had been achieved, but they pressed on and a week later captured Myitkyina (pronounced Mich-en-ar), while the bedraggled British, Indian, Burmese and Chinese forces trudged north to the relative safety of Imphal and Kohima in upper Assam. Here heavy monsoon rains rather than military might put a stop to the Japanese advance. Burcorps was disbanded on 20 May.

If Calvert had hankered after a more active rôle away from training units, the arrival of the Japanese in Burma more than fulfilled his wish, and for the next two and a half years he was to be involved in as much direct action against the Japanese as any other British soldier. When the retreat from Rangoon started, Calvert, still at the Bush Warfare School, though many of his staff had left to join their units or to go up to Chungking, decided in his unconventional way to take some action himself.

Through his Australian contacts he knew that an Australian division might be diverted to assist the British forces in Burma. There were several Australians at the school, and all the staff there wore the Australian bush hat. Calvert, assuming the Japanese would know about the possible arrival of the Australian division, reckoned that, if they discovered a group of Australians in the fighting, they might be confused and assume the division had arrived. Therefore, with seventy of his staff he set off down the Irrawaddy to Prome, about 150 miles north of Rangoon, where he reported to the HQ of 17th Indian Division, then under the command of Major General "Punch" Cowan. A depressed and harassed staff officer suggested that Calvert and his group should operate towards the west bank of the Irrawaddy. After the Burma Retreat, he observed that, in the often chaotic conditions of a retreat, when everything was unpredictable, the majority of officers and soldiers look desperately for their own unit or HQ. Calvert took an opposite view, and welcomed such a vague instruction, which gave him a free hand to use his small force as he thought fit.

Fortunately for him, as he left the HQ and went towards the river he met a Royal Marines officer who, in his small unit, had a motor launch. Calvert was now in his element. Through his military contacts and by using his initiative, he managed to appropriate a double decker river steamer, which normally plied up the river to Mandalay, and to load it up with food, water, ammunition, machine guns and explosives. He had another stroke of good fortune when the English captain of the craft, Captain Rae, appeared happy to go along with his scheme. Calvert did not expect to halt the advance of the Japanese, but he felt that he might achieve something that would confuse or delay them, and possibly give more time to Slim, Cowan and 17th Indian Division to prepare their defences. He calculated that most of the Japanese forces would be travelling as fast as possible up the roads, and the river would not be heavily patrolled.

The quaint craft, skilfully steered by its experienced captain, sailed down the river, stopping only to blow up any promising targets like railway bridges, oil installations, or boats that could be used by the Japanese. Each escapade on shore was carried out in a thoroughly military fashion, with covering fire ready to support the demolition parties as they returned to the boat. Other groups went ashore to talk loudly about the powerful additional brigades arriving, or to loiter in order to give the impression of large numbers of Australian forces.

Helped by the current, the boat quickly travelled about 60 miles downstream to the town of Henzada where, after securing the boat to a flood bank, Calvert set off to investigate the town. His group went to the main square where quite a crowd turned out to see them. Calvert made a brief speech saying they were the advance party of a large Australian army which would drive out the Japanese and restore Burma to its people. This appeared to go down quite well, when a voice interrupted in English saying, "Lay down your arms. You are surrounded." They had been caught by a unit of the pro-Japanese Burmese Independence Army, which was led by Japanese officers. The tricky situation was saved by a quick-thinking corporal who shouted "Balls", and opened fire with a tommy gun. The local people fell flat as a brisk fire fight ensued and Calvert led his group rapidly back to the boat. They outpaced their pursuers and then, as they reached the river, the covering fire of their support group stopped the enemy and caused heavy casualties. As they began to move off, Calvert learned that one section of the cover party had not got aboard. He then made the craft tie up again and, putting as many well-armed men as possible on the roof of the boat to give covering fire, he led a small group ashore to collect the stragglers.

Captain Rae had the craft ready to move, but it had to turn round in the river under a hail of fire from the enemy on the banks. Having previously had to jettison their sandbags, the crew had stored a lot of food in sacks and tins on the upper deck to give them some cover. This proved effective and some men kept as souvenirs bullet-riddled tins of meat which had perhaps saved their life. Although it had to travel against the current of the river, the boat managed to out-pace any pursuers and ploughed steadily back up the river. Later, it was less fortunate and suffered some heavy casualties before returning to Prome.

Feeling considerable satisfaction at the success of his raid, Calvert reported the details by wireless to 17 Division HQ, and was told to report back at once. He was extremely unhappy at having to leave his men on the boat, since the whole project had been his personal concept, but as a major he had to obey a direct order, so he left the boat and reported back to Prome. Instead of receiving congratulations on a successful raid, he was sharply rebuked for endangering the lives of the boat crew and for damaged property, including that of the Burma Oil Company, whose installations had been damaged by explosions. Years later Calvert was grateful when Slim, in his book *Defeat into Victory*, wrote about Calvert's daring raid by river into Henzada. However, Calvert's immediate reaction to the rebuke was to return to Maymyo in a mood of fury and resentment. Arriving there, his mood was not improved when he was told there was a senior officer visiting the unit and waiting for him.

When Calvert reached his office he saw, sitting in his chair, a rather scruffy officer wearing the badges of a full colonel. A curt and tense conversation followed. "Who are you?'" "Wingate". "Who are you?" "Calvert". Then Calvert said "Excuse me, that is my chair," and Wingate politely got up and moved to another chair.

Among Calvert's colleagues at the Bush Warfare School were several outstanding leaders who had served in the SOE, the Commandos and other irregular units in the Middle East and Burma. Among these were Count Bentinck and Courtney Brocklehurst who had been in Ethiopia in 1941. They knew Wingate and were familiar with the detail of his crisis in Cairo in 1941 when he had tried to commit suicide, and they shared the widespread regular army prejudice about him. They reacted adversely to the rumours circulating in Maymyo that Wingate was to be put in charge of all irregular operations against the Japanese. Their views fortunately did not influence Calvert who has described his first meeting with Wingate after they had settled in their chairs.

"In spite of my unpleasant mood I was impressed. He showed no resentment at this somewhat disrespectful treatment by a major. He began talking quietly, asking questions about the showboat raid. And, to my surprise, they were the right sort of questions. Tired as I was, I soon began to realize that this was the sort of man I could work for and follow. Clearly he knew all that I knew about unconventional warfare and a lot more; he was streets ahead of anyone I had spoken to, including the Lochailort boys. Suddenly I no longer felt tired. For even at that first meeting something of the driving inspiration inside Orde Wingate transferred itself to me."

At this time Maymyo, the pleasant summer station for Burma, became briefly a most significant headquarters. General Hutton, soon to be replaced by General Alexander as Commander-in-Chief, was a neighbour to the Bush Warfare School. On 6 April, 1942, Wavell and Alexander met Chiang Kai-shek in Maymyo to discuss the operation of the Chinese divisions under Stilwell's command, and also to decide the future rôle of the groups Calvert had been training. Calvert now had many contacts with the Chinese and managed to arrange for Wingate to fly up to Chungking when Chiang Kai-shek left. Wingate returned to Maymyo on 16 April and spent some time travelling around central Burma with Calvert, who was amazed at the way Wingate studied the ground and the countryside. Calvert wrote, "Listening to him I realized I had been looking at the countryside with unseeing eyes ... It was a humbling experience."

During their travels Calvert took Wingate to see Slim in his Corps Headquarters at Prome, and soon after this Wingate appointed

Calvert as his second in command. They worked together planning possible operations, but by then the Japanese had advanced so quickly that there was little prospect of organizing any guerrilla activities before the Japanese arrived. Wingate was then called to GHQ in Delhi, but Calvert had other adventures before they were to meet again.

By the end of April, 1942, the Japanese advance had threatened to engulf Maymyo, and Alexander ordered Calvert to take his remaining staff, to gather any troops who were separated from their unit, and to try and hold the Gokteik viaduct, an important crossing on the road between Mandalay and Lashio. Already many of the roads were choked with terrified civilians clutching their few pathetic belongings and with equally frightened troops whose units had disintegrated under the force and speed of the Japanese attack.

Calvert collected a fair number of men, including some from a convalescent camp and a detention centre, and did his best to carry out Alexander's orders. The troops were hopelessly unreliable: sentries fell asleep, they panicked at the sight of the enemy, and one group stole a unit truck and made off – *sauve qui peut*. In a fury Calvert tried to catch them, everyone convinced he was going to shoot them. He failed to find them, but the rumour of his wrath helped to stiffen up the remainder, and soon they reached Gokteik and took up defensive positions.

They stayed there several days and Calvert frequently sought permission to blow up the viaduct, but each time his request was sternly refused. Much later and after the retreat, Alexander asked Calvert if he had blown it up. Totally baffled, Calvert replied that of course he had not. Alexander then explained that for political reasons he could not order it to be blown up, but thought that Calvert would be the person most likely to disobey orders and blow it up anyway. Calvert apologized, adding, "He seemed disappointed that I had let him down by doing what he told me to do."

After Gokteik, he was sent with a small group to ascertain the situation in Mandalay. His nervous troops were alarmed to be going back into Mandalay when everyone else was desperately moving out. Having reached the town, he improved morale by making a stop at a brewery which had been abandoned. Mandalay was virtually deserted, but the Japanese were fast approaching. After reporting this information, he took his dwindling band and crossed the famous Ava bridge over the Irrawaddy, moving on northwards with half-a-dozen delapidated trucks which were kept going by the brilliant work of a REME officer who had joined the group. After some of the petrol pumps had packed up, he fixed a petrol tank on the roof of the cab and fed petrol straight into the carburettor.

As they moved north among the crowds of refugees, they suddenly found a group of women and children clearly waiting to be picked up. Most of the children were British, loyally looked after by their servants, and in charge of the group was a formidable elderly lady who explained that a Colonel had said that he would send transport for them, so of course it would come. After some delicate discussion, she agreed to accept Calvert's offer to send the group in his lorries to the next town where they could be properly cared for. He ordered the trucks to be back in twenty-four hours, and, after posting sentries, he let his unit rest.

As he settled down to rest, an agitated orderly approached to tell him there was a large staff car in the village and that two officers were looking for him. Then a familiar voice said, "Get on your feet you lazy old so and so." It was Peter Fleming, whom he had last seen when they were planning the defence of Kent and Sussex. Fleming, still operating with Military Intelligence, and accompanied by Wavell's ADC, was carrying out a serious and complicated scheme to mislead the Japanese forces. He was clutching a briefcase which contained high-level top-secret documents which gave details of powerful newly arrived forces including battleships, armoured divisions and RAF squadrons. These units were entirely fictitious and it was planned that this information would fall into Japanese hands and mislead them into diverting their forces from the real battle area. To make the whole thing authentic the case also contained personal letters from Lady Wavell. Every detail had been carefully worked out. They hoped it would appear to the enemy that the case was being carried by Wavell's ADC to front-line unit commanders. Then he was suddenly to realize that he was too close to the enemy, and, in a panic, turn round to escape and crash the car. To carry out the subterfuge Fleming, Calvert and the ADC would have to go back along the road and over the Ava bridge in order to get close to the Japanese. They knew the bridge was due to be blown that night. Calvert, who knew the area best, drove the car and passed many units hurrying north, doubtless wondering why a large staff car should be racing south. He drove over the bridge, looked down at the menancing river below, and went on for some distance until they sensed the Japanese were close. They stopped the car at the side of the road and were greeted by a burst of enemy fire. They jumped back in, swung the car round and raced off as they saw the Japanese a couple of hundred yards away. As they came to a corner, Calvert jammed on the brakes and skidded into a ditch and over an embankment so that the car rolled over. As they broke clear, carefully leaving the briefcase close to the car, the advancing Japanese started firing. They returned the fire and were soon able to break away and lose contact with their pursuers. It is thought that this scheme was the idea of General Wavell, the best-read of British generals, since a very similar ruse had been used by Captain Meinertzhagen during Allenby's campaign in Palestine in 1917.

Using his compass, Calvert hurried off through the darkness, hoping to be able to cross the Ava bridge before it was blown up. They reached the river, crossed the bridge, and as they hurried on they heard the explosion which would certainly delay the Japanese for some time. Fleming and the ADC returned to their headquarters while Calvert returned to his group. He snatched a few hours' sleep and, when the trucks returned, they set off again. Years later, in 1964, when Calvert described this episode in *Fighting Mad* he was reprimanded because the whole incident was still considered top secret.

Calvert's escapade at the Ava bridge had delayed his group and they were now in danger of being cut off by the advancing Japanese. They therefore tried to get off the main roads which were still clogged with refugees, and to make haste through the jungle. When they reached one village, they received a message that a group of Gurkhas, with some wounded, were in a long house and needed help. Calvert went off with a couple of NCOs and soon found the house. Realizing that the Gurkhas might be a bit trigger happy after all their fighting, they spoke loudly in English as they approached the house. Calvert barged in to greet the Gurkhas, but to his amazement found himself face to face with a room full of Japanese officers studying maps and plans. He described the moments of suspense, adding, "I suppose Errol Flynn would have killed the lot, but we just stood like statues". He came to, grabbed his two companions, bundled them out and ran for the cover of the jungle. They kept going for a mile or more, then, hearing no sound of pursuit, collapsed, gasping for breath, and as a reaction to their narrow escape started roaring with laughter. Near the village he found the Gurkhas who had left the house shortly before. He patched up their wounded, gave them some food and sent them on their way.

After this they spent days of hard slogging with very little food, trying desperately to distance themselves from the Japanese and to reach Assam before the monsoon rains started in the middle of May. At last they reached the Chindwin, a sure sign that they were close to their destination, and Calvert decided that they could afford time for a swim. Feeling that his men might like a relaxed swim without him present, he wandered off to a quiet cove round a bend in the river. He stripped off his clothes and plunged in. As he surfaced he saw a Japanese officer who, perhaps like him, had left the men of his patrol and had come for a quiet swim by himself. Both hesitated, wondering whether they should call for their men, but not knowing whose group would be the stronger. Then the Japanese clearly decided that he would despatch his enemy in single combat and advanced into the water. In several feet of water they started what had to be a fight to the death. Physically, Calvert was immensely powerful, but his Japanese opponent was obviously trained in ju-jitsu and wrestling. The Japanese tried to claw Calvert's eyes, but he grabbed the smaller man and, in spite of frantic blows and kicks, slowly pushed him under the water. After a final shudder the body went limp. Calvert released it and it slowly floated off, as he said, "Like a ghastly yellow Ophelia." Feeling physically sick and totally drained, he staggered back to his men who, unaware of his fight to the death, were splashing and laughing in the water. He sent them off as soon as possible to attack the Japanese patrol. They took them by surprise and killed them all. Just as the clash finished, the body of the Japanese officer floated past. Considering all the violent action he went through in Burma, Calvert admits that this is the incident that stays in his mind and haunts him.

He now realized that the leading forces of the Japanese advance had overtaken his group and he decided that the time for taking offensive action was past. He spoke to his men and stressed that their main priority must now be to reach safety, which involved a journey to Kalewa nearly 200 miles away. He gave them clear instructions that if they got split up everyone was to use their initiative to get back by themselves. Soon after this they had a serious clash with a

Japanese patrol, and after that Calvert found himself alone with a cheerful cockney private called Medally, and Corporal Sergeant who had been with him when they burst in to the hut full of Japanese officers. Between them they had two revolvers, a Sten gun, a few grenades and no food or water.

After two days of hard marching, suffering desperately from thirst, they reached the point where they had to cross the Chindwin, but realized that Japanese patrols were active in the area. At the same time it started to rain. This gave some relief to their thirst and to their aching bodies, but created an added hazard, that shortly the Chindwin, already 400 yards wide, when swollen with monsoon rain would become a raging torrent. Calvert was a strong swimmer, but Sergeant and Medally could hardly swim at all. They found a rowing boat, but it had been wrecked, so they were forced to swim across. They pushed off into the water with Calvert holding the pack containing their weapons and most of their clothes, and trying to help the other two. Half-way across Sergeant cried out, "I can't go on," and, in trying to help him, Calvert lost his grip on the pack which floated off and sank. They eventually reached the far bank, with Sergeant totally exhausted and all three without weapons, proper clothes or boots. The enemy must have witnessed their crossing, for almost at once they came under fire and had to rush off into the jungle. Calvert had a pair of shorts and about 1000 rupees, Medally had a pair of shorts, and Sergeant had a shirt and a pair of socks. Wisely, they decided to find dry shelter in the jungle and sleep till morning.

Barefoot, inadequately clothed with no food or water, they set off slowly walking northwards. Soon they found a path where many people had passed, and sometimes they found discarded food – peanuts, sugar and pieces of chapatti – which helped to stave off the worst of their hunger. In their emaciated state, they suffered even more at night when they had little cover from or resistance to the intense damp cold. They were totally exhausted and wondering whether they could go on for another day when they came upon a fairly large group of Indian refugees. These were Oriya Indians, many of whom had worked in Burma on the railways and in timber firms. This group, at considerable danger to themselves, looked after Calvert and his companions, gave them food and hot sweet tea, and even provided warm places for them to sleep. Later, Calvert paid an impressive tribute to these fine people. "I sometimes think of these Oriya people when I hear talk of the oppression suffered by the Indians under the British and how much we were hated. These people need not have helped us. We were unarmed and physical wrecks. They knew we were part of the British army which was being ignominiously kicked out of Burma. They may have guessed that this was the beginning of the end of the British Empire, but their insistent offers of help were instantaneous and open-hearted. We were at that moment poorer and weaker than they were, entirely dependent upon them, and they could have had no thought of gain. Yet they risked their lives and the lives of their womenfolk to help us – the hated British!"

The Indians had been threatened with death by a Japanese patrol if they helped any British survivors, but they insisted on helping, the only stipulation being that the three men would dress as women in order to hide their colour and their beards. So, wearing sandals, and covered from head to foot in their saris, they set off again with their new-found helpers. The Indians were heavily laden with cooking utensils, bedding, and even carrying some elderly and infirm people on their backs, and only managed to walk about six miles a day. Calvert warned his two companions, whose strength had begun to return, helped by the leisurely pace and some reasonable food, that if a Japanese patrol started to interrogate them, they should run off into the jungle giving high-pitched screams as if they were women about to lose their honour. Fortunately they never had to do this. After a few days Calvert thanked their hosts, left them most of his 1000 rupees and headed off with Sergeant and Medally. They kept their Indian disguises and managed to reach Kalewa and report to 17 Division headquarters. A staff officer who knew Calvert took him, still in disguise, to see General Cowan. When the disguise was removed he said, "Calvert! What the hell have you been doing? We thought you were dead."

The demoralized troops and refugees pouring north to evade the clutches of the Japanese eventually reached Imphal, Kohima, Tamu and other towns in northern Burma and upper Assam. During their ordeal they had sustained themselves by the thought of the warm welcome they would receive when they reached the haven of India, but they were to be sorely disappointed. The civil authorities had no time and no resources to prepare for the avalanche of sick, hungry, destitute people who were about to arrive. The military forces were no better prepared, and, following the lead of the unsympathetic and abrasive General Irwin, who was later sacked, did little to help the remnants of Burcorps when they reached hospital. Cowan, offered a bare hillside with monsoon rain cascading down it as accommodation for his division, had a blazing row with Irwin, and was fully supported by Slim. These towns, sleepy provincial towns in peace-time India, where the well-to-do British residents still kept up their normal social life with dinner parties, dances, tennis tournaments and polo, generally reacted well when they eventually realized the scale of the disaster which was engulfing them.

From Imphal Calvert travelled for days in a cattle truck on a train with virtually no food or water, and no toilet provision except for a rope over the side of the truck. He finally arrived in the large military centre of Ranchi which lies north-west of Calcutta. This was a considerable distance from Imphal but the conditions were little better. While men, severely wounded and suffering from malaria, dysentery and cholera, were lying in make-shift hospitals with few facilities and fewer staff, a short distance away dinner parties and elegant balls still continued, the dancers and diners unaware of the tragedies all around them. When alerted to the problem, most people offered help, but not before a large number of wounded and seriously ill soldiers had died. Calvert experienced these conditions as he searched for George Dunlop, a colleague from Maymyo, who had cholera. He found him lying in a ward which had no staff and with corpses occupying many of the beds. In desperation, and with Slim's help, Calvert found a formidable matron who rounded up her friends and started to put things right.

Wingate had heard of Calvert's arrival in Ranchi and summoned him to Delhi. Wavell had just given Wingate authority to raise and train a brigade to operate his plan of Long Range Penetration behind the Japanese lines in Burma. Both Calvert and Dunlop agreed at once to join this new venture. However, Calvert did enjoy a brief period of sick leave with his sister Eileen who was then living in the pleasant hill station at Bangalore in southern India.

CHAPTER FIVE

# OPERATION LONGCLOTH

When Calvert travelled back from his leave in Bangalore in August, 1942, to join Wingate at the training camp at Gwalior, 150 miles south of Delhi in central India, he was about to embark on the most decisive phase in his career. Still in his twenties, he had an immensely powerful physique and was then reaching the peak of tough physical maturity. His boxing, swimming and water polo training had always made him an outstandingly fit man, and now he had been toughened and hardened by the years of Commando training and by the rigours of war. His experience of war, stretching from Shanghai to Norway and the Burma retreat, had built up his confidence and enabled him to formulate effective ideas on guerrilla war.

He had spent considerable time with Wingate at Maymyo and, perhaps fortunately for them both, they had immediately established a close rapport. Yet, in spite of his wide military experience, Calvert realized that Wingate outshone him both in direct experience of war and in original thinking. Wingate had won his first DSO in Palestine in 1938 when, contrary to British military establishment thinking, he had led the Jewish settlers against the Arab terrorists. Then in Ethiopia in 1941 he had shown further brilliance when he led a guerrilla force in the Gojam area and capped this by leading Haile Selassie's victorious procession back into his capital, Addis Ababa. In all these operations he had proved himself a brilliant and original thinker, and a determined and abrasive leader. He had also established a reputation with the regular army establishment as a dangerous and unbalanced character.

Calvert was aware of Wingate's unpopularity, since several of his colleagues at Maymyo had arrived there after serving in other clandestine operations in Ethiopia. Thus, in the close-knit brother-hood of Special Forces, as well as in the military establishment,

Wingate was viewed largely with dislike, suspicion and even hostility. This did not deter Calvert, who had already weighed up the potential of Wingate's ideas. So many of these fitted into his own philosophy and mirrored much of the detail he had produced in his paper "Operations Behind the Enemy Lines" which he had written in the spring of 1940 before joining up with Peter Fleming in Kent and Sussex. He was soon to experience the practical effect of Wingate's unpopularity.

When Calvert reached Gwalior Wingate had already established a fearsome training régime. Some time later Wingate noticed the figure, half lion and half eagle, which stands at the entrance to Burmese temples. He felt that this figure best symbolized their need for strength both on the ground and in the air, and, through a mispron-unciation, coined the name "Chindit". This name came later, but will be used from now onwards. Calvert assessed the training of the Chindits under Wingate and commented, "Training with this human dynamo was tough but stimulating. After marching for miles and fighting mock battles in thick bush we would strip to the waist in the steamy rain and listen to Wingate propound his new lore of the jungle." After only a few days training Calvert was sent off to GHQ in Delhi to attend a conference on Long Range Penetration. Wingate had given a lecture on this subject a few weeks before, but, signifi-cantly, he was not present at the conference, and it fell to Calvert to report back to him. He stayed at Maidens' Hotel near GHQ and wrote in detail to Wingate. He explained that the majority of senior officers opposed the idea of Long Range Penetration and considered that Wingate was not a sufficiently balanced commander to lead such an operation. In Cairo, after the Ethiopian campaign in 1941, while suffering from cerebral malaria and its antidote atabrin, which taken together cause suicidal tendencies, Wingate had tried to cut his throat. His opponents held this against him for the rest of his life, and long afterwards. Calvert now had to handle the effects of this prejudice and use his tact in conveying this message to Wingate. In this sensitive situation they established a deep and loyal rapport which was never damaged or broken. In a letter of 6 August, 1942, Calvert quoted one General who had said that some of Wingate's ideas were brilliant but that more than 90% were dangerous and absurd. Calvert added, "I think the phrases 'impractical' and 'not fit to command' is the attitude of those few who, due to jealousy, listening to gossip, and guilt over their own unpreparedness and inefficiency have put themselves against you. Their minds must be small." (Letter August, 1942. Calvert Papers)

Wingate replied by return, giving Calvert detailed information to argue his case. He pointed out that he had commanded over 2000 troops in over seventy different actions against the enemy. He added, "It is because I am what I am, objectional though that appears to my critics, that I win battles." Calvert understood well enough that, apart from Wingate's personal unpopularity, most of the army in India, which was short of supplies and weapons of all sorts, resented the extra supplies that the Chindits needed. They both realized that their hopes of arranging a Long Range Penetration attack depended almost exclusively on maintaining the backing of Wavell. He had supported Wingate both in Palestine and in Ethiopia and had requested his posting to India to take over guerrilla activity. Their assessment of the situation was realistic, for Wavell incurred considerable unpopularity by giving priority to supplies for the Chindits and by refuting the opposition of those who maintained that real fighting and the effective destruction of the enemy had to be achieved by regular divisions and not by madcap groups propounded by the likes of Wingate.

As second-in-command to Wingate, Calvert had to handle much of the antagonism towards their venture and at the same time plan for the actual operation and train the whole force in every aspect of demolition. His passion for blowing things up had never left him, and he managed to imbue most of the Chindits with his enthusiasm.

After doing his best to fight their corner in Delhi, Calvert returned to the rigours of Chindit training at Gwalior. Their unit, 77 Brigade, included 13th King's Liverpool Regiment, the 3/2 Gurkha Rifles, the 2nd Battalion Burma Rifles and 142 Commando. Several serious problems emerged during the urgent attempts to bring the Brigade up to an acceptable level of fitness for their campaign. The King's Regiment, composed of older men than was normal in an infantry battalion, illustrated Wingate's maxim that any unit could be trained up to the necessary standard, but initially large numbers went sick. At one stage 70% were absent from duty and the unit was reduced in numbers, but those who remained became a fit and confident unit. The Gurkhas presented different problems. A very proud fighting regiment, their officers did not take kindly to being told by someone they regarded as a showman and an upstart how to fight in the jungle. The Gurkhas faced an added problem. Hailing from the fastnesses of Nepal where the rivers cascaded down mountainsides, they were never at their best in water, and they found the constant Chindit training in river crossings, preparing them for the Chindwin and Irrawaddy, to be very difficult. In contrast, the Burma Regiment excelled at all types of work, and their skills in tracking, in moving through the jungle and living off the jungle was a great advantage to all units in the brigade. Many of these problems came to Calvert to be solved and, while he sympathized with some of the Gurkhas, he was able through his personality, reputation, experience and his loyalty to Wingate, to smooth out most of the difficulties, and to overcome the unfortunate effects of Wingate's well-known criticism of the Indian Army in general.

During August, 1942, the Brigade faced a serious crisis when, because of an unexpectedly heavy monsoon downpour, the whole of their jungle camp was flooded and the river which flowed through the camp rose by 30 feet. Calvert's swimming prowess proved invaluable, and Wingate, swimming up and down in his topee, remained unperturbed. Several men were lost in the flood, and the incident gave valuable ammunition to their critics. Command sent grossly exaggerated reports to over forty departments at GHQ. In spite of this setback, vigorous training continued and, as the time of their operation approached, Wingate and Calvert briefed the units in detail on both their strategy and tactics.

The Brigade would infiltrate through the Japanese lines in an area forward from Imphal, and march up to 200 miles in the direction of Indaw. Supplied by air, they would roam the area in order to attack and destroy roads, railways, bridges, storage depots and every part of the enemy lines of communication. The Chindit Brigade was divided into eight columns of about 400 men, and these operated as completely independent units with their own mule transport and their own wireless communication system. Extremely high standards of signal work, compass work and map reading were established, since the very existence of the unit would depend on the accurate air drop of both food and ammunition. Equally important was the processing of intelligence information about the enemy.

These detailed plans for movement on the ground were to be part of Wavell's wider strategy for north Burma in 1943. The British 4th

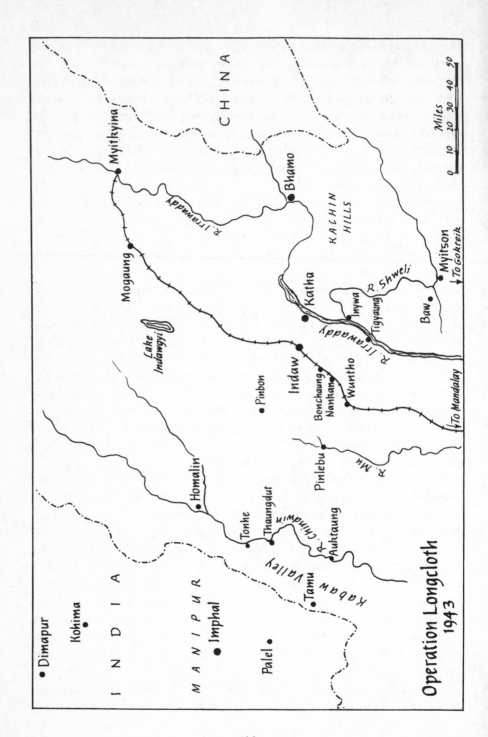

Operation Longcloth
1943

Miles
0 10 20 30 40 50

Corps, based on Imphal, was to advance southwards towards the Chindwin. From Ledo in the extreme north of Burma, General Stilwell and his Chinese divisions were to attack the Japanese and advance towards Myitkyina. Chiang Kai-shek would advance in Yunnan, while, in the Arakan the 15th Corps would advance towards Akyab. During these three major attacks the Chindits would destroy the communications of the Japanese divisions facing Stilwell in the north as well as those facing 4th Corps at Imphal and Kohima. It had been agreed as early as September, 1942, that the purpose of 77 Brigade's operation was to assist the major advances by the main British and American/Chinese forces "so that each helped the other".

Weeks of arduous training reached a climax in December, 1942, with an exercise for the whole Brigade – over 3000 men organized into eight columns – in which every aspect of Chindit activity was tested. The Army showed great interest in this novel development of warfare and Wavell himself attended the exercise. Some things went wrong, but the operation and control of eight separate columns, the airdrop of food and ammunition to each of them, the RAF liaison, the wireless communication and the sabotage squads, personally trained by Calvert, all worked well. Wingate himself, ever the perfectionist, was highly critical of some of the standards achieved, but was reassured by both Wavell and Calvert.

After the exercise Calvert accompanied Wingate on further reconnaissance in the 4th Corps area at Imphal. He had grim memories of passing through Tamu and Imphal as a half-starved physical wreck, but now things were different and he was to be among the first to hit back at the Japanese. As part of the final preparations Calvert travelled with Wingate to a high-level briefing at the end of which they had a hair-raising trip in a chartered Indian aircraft piloted by a civilian. First the pilot took off without them, and when he was called back his nerve seemed to break. He had to land at an airstrip to pick up another passenger, and he landed on the runway just as a Dakota was taking off in the opposite direction. Finally, as they landed at Imphal there was an alarming bump and the plane came down festooned with bushes and creepers. Calvert commented, "A foot or two lower and the Chindits might have been without their commander."

In January, 1943, all was ready. 77 Brigade moved by train to Dimapur and then marched 130 miles up to Imphal, moving mostly at night because of the heavy traffic along this vital but precarious road supplying the whole of 4th Corps. Calvert now reverted from second-in command of the Brigade to being a Column Commander, and relished the opportunity during the long march to try out all the techniques for the effective control of the Column. The pre-Christmas exercise had proved the need for more good signals staff, and to some extent this had been remedied by the time they moved, but the signallers still carried a very heavy burden of responsibility.

When the Brigade was installed at its camp about seven miles from Imphal, Wavell came to see them on 5 February. He brought bad news. The proposed advances by 4 Corps, by Stilwell, by Chiang Kai-shek, and by 15 Corps would not take place because none of them was ready. Wavell, out of genuine concern for the Chindits, felt that the operation should be called off because the Japanese, instead of facing major attacks on four different fronts, would be able to concentrate their entire force on destroying the Chindits. Wingate argued that, after intense specialist training, the whole Brigade was keyed up and ready for battle, and if the plan was called off it would give renewed ammunition to their critics and the whole concept of Long Range Pentration might be lost. It was essential, too, that lessons should be learnt about communications behind enemy lines and about the techniques of supply drops, close support bombing and air attacks in support of the Columns.

Calvert has always loyally supported Wingate's decision that Operation Longcloth should go ahead in spite of the failure of all the other commands to carry out their planned attacks. He has rigourously refuted the criticism from which Wingate has suffered over many years. He points out that, in spite of all the promises and all the plans, out of a million men under arms in India, 77 Brigade alone was the only unit ready and eager to attack the Japanese in 1943. Wavell, then a Field Marshal, when he had finally agreed to the Chindit operation going ahead, gave the order to move, and in a shy and moving gesture he saluted them on their way. The Brigade moved off to Palel, south of Imphal, and then on to Tamu, which brought them to the enemy front line. Here Wingate issued his order of the day, beginning, "Today we stand on the threshold of battle." It concluded, "Let us pray that God may accept our services and direct our endeavours, so that when we have done all, we shall see the fruit of our labours and be satisfied." Chindit veterans have treasured his words to this day, and feel that this alone refutes the allegations of Wingate enemies that he was a phoney or a charlatan.

The Chindit Column, a completely new formation for the British Army, cut across the traditional platoon, company and battalion organization and they soon proved that they could operate effectively as independent units. After they moved off on 13 February, 1943, they quickly melded into fighting units. They developed their own characteristics and reputation. Bernard Fergusson's Column, well known through his book, *Beyond the Chindwin*, was soon regarded as unlucky: for example, in missing the rendezvous for airdrops which meant short rations for several days. In contrast, Calvert's No 3 Column which he had put through much more demanding training than the other Columns, especially on digging slit trenches, tended to be lucky and to be in the right place at the right time. Here, at last, was the climax of his years of training and the study of war, and he could hope to avenge some of the suffering he had endured during the retreat from Maymyo.

Operation Longcloth started with a brilliant deception. The main thrust was aimed at Indaw, almost due east of Imphal, but on 14 February two Columns of nearly 1000 men crossed the Chindwin, moved south from Auktaung, and the following day took an air-drop in broad daylight. Burma Rifles intelligence had discovered where there were pro-Japanese villages, and here a Chindit officer, dressed up with beard, topee and a brigadier's red tabs to resemble Wingate, loudly ordered substantial air-drops at points further south. This deception distracted the Japanese, while the six remaining Columns moved forward during the night of 14 February completely undetected. They were able to advance fairly quickly through the extensive teak forests lying between the Chindwin and the Irrawaddy rivers, and for several days most Columns saw little sign of Japanese forces. This helped the Columns to gain cohesion, but to complete their initiation they badly needed a successful clash with the enemy.

On the third day, when reports of a body of Japanese troops came in, Wingate ordered Calvert's Column, supported by two others, to attack. They moved off at night. The Burmese officers with the Columns were generally welcomed by the local people who readily passed on information. When Calvert's group reached the target area they found it deserted, as if the Japanese had left in a hurry. They also found Burmese servants ready to serve breakfast, and, hating to disappoint them, the Column tucked into a hearty meal. They also captured a horse and an elephant complete with its driver which proved invaluable for carrying the ammunition and heavier equipment or for forcing a way through some of the denser jungle they subsequently faced. Calvert's passion for explosives now came into play. Before they moved off they discovered from the local people which paths were frequented only by the Japanese and left many types of booby traps on them.

Leading a Column behind the enemy lines puts huge pressure on the commander and is the ultimate test of leadership. Calvert emerged from this as the most successful of all the Chindit leaders. Some commanders just could not cope with the pressure, and by imagining a Jap behind every tree reduced their units to pitiable ineptitude. There were several examples of this during the second Chindit campaign, but during Longcloth, with the inspiring examples of Calvert, Scott and Fergusson, the majority measured up to the exacting standards required. But even these leaders were not unaffected by such pressures. In an early skirmish 3 Column suffered its first casualties and several British soldiers panicked under fire and had to be restrained by force. Several mules and some equipment were lost in this encounter and Calvert confessed, "During one period I became depressed and rather useless, but my officers carried on excellently." (3 Column War Diary)

The relatively trouble-free progress of Calvert's group had not been matched by the other Columns and, before the proposed major attack on the railway, Wingate faced a serious crisis. 2 Column, which had taken part in the deception south of Auktaung, had itself been ambushed by a strong Japanese force. This incident again illustrates the intense pressure on the Column Commander. 2 Column, far from seeing a Japanese behind every tree, had foolishly marched down the railway and had bivouacked near the track. When they moved out of the bivouac they walked straight into a well prepared ambush. The CO changed his rendezvous plans in the middle of the action and, as a result, mules, weapons and equipment were lost. The Column broke up, failed to assemble at the rendezvous and ceased to exist as a fighting unit. A few remnants subsequently reached Imphal. About the same time 4 Column, which was ordered to ambush the road north of the main body, were themselves ambushed. In this incident some young Gurkhas broke under fire, with disastrous results. The Column broke up, the mules panicked and ran off with the ammunition, the reserve weapons and, most damaging of all, the wireless. This unit too ceased to function. In addition, 1 Column, which had also taken part in the initial feint to the south, had completely lost contact, so Wingate was left with only four of his original eight columns with which to carry out the main attack on the railway.

He established his HQ in fairly pleasant hilly country south of Pinbon, and from here he planned the main Chindit attack. Two columns went north to attack Pinlebu, to draw any Japanese forces to that area and to prevent any forces coming south towards Nankan and Bonchaung where the main demolitions were planned. There the main railway from Mandalay to Mitkyina, the main supply route for the Japanese divisions facing Stilwell, crossed two bridges and then snaked along a precarious ledge through the Bonchaung Gorge. It was intended to destroy the bridges and then, by a huge explosion at the gorge, to put the railway out of action for a long time.

Any hopes of a Chindit success rested substantially on Calvert and 3 Column which set out towards the village of Nankan. They reached the outskirts of the village on 4 March and Calvert, partly to rest his men prior to the attack, and partly to co-ordinate the timing with Fergusson's attack on the Bonchaung Gorge, made a secure bivouac. The approach to Nankang brought back vivid memories to Calvert for it was littered with rusting cars and lorries and abandoned guns and equipment from the 1942 retreat. While most of 3 Column rested, active recce patrols discovered that there were some Japanese units in the area, though several had been sent off to deal with the Chindit diversion further north. It was also discovered that a major Japanese unit was located at Wuntho on the railway about ten miles south of Nankan and Calvert was able to order an RAF bombing attack on it to coincide with his own attack on Nankan.

He made a careful plan for the attack which aimed to destroy the railway and in particular two railway bridges, one with a span of 300 feet, close to Nankan station. First, one group of Gurkhas was sent off to establish a road block to the north of the village, and another to block the road to the south. He carefully sited the rendezvous just a few hundred yards to the south-east of the village and established here a "Keep in touch party" which included the mules, Flossie the elephant and Flight Lieutenant Thompson who controlled the wire-

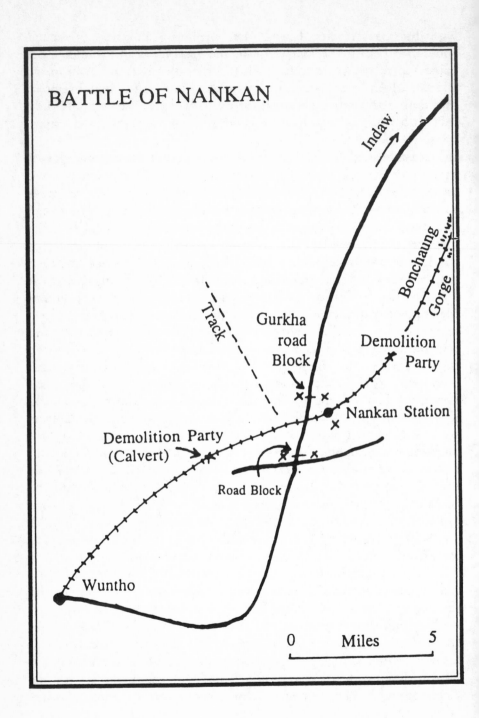

# BATTLE OF NANKAN

Indaw

Bonchaung Gorge

Track

Gurkha road Block

Demolition Party

Demolition Party (Calvert)

Nankan Station

Road Block

Wuntho

0    Miles    5

less (later Sir Robert Thompson who became a world expert on counter-insurgency and wrote *Make for the Hills*). The remainder of the Column was formed into two carefully trained demolition teams.

The action started at 12.45 hours when the road blocks were in position. Then the demolition teams – the first commanded by Calvert himself – moved on to the railway to the north and south of the station and started laying mines and booby traps. It occurred to Calvert that he was considerably better equipped for this sort of activity than he had been in Norway. Both groups worked carefully but swiftly along the track towards the station and laid over seventy mines. Everything went smoothly until about 13.15 hours when two trucks loads of Japanese troops, apparently unaware of the Chindit activity in the village, blundered into the northern road block. The Gurkhas inflicted heavy casualties on the Japanese, but then another truck arrived and soon the Gurkhas were outnumbered. The two demolition teams and the "Keep in touch party" all sent men to help the Gurkhas, while Calvert and the rest of the demolition teams worked frantically to complete the demolition work on the two bridges in spite of intense Japanese fire. As soon as the demolition charges were ready, Calvert returned to his command group and was able, by re-siting the 3-inch mortar, to bring its fire down on to the Japanese. With remarkable luck, the first bomb hit the Japanese truck and very soon the enemy fled. Both the bridges were effectively blown up and a very long stretch of railway was completely destroyed.

Having successfully completed their mission and defeated a Japanese unit, the Column was ready to move off, but Calvert insisted on placing booby traps all round the station to welcome the Japanese when they returned. At this stage one of the strange coincidences of war took place, when a Captain Peterson, a young Danish officer who had a deep grudge against the Japanese and who had heard the noise of battle, suddenly appeared out of the jungle and joined in the action. Calvert quickly organized the roll-call at the rendezvous and discovered that in this action, which had completely wrecked the main Myitkyina railway and had inflicted heavy casualties on the Japanese, his Column had not sustained a single casualty. It was 6 March, his 30th birthday, and for his outstanding leadership he was awarded the DSO.

In order to wreck the railway completely, while Calvert attacked

Nankan Fergusson led his Column a few miles further north to Bonchaung Gorge where another large railway bridge was blown up and a large explosion, heard by other Chindit units ten miles away, brought down hundreds of tons of rock and earth on to the railway where it went through the gorge. Although Fergusson achieved his demolition objective, his Column suffered several casualties when it clashed with a Japanese patrol. Some men were killed and some who were wounded had to be left behind.

From Nankan 3 Column moved off eastwards towards the Irrawaddy. This was a difficult task for such a large group of men to accomplish while the Japanese were fully alerted and definitely out for revenge. As the Column tried to distance itself from the railway, the jungle got denser and denser and made progress dangerously slow. Calvert has described amusingly how, as the Column leaders were laboriously hacking their way through the elephant grass, the idea suddenly came to him that the elephant could help them to move much more swiftly and easily. He ordered a corporal to ride up on the elephant with the mahout (driver) and, by reading the compass and shouting instructions, Calvert was able to maintain the right direction.

With the help of Flossie, the Column managed to evade the attentions of their Japanese pursuers and soon were able to stop in relative seclusion and take an air drop. Now a major decision had to be taken, and over a period of several days Wingate discussed matters with Calvert, Scott, Fergusson and other Column Commanders. The issue was whether the Chindits, having accomplished their main mission, should now return the way they had come and recross the Chindwin or march on eastwards and cross the Irrawaddy. Every solution to the problem posed serious dangers. The Japanese were now fully alerted to the Chindit presence and to retrace their steps as a force of 3000 men could invite catastrophe. Intelligence had suggested that east of the Irrawaddy the country would be easy to traverse and the local Kachin people were thought to be loyal, but this was later found to be incorrect. On 8 March Wingate asked Fergusson and Calvert for their view and both strongly suggested that the whole force should cross the Irrawaddy and go east. They added that, in view of harassment by the Japanese, they would like to move off as soon as possible. Wingate then made the decision for the whole force to cross the river. He has been severely and unjustly criticized for this decision, notably by Kirby, the biased editor of the Official History, who maintained that Wingate had a preconceived notion to cross the river. It is significant that both Calvert and Fergusson, on the spot at the time, strongly supported Wingate's decision.

Fergusson's Column got away first, with the result that Calvert had to lead his Column about five miles down the river, knowing that the Japanese were hunting for them. He did not get away lightly. When they reached a possible crossing point near Tigyaing, where the river was nearly a mile wide, the Japanese attacked. The river crossing techniques practised in training proved inadequate and were certainly irrelevant to crossing such a wide river against stiff opposition. The leading men of the Column managed to get to an island and then, as the enemy closed in, were in real peril. Any military commander needs some luck and Calvert's luck did not desert him now. As his Burma Rifles officers tried desperately to get hold of some boats, a group of Burmese sailing boats appeared and these Calvert commandeered. He took command of a strong rearguard to fight off the Japanese while the main body crossed the river. This succeeded, but when the time came for the rearguard to cross, now with covering fire from the far side, it became clear that some of the heavier equipment would have to be left behind, but they managed to keep all their weapons, the wireless and their demolition explosives. In the action seven men were killed, and six, a Burmese Rifleman and five Gurkhas, were wounded. These were taken across the river and, fairly close to the far bank, were left in a Burmese village. Here Calvert's knowledge of military history came into play. Realizing the Japanese would probably find them, he left a note for the Japanese Commander saying that the wounded men had fought bravely for King and Country, just as he had, and had been wounded. He added "I leave them confidently in your charge knowing that with your well-known tradition of Bushido [Chivalry] you will look after them as well as if they were your own." It was learned later that this message was effective and the men survived. (Wingate Papers)

All the other Columns, as well as Wingate's HQ, crossed the river with varying success, Fergusson being bundled unceremoniously into the back of a boat and crossing crouched on all-fours. By 15 March they were clear of the bank and were not too closely pursued by the Japanese. Almost at once it was found that the Intelligence information about the country east of the Irrawaddy, which had been a major factor in the decision to take the whole force across the river was false. The suggested pleasant country, peopled by scattered villages full of friendly and hospitable people, turned out to be a harsh waterless plain crossed by numerous roads which were frequently patrolled by the Japanese to hunt down the Chindits. This also meant that it was increasingly difficult to arrange an effective airdrop because it drew attention to their presence, and some of the columns which were near exhaustion suffered from a shortage of food and water.

Calvert's and Fergusson's Columns, which had crossed the Irrawaddy ahead of the main force and were lying some miles to the south, were now ordered to move further south, and for Calvert to attack the Gokteik viaduct on 17 March. What an irony for Calvert to receive this order after the days of frustration he had suffered while actually sitting on it during the early days of the retreat! Now he was faced with a more daunting task. The viaduct was over 100 miles away, the country was inhospitable, the Japanese were out in force, and were able to concentrate their troops whenever a Chindit unit was located.

Calvert led his troops off towards Myitson but had to move with great care in order to avoid Japanese patrols, though, once again, the Burma Regiment officers provided up-to-date and accurate information which they culled from the local people. After several days of strenuous effort the Column reached the area of Myitson, which was about a third of the way to Gokteik. Here Calvert received fairly detailed information about a Japanese unit which was regularly patrolling the river approximately where they wanted to cross.

Because the Column had moved so carefully through the jungle, the Japanese appeared to be completely unaware of their presence. He therefore decided that he would ambush and destroy the Japanese unit, thus inflicting a defeat on the enemy and at the same time clearing a stretch of the river which his Column needed. He set up the ambush with meticulous care. His mind went back to his days with Spencer Chapman at Lockailort and in Australia, and he established three ambush points in line and ensured that everyone in the unit was fully briefed. After several hours of waiting, a Japanese unit of company strength came along and walked straight into the ambush. A majority of the enemy, estimated at over 100, were killed when the Chindits opened fire. "We just shot them to pieces," said Calvert, who commented that it was the most one-sided action he had ever fought in. The Chindits sustained only one casualty. As soon as the action was over they crossed the river and established a secure base away from the Japanese in order to have a day's rest before moving to Gokteik.

During this brief pause Wingate, on 24 March, signalled an order which completely changed the plans. Two days earlier 4th Corps HQ had ordered Wingate to bring his whole force back to India, largely because it was becoming increasingly difficult to sustain the air supply at such a distance and with the Chindit units so scattered. Because he was so much further south than any of the other columns, Calvert was ordered to move independently of the rest and for him to decide on the route.

Wingate had lengthy discussions with all the Column Commanders before taking the decision how best to return. There were several options. If the Force stayed together it would make air supply easier and would enable them, with close support from the air, to concentrate enough fire power to brush aside any Japanese unit they were likely to meet. If they broke up into small units they could use the cover of the jungle and might return over the Chindwin relatively unmolested. Fergusson strongly urged that they should stay together as a unit and march out to safety via Myitkyina.

Having weighed up all the possibilities, Wingate made his decision. He ordered the main force to return to Inywa, where he had crossed, and he reasoned that the enemy would not expect them to return to the same place. At Inywa they would abandon their heaviest equipment, kill most of the mules, and then, once they had recrossed the Irrawaddy, they would disperse into small groups and make for the Chindwin. Within this general plan Wingate allowed very wide discretion to the Column Commanders. His overall view was that Longcloth had now achieved most of its aims, and the highest priority must be given to getting as many men as possible safely home with their invaluable experience. On 27 March Wingate with his HQ and three Columns moved off towards Inywa. They had several clashes with the enemy and, after one of these, Fergusson's Column lost contact and never regained it. Many of the Chindits were now at the end of their tether as the result of the prolonged stress of being behind the enemy lines and in constant contact with the Japanese. When Fergusson tried to cross the Shweli River some of his men were too scared and too exhausted to attempt it, and despite orders, entreaties, encouragement and threats, they would not move and had to be abandoned. They were later captured. Most of the different groups faced similar problems before they reached safety.

Lying many miles south of the main force, 3 Column, too, was being harassed by the Japanese. On the way south Calvert had buried a supply of food and ammunition near Baw, and he now returned there and replenished his stores. Although his Column fared better than the others, his men, too, were in a poor state. As they passed one river crossing, they just could not face it. Calvert himself wrote, "My own spirits dropped to zero." (Calvert Report) Then he had a long discussion with all his officers about what they should do. During training, all the Chindits in contemplating such a situation, had practised a drill for breaking up into small units, but Calvert, deeply conscious of the duty and responsibility of a commander, initially opposed this idea. He felt that it was shelving the commander's responsibility just when the men needed him most. If the unit was to break up into ten groups, he doubted if there were ten men with sufficient confidence, ability and leadership qualities to undertake the awesome responsibility of leading a group back to safety. He also recognized that the morale of some of the men was so low that they just would not fight. In the discussion with his officers he used the analogy that it was like leaving a ship with its heavy guns and taking to the boats in the middle of a storm. After much anguished thought he accepted the majority view that they should split up; he then planned the withdrawal.

His orders to the group leaders are a model of sound sense built on wide experience and probably account for the fact that a high proportion of 3 Column arrived safely home. First he tackled the problem of tiredness, saying, "Tiredness makes cowards of us all," and he ordered them to march methodically and not to get overtired. Then he added, with homely and sound sense, "If you are really up against it, sit down and make a cup of tea, and the problem will usually get solved." Then, on another plane, he warned them not to let the hunted feeling get to them, and advised them not to go so far out of their way to avoid Japanese patrols that they suffer more casualties through drowning or through the lack of food and water.

There were many rivers to cross, and here too he gave sound advice: "If you can't get boats in one place, then get them in another, and if all else fails make big rafts of bamboo and push off at night. Remember, it doesn't matter how far you drift down river." Realizing that the new groups might themselves be split up, he ordered the unit commanders to ensure that every man had a map giving directions and distances. He concluded his orders by saying, "When you come in, don't look like a defeated army as you pass the frontline troops. Overdo the drill and saluting. We have been under great strain. Let us keep our dirty washing to ourselves on our return."

There was concern in most of the columns at the wasteful abandonment of expensive equipment, but 3 Column carefully wrapped up and buried mortars, machine guns and heavy items which could no longer be carried "in case they come back next year." When this was completed they had an excellent airdrop with food, ammunition and boots, and carefully divided it between the groups. Finally, after giving time for each leader to organize his group, "they used up some of the remaining rum ration, drank the health of the King, wished each other luck, and departed in various directions but not very far, due to the rum!" (Calvert Report)

Before moving off Calvert sent a detailed message to 4th Corps HQ: "Am near Baw. Brigade orders return to Chindwin. Japs have ringed Irrawaddy and mountains. Sending reinforcements from Mandalay. Column will move to Chindwin in groups of 40. Please help returning groups. Warn Kachin Levies and Chinese. Regret troubling you." Although he was going to lead one of the groups, he felt deflated that this was now the end of No 3 Column which he had commanded so proudly.

Thinking that they might need nursing along more than the riflemen, Calvert kept most of the cooks and orderlies in his own group, and he also had the support of a remarkable Scotsman, Jeffrey Lockett, who insisted on wearing a kilt at all times. As the groups moved off northwards Calvert led his men a little further south to draw off any Japanese and to give the others a good start. Then they moved north-west and when they reached the Irrawaddy they were fortunate to find a clear spot and were able to cross unopposed.

Few men have ever suffered such prolonged privations as the Chindits endured during the next weeks. They had gone into Burma as outstandingly fit, strong men, and the majority came out as emaciated skeletons hardly able to walk, their muscles wasted away, leaving brittle skin and bone. Calvert's group suffered as much privation as the rest, but his leadership and training often made the difference between success and failure. Calvert often described incidents in a self-deprecatory, almost flippant, way, but this should not disguise the grim reality of the situation. Lockett gave a vivid description of their return journey, including the moment when they re-crossed the railway near Nankan. He was all for hurrying over, "but not Calvert. He insisted on blowing it up." Calvert, too, described this incident. He had taken Lockett with him to set the final timed fuses for the detonators when he realized that he had failed to follow his own orders to mark the different timers so that they could be recognized in the dark. With Japanese patrols in the area they dared not light a match to check this. Calvert then had the idea of lighting a match under Lockett's kilt, which would effectively hide the light. Lockett did not like this idea, but reluctantly agreed.

From the railway there was still a long and dangerous trek of 80 miles back to the Chindwin. The group moved mostly at night and tried to eke out their meagre rations by eating snake or reptiles or sometimes food from friendly villages, but, on most days it was a monotonous diet of rice gruel. The men became more and more emaciated and exhausted. Lockett made the remarkable admission that he only kept going by taking a dozen benzedrine tablets a day. At length, on 15 April, the group reached the Chindwin and were welcomed back to the luxury of clean hospital sheets and generous supplies of food.

Calvert's group, though shattered and exhausted, was the first Chindit group to return, a tribute to his tough and professional leadership. Wingate's group which he led "with unrelenting ferocity, allowing no one to drop out of line," returned on 25 April. Other groups suffered for longer periods. One which went north could make hardly any progress because of the number of sick and wounded. One day they found a long, flat stretch of land where they were to take an airdrop, and they spelt out on the ground – PLANE LAND HERE NOW. The brave pilot landed and took off all the sick and wounded, thus enabling the rest to get home safely.

A part of 7 Column under Major Gilkes kept going due east and eventually reached the Chinese forces in Yunnan who treated them as heroes. They were doubly fortunate, for after lavish hospitality from the Chinese, in early June they were flown home by an American aircraft which was returning empty over "The Hump", after delivering supplies to Chiang Kai-shek.

During May and June, 1943, everything changed for the Chindits. Overnight they became heroes. Alone among the military forces in India they had gone into the jungle, attacked the Japanese, inflicted untold harm on their communications, destroyed many of their units and returned safely. Wingate held a press conference in Delhi on 20 May, 1943. Reuters struck the mood of the media in a report which included: "This must surely rank as one of the greatest guerrrrila operations ever undertaken ... the Japanese were harassed, killed, bamboozled and bewildered through a vast area of Burma." At a time when news of nothing but defeat and disaster was coming out of Burma it was natural that the press latched on to this one great success and perhaps overdid it. Louis Allen, the doyen of military historians of the Burma campaign, referred to the depressing reports in early 1943 from the Arakan "of untrained, undisciplined gutless British soldiers," and contrasts this with Wingate who infused a new spirit into the Services. His first expedition "had panache, it had glamour, it had cheek, it had everything the successive Arakan failures lacked" (*Burma, the Longest War*, p. 118).

Wingate and Calvert, already aware, even before Operation Longcloth, of the antagonism of the military establishment towards the Chindits, nonetheless enjoyed the success and euphoria, though they realized it would not last. The most unfortunate aspect of the first Chindit operation, and indeed of all their subsequent campaigns, is the grudging and dismissive attitude of the military establishment, an attitude illustrated above all in the unbalanced and biased Official History. The establishment version can be summed up roughly as follows: "The Chindits went in and milled about in the jungle for several weeks. They blew up railways and bridges which were soon repaired, then at a huge cost in lost equipment and men's lives, they got out having suffered one third casualties. Many of those who got out were never fit for service." The Official History concluded: "*The operation had no strategic value.*"

In reality, the Chindit achievement gave a tremendous boost to morale in the Services throughout India, in contrast to this negative, grudging criticism. The Chindits had shown that British soldiers, well-trained and well-led, could beat the Japanese in the jungle, and they destroyed the myth of the invincible Japanese jungle fighter. The effect of Operation Longcloth on the Japanese was only discovered later, and then it completely refuted the view of the Official History. From March to June, 1943, the Japanese deployed their 18th Division, the crack Chrysanthemum Division under General Mutaguchi, as well as the 33rd and 56th Division, to hunt and destroy the Chindits. Thus three excellent well supplied divisions, which should have been defending themselves from attacks from Imphal, the Arakan, Myitkyina and Yunnan, were free to pursue the Chindits. Significantly, it was the same number of divisions which were later used in the Japanese attack on Slim and the whole 14th Army at Imphal and Kohima.

Interviewed after the war, Mutaguchi, who commanded the entire 15th Japanese Army in the Imphal attack, agreed that not only had the Chindit operation completely disrupted his campaign plans for 1943, it had changed his whole assessment of Burma. The Chindit incursion showed that crack troops could operate independently in the jungle and could carry out attacks on an east-west axis. This forced him to rethink his whole strategy and made him decide to attack Imphal and Kohima in March, 1944. So much for the Official History view that the Chindit operation had no strategic value!

Calvert would not have been surprised by this view, but in the immediate aftermath of Operation Longcloth he was happy, as were all the Chindits who had returned, to struggle back to fitness and to enjoy some well-earned leave.

He was at a leave centre in Calcutta enjoying a swim when Jeffrey Lockett brought him an urgent message from Wingate. It read: "I am off to England. You will be Second-in Command of 77 Brigade as full Colonel and will probably command it. Get fit and get fat as you will have a lean, hard winter's hunting ahead of you. Orde Wingate.'

# CHAPTER SIX

# OPERATION THURSDAY

## *Preparation*

Wingate's dramatic message led Calvert into a frantic whirl of activity. At the same time he succumbed to a severe attack of malaria, but in spite of this he had to go off to Delhi, and then to organize a new training programme for what was to become his command, 77 Brigade. Three battalions, 3/6 Gurkhas, 1st King's Liverpool Regiment and 1st Lancashire Fusiliers, soon arrived at the training camp at Orchha in Central Provinces. Then, as serious Chindit training got under way, a fourth battalion arrived – the 1st South Staffordshire Regiment, which had fought at Tobruk. Calvert revelled in this new challenge of welding a team together, backed up by the confidence and prestige of his leadership in the first campaign, bolstered too by the support of some, like Bobbie Thompson who had looked after the mules and the elephant at Nankan, and who had been through that campaign with him.

While Calvert set up the training and administration for 77 Brigade, Wingate was engaged in one of the most remarkable enterprises of the war, which was to change the whole aspect of Chindit operations and Calvert's career with it.

Churchill considered Wingate a man of genius and audacity, whose actions contrasted starkly with the welter of inefficiency and lassitude which characterized most operations in India. He therefore sent for Wingate who reported to him in Downing Street on 4 August, 1943. Churchill invited him to dinner, and over the meal Wingate put forward his views on Long Range Penetration. The next day Churchill was due to leave for the Quebec Conference for discussions with Roosevelt and the Joint Chiefs of

Staff. He decided to take Wingate with him, and even had Lorna Wingate taken off the overnight Aberdeen express so that she could join her husband with Churchill's party on the *Queen Mary*.

At Quebec Wingate presented his plans to Roosevelt, Churchill and the Joint Chiefs of Staff. The Americans, influenced to some extent by Stilwell's pungent views of "Limeys", were critical of general British failure and inertia in the Far East. Since 1942 the Americans' main priority in Burma had been to drive the Japanese out of north Burma. They aimed to open the old Burma Road so that supplies of munitions and oil could be sent up to help Chiang Kai-shek raise a large army to drive the Japanese out of southern China. At the same time this would enable American bombers to have bases there in order to bomb Tokyo and mainland Japan. At Quebec, rather to their surprise, they saw an outstanding and confident British officer who had clear ideas and who seemed eager to attack and destroy the Japanese. He appeared to be the best opportunity they had to get rid of the Japanese in north Burma and to achieve their strategic aim of assisting the Chinese. This was the background to the decision by those great American leaders, General Marshall and General "Hap" Arnold, and the Chiefs of Staff to back Wingate in a way he had never contemplated.

As a result of the decision made at Quebec, Wingate was promoted to Major General and six brigades were allocated for training in Long Range Penetration. The Americans had responded to Wingate's enthusiasm and had allocated him, in addition, the support of the 1st Air Commando, a very large force of Mustangs, Mitchells, Dakotas, 100 gliders, many Sentinel light aircraft, and even some early Sikorski helicopters. This meant that instead of an exhausting plod through the jungle, the Chindit brigades could be flown to their destination.

Wingate himself was amazed at the scale of support he had received, but all too soon he was brought down to earth when Auchinleck, who had succeeded Wavell when the latter became Viceroy of India, cabled to the Chiefs of Staff that it was quite impossible to provide six brigades for Long Range Penetration. His strongest argument, and one which represented a deep gut feeling shared by most of the British army, maintained that he was not prepared to break up a tried and tested British infantry division – the 70th under Major General Symes – in order to provide extra Chindit brigades. Auchinleck offered, instead, the 81st West African Division which had recently arrived in India. Auchinleck, who to his great credit remained very supportive of the Chindits, was overruled on this issue and 70th Division was broken up to form the new enlarged Long Range Penetration Force.

At Quebec the young Mountbatten, in another clever move by Churchill, was appointed Supreme Commander of South East Asia Command, over the heads of many more senior officers who had squabbled among themselves, and many of whom remained positively unhappy at the new arrangements. It would not be far from the truth to say that the two young upstarts, Mountbatten and Wingate, obviously Churchill's protégés, were likely to face formidable opposition from phalanxes of establishment top brass when they arrived at their new commands. Wingate suffered the most, and at GHQ Delhi was faced with absolutely puerile opposition. For example, there was no staff car for him, and there was no office available, so he had initially to work in the corridor. This in a headquarters where there were over fifty brigadiers, and, as one disgruntled Chindit commander put it, "Curry colonels by the dozen". This unrelenting opposition above all affected supplies which were needed urgently for a campaign to start in January, 1944, and it was already September, 1943, when Wingate returned from Quebec. The worst of these struggles took place in Delhi, but the resulting frustrations filtered through to the training grounds where Calvert was getting his brigade to a high pitch of readiness.

Of all the Chindit leaders, Calvert was the most loyal and the most totally in tune with Wingate's ideas and concepts. This meant that 77 Brigade – Calvert was now a Brigadier aged 30 – was the doyen among the Chindit brigades and set the standards for the rest. It was, after all, Wingate's own brigade; they had shared the triumphs and disasters of the first campaign and had built their new training on the grim lessons they had learned there.

As the force prepared for a new campaign, the attitudes in the other brigades, notably 111 Brigade under Brigadier Joe Lentaigne, were very different. This brigade had transferred reluctantly from 70 Division under Symes, who set a splendid example by giving loyal support to Wingate, his junior in both rank and service. In contrast, Lentaigne and many of his officers did not take kindly to Chindit methods and were most reluctant to accept Wingate's tactical principles which had been hammered out in the harsh experience of Longcloth. Tragically, this rejection was a major factor in the disasters which later befell 111 Brigade.

The Chindit concept of independent units supplied by air and operating behind the enemy lines was a completely new form of warfare, made possible by effective wireless communication and by air domination of the battle area. Longcloth had proved this, but there now fell on the Chindits yet new demands. They had to adapt their existing training to the totally new concept of the whole unit, with all its weapons, equipment, ammunition and supplies, including the mules, being loaded on to Dakotas or gliders, and landed on rough uneven airstrips up to 200 miles behind the enemy lines. All of this, together with glider training, loading and off-loading techniques, and airfield construction, fell largely to the ever-loyal and supportive 77 Brigade under Calvert.

He and Wingate had also to work out the practical implications of yet another of Wingate's brilliant ideas – the Stronghold. Wingate had presented the idea in a typical memorandum: "Turn you to the Stronghold ye Prisoners of Hope". (Zechariah, ix, 12). The idea was clear. A Stronghold of brigade strength would be established behind the enemy lines in an area remote from main roads and railways to preclude attacks by tanks or heavy artillery. The Stronghold would have a supply of clean water with sufficient flat land for an airstrip which could take both light planes and Dakotas. These would take in supplies and fly out the wounded, the most traumatic issue of the first campaign. The Stronghold would have a garrison battalion and two troops of 25-pounder guns to form a secure base, with earthworks, minefields and barbed wire backed by detailed fire plans for the artillery, machine guns, 3-inch mortars and small arms fire. From this secure base Chindit Columns would range far and wide destroying the Japanese lines of communication, transport and supplies to all their divisions in north Burma.

Calvert and his Brigade were proud to be chosen to establish the first Stronghold and had responded eagerly to the challenge. Calvert in his book, significantly called *Prisoners of Hope*, wrote:

"This belief in Wingate's ideas and the determination to put them into effect kept us going through most of the campaign, when otherwise we might have cracked up. We were 77 Brigade, Wingate's Brigade, and we had to do our stuff."

The layman has often found the Burma Campaign to be both complex and confusing, and this is no wonder, for from September, 1943, when Wingate was given his orders for Operation Thursday, until March, 1944, when it started, his orders had changed, often week by week. Strategic decisions directly affecting the operation were made by Roosevelt, Churchill, Stalin and Chaing Kai-shek, and were not even reported to Wingate. Less than a week before the operation, the Chiefs of Staff were still dithering, and Lord Ismay, Churchill's military adviser, said, "The waffling that has gone on over our Far East strategy will be one of the black spots in the British higher direction of the war". (Ziegler, *Mountbatten*, p. 277).

In spite of this dangerous uncertainty, Wingate and the Chindits loyally adhered to the original plan for 77 Brigade to fly in and establish a Stronghold. From the Stronghold they would attack and destroy the communication to Japanese forces facing Stilwell, and also those attacking 4th Corps at Imphal and Kohima. As had been planned in 1943 (but abandoned) this operation was to be linked with major attacks by 4th Corps, by Stilwell and by Chiang Kai-shek, with the object of eliminating all Japanese forces from Burma north of a line roughly through Indaw. The military establishment have always criticised Wingate for his abrasive and aggressive demands, yet, against strong opposition he had prepared the Chindits for Operation Thursday, and they were ready by February, 1944. Then, he was once again told that none of the advances which were part of the strategic plan could take place. Almost in despair, he was rescued not by some aggressive British plan, but by a major attack of three Japanese divisions under Mutagushi on Imphal and Kohima. Mutagushi's idea for this attack had been prompted by Operation Longcloth the previous year. Wingate and Calvert saw at once that a major attack by the Japanese gave the Chindits an even better opportunity to harass and destroy the Japanese supply lines.

Operation Thursday, in which 77 Brigade played a leading rôle, had wide strategic implications. On 10 February, 1944, 16 Brigade under Brigadier Bernard Fergusson, who had commanded a Column in 1943, had started an epic march from Ledo at the Assam railhead where they had some initial support from Stilwell's forces. 16 Brigade aimed to march south, set up a Stronghold, codename Aberdeen, and to make a swift attack on Indaw. The main spearhead of Operation Thursday was the fly-in of 77 Brigade (Calvert) and 111 Brigade (Lentaigne) to three landing grounds, codenamed Broadway, Piccadilly and Chowringhee. Lentaigne was to take 111 Brigade into Chowringhee and to block the road and railway coming up from the south so that the Japanese could not send reinforcements to attack 77 Brigade at Broadway. Two further brigades, 14th and 3rd West African, were ready and prepared to follow up the initial fly-in.

By the beginning of March, 1944, when 16 Brigade had already been on the march for three weeks, all was ready for the main launch of Operation Thursday, the biggest allied air operation which had ever taken place. 77 Brigade, which led the operation and needed a very swift build-up of forces, was due to fly to Broadway and Piccadilly. The two brigades, 77 and 111 trained, equipped and ready for action, were concentrated at Tulihal and Lalaghat airfields near Imphal.

The launch was planned for 1700 hours on Sunday, 5 March, 1944. The significance of the occasion was illustrated by the presence at Lalaghat airfield of a large number of British and American senior commanders: General Sir William Slim, GOC 14th Army, Air Marshal Sir John Baldwin, Commander of the 3rd Tactical Airforce, General Stratemeyer and General Old, USAAF, together with many high-ranking officers and war correspondents. Security had been very tight, but there was some concern since the Japanese had shown that they knew considerable detail about Fergusson's march; they even named him in a radio broadcast the day after he had started. There was also the danger that information might have leaked out from the lax and inefficient Chinese headquarters. Wingate had even banned all recce flights over the area for three weeks so that the Japanese could not possibly be alerted.

On that sunny Sunday afternoon, months of training and preparation came to a climax. The close-knit team of Wingate and Calvert, working in harmony with Colonel Alison and Colonel

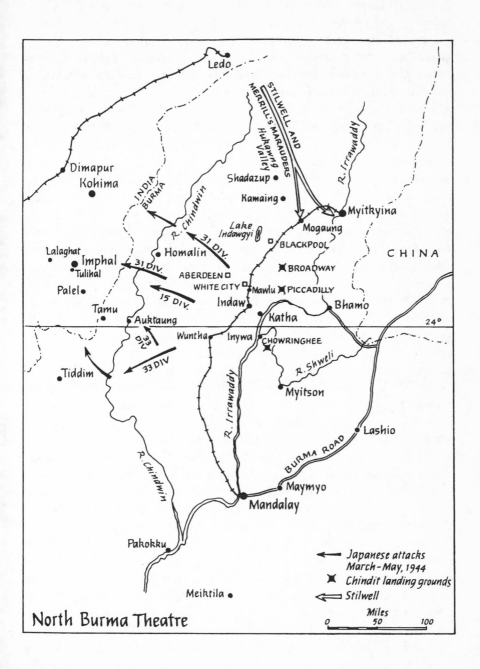

Ledo

Dimapur
Kohima

Shadazup
Kamaing

STILWELL AND
MERRILL'S MARAUDERS
Hukawng Valley

R. Irrawaddy

Myitkyina

INDIA
BURMA

R. Chindwin

Lake
Indawgyi

31 DIV.

Mogaung

BLACKPOOL

CHINA

Lalaghat
Imphal
Tulihal
Palel

Homalin

31 DIV.

ABERDEEN

BROADWAY

WHITE CITY
Mawlu
PICCADILLY

15 DIV.

Indaw

Bhamo

24°

Tamu

Auktaung

33 DIV.

Wuntha

Inywa

Katha

CHOWRINGHEE

R. Shweli

Tiddim

33 DIV

Myitson

R. Irrawaddy

Lashio

BURMA ROAD

R. Chindwin

Maymyo

Mandalay

Pakokku

⟵ Japanese attacks
March–May, 1944
✷ Chindit landing grounds
⟸ Stilwell

Meiktila

Miles
0    50    100

North Burma Theatre

Cochran, brilliant American pilots in charge of the Air Commando, had built a tremendous feeling of confidence. Although there was the usual atmosphere of tense excitement which precedes any major attack, the Chindits sat calmly in the shadow under the wings of the Dakotas and gliders, with the tow ropes carefully laid out and fastened.

Less than an hour before the start, a Sentinel light aircraft of the Air Commando landed and the pilot, Major Russhon, hurried over to Cochran. He handed over photographs taken two hours earlier which showed that the landing strip at Piccadilly was blocked by teak tree trunks. At first Wingate reacted angrily because his order had been disobeyed, but he quickly realized that this information had prevented a certain catastrophe and he apologized to Cochran for his outburst. The immediate tension in the command group can easily be imagined. The most urgent question concerned a possible security leak and whether the Japanese forces would be waiting to ambush the landing at Piccadilly, or perhaps at the other two as well. Did this information mean that the entire operation should be called off? Wingate and Calvert realized that their critics back in Delhi would relish a débâcle and would rejoice if the whole LRP concept was abandoned. From another point of view, it could be argued that the tree trunks on Piccadilly were just part of routine precautions, or that there was a totally innocent explanation. All these issues had to be considered in moments, because a decision had to be made which could cost the lives of thousands of men. All the senior commanders present have described these events: Slim, Baldwin, Calvert, Cochran, Alison, Tulloch and Scott. Six of them tally in almost every detail. Only Slim's account differed from the rest and was fiercely critical of Wingate. The others paint a picture of immediate and urgent discussion, weighing most heavily on Wingate. Scott wrote that if he ever saw real greatness in a human being it was in Wingate at that moment. He had to consider whether his decision would put the lives of both brigades of Chindits into immediate jeopardy. He had always led the Chindits into battle and now he had to decide to send them on a highly dangerous mission which he was not to lead. It was decided that the operation should go ahead, but swift changes had to be made since Piccadilly could not be used. Wingate had to make grave decisions, but so too did Calvert who showed bravery of the highest order. After hurried consultation with Wingate and Cochran, Calvert agreed that 77 Brigade would fly in, provided that the entire brigade went into Broadway. The best description of these momentous minutes came from Scott (Lieutenant-Colonel Scott, commanding the 1st King's Liverpool Regiment) who was to fly in the leading glider. He described how Slim, Wingate, Baldwin and the American commanders briefly conferred, then, "Wingate turned away, with his head bent and his hands clasped behind his back: he looked a forlorn and lonely figure. After going about 30 yards, he turned and called Brigadier Calvert. They talked, then walked to where the Allied Commanders were standing. A brief vital conference took place, after which General Wingate and Brigadier Calvert returned to me, and I received fresh orders which were so clear and so concise that it was hard to realize that 'Piccadilly' had ever existed."

As soon as he had agreed to fly in, Calvert had to make other urgent decisions. Most of the flight plans had to be changed and some gliders reloaded. He was helped by the relaxed confidence of Cochran who went back to his pilots and said, "Hey, you guys, we've got a better place to fly to". Later Calvert wrote, "We knew we had to go. We could never again be keyed up to such a pitch, morally, physically or materially." (*Prisoners of Hope*) The first Dakota took off one hour and twelve minutes behind schedule.

The weather and the phase of the moon played a large part in the timing of Operation Thursday. After Sunday 5 March there were five nights of good moonlight during which three brigades – 12,000 men, 2,000 mules and all their guns and equipment – would have to be landed. Ironically, as the Chindit aircraft took off and thundered eastwards, the Japanese division which was about to attack Kohima was waiting by the Chindwin. A young Japanese platoon commander crouching by the river heard the sounds of the huge air armada and was filled with foreboding.

# Broadway

The success of the operation now depended above all on Calvert and his colleagues in 77 Brigade. Scott and Alison and their advance parties were in the first four gliders. Calvert flew in the fifth glider, and the remaining aircraft of the first launch carried men of the King's Regiment, the Lancashire Fusiliers and the South Stafford Regiment.

When the Dakotas took off from Lalaghat towing two gliders, they had to climb quickly and clear mountains of over 7,000 feet before locating the exact position of Broadway. It was fairly familiar territory for Calvert who had crossed the Chindwin and the Irrawaddy several times and was now returning to wreak vengeance on the Japanese. As the gliders approached Broadway, no one knew whether the Japanese would be waiting for them. When Calvert's glider crashed to a halt, an NCO was injured, but the majority were able to leap out, take up defensive positions and prepare the strip for aircraft coming in.

There were no Japanese. Indeed, it was discovered later that the tree trunks on Piccadilly were the perfectly normal way in which the local farmers dried out their logs, but there was great danger. The air photographs which they had studied so carefully had not revealed several deep ditches running across the strip, nor two fairly substantial trees. These unexpected hazards had wrecked some of the earliest gliders. By the time Calvert landed the most urgent task was to put out petroleum flares to guide the remaining gliders. To their horror, before this was completed, they saw and heard more gliders approaching. There was no way of stopping them, and soon the gliders were coming down and crashing into wrecked gliders already on the strip. Some pilots, when they saw the wreckage, did try to make a second turn, but of these several crashed into the jungle. The Chindits on the ground worked frantically to succour the wounded, to set up a first-aid dressing station, to remove the crashed gliders and to rescue those trapped inside, the whole ghastly scene lit by the burning flares and rent by the screams and cries of the wounded. This scene has been immortalized in the painting "Chindits – Broadway" by

David Rowlands which is in the possession of the 1st Battalion, The King's Regiment.

Before he left, Calvert had arranged a signal with Wingate's Headquarters: "Pork Sausage" if things were going well and could continue, or "Soya Link" (a hated element of their rations) if things had gone badly and should be stopped. As he surveyed the disastrous scene, made more macabre by the smoke and flames of the flares and by the continuing cries of the wounded, at 0400 hours on 6 March, his 31st birthday, he signalled "Soya Link". Even after this, two more gliders came in, but they landed safely. Assuming that no more gliders would arrive, Calvert tried to grab some sleep, but was awoken by the arrival of thirty Lancashire Fusiliers. Their glider had missed the strip but had landed safely in the jungle. Then, to his amazement he heard the sound of an engine and a small bulldozer drove on to the strip. This vehicle had been in a glider which crashed into trees off the strip but in the impact the crew had been flung aside and the bulldozer had catapulted through the front and had landed safely and relatively undamaged in thick brushwood. This happy accident virtually saved the operation, for, with the bulldozer working and with the help of every available man, the Americans assured Calvert that they would have a Dakota landing strip ready by that evening. He found this hard to believe, but, reassured by Alison, he signalled "Pork Sausage", to the great delight of Wingate, Slim and Tulloch who had waited in tense anticipation in the command tent during the night. A later assessment showed that fifty-four gliders had taken off, thirty-seven had landed at Broadway, six landed in Japanese territory, and eleven landed behind our own lines. On the ground at Broadway thirty men had been killed and twenty-one wounded.

During the first day most of the Chindits worked under Alison and the American engineers to clear the strip. Calvert had to recce for his actual Stronghold site. Others had to search for survivors in nearby gliders and occasionally to arrange a funeral pyre. A comforting aspect of that first day was the arrival of the Sentinel light planes. Their indomitable pilots flew their unarmed aircraft across 400 miles of enemy territory in order to take out the wounded.

That night sixty-four Dakotas landed and took off. Air Marshal Baldwin, who flew in, later wrote, "Nobody has seen a transport operation until he has stood on that jungle runway under the light of a Burma full moon, and watched Dakotas coming in and taking off in different directions on a single strip all night long, at the rate of one landing and one taking off every three minutes." Baldwin remained a steadfast supporter of the Chindits, and strongly countered the disgraceful denigration propounded by Kirby in the Official History. The system which Baldwin saw and praised worked so well that within a few days all the men, mules and equipment had been safely landed.

The complete absence of enemy interference certainly helped the swift establishment of the Stronghold at Broadway. Trenches were dug, barbed wire erected, minefields laid, fields of fire established for 25-pounders, 3-inch mortars, machine guns and small arms fire, and a field hospital established. The Burma Rifles quickly established rapport with the local people and offered medical help and barter facilities. Many a Burmese girl had a new dress or nightie from torn parachute silk. The signals centre, so crucial to the whole operation, was linked to the powerful Chindit Station in India which could pick up weak signals and relay them when necessary. The Stronghold had to be powerfully defended, and from the second day the 3/6th Gurkhas became the garrison battalion, but its main role was offensive, and from the start Calvert despatched floater columns in an attacking role. The King's, the Lancashire Fusiliers and South Staffords in floater Columns ranged east, west and south to dominate the whole area. One Column went south to the Irrawaddy, established a mock gun emplacement and ensured that no craft could move up or down river without their permission.

To the delight of the Chindits, on 7 March, when all this preparatory work was at its height, Wingate flew in to see them. His visit gave them a great boost, and it was deeply satisfying for him to see his concept of the Stronghold work so well in practice. Calvert heard the news that he had been awarded a second DSO for his outstanding bravery and leadership at the launch of Operation Thursday. The new Chindit expedition had received much publicity, and the press, which, after Operation Longcloth, had dubbed Calvert "Mad Mike", were now able to follow his exploits again. The nickname "Mad Mike" has been widely misunderstood. Writing in 1951, his friend Peter Fleming who had shared in several wild escapades, stated that "Mad" was an inaccurate description of an unusually imaginative and vigorous fighting commander. His keen sense of humour might have earned him an aura of lunacy, but "If in moments of peril he had not so often giggled, he might not live in the popular imagination as a sort of hare-brained tiger". More recently the distinguished author George Macdonald Fraser, in *Quartered Safe Out Here*, who served in the Border Regiment in Burma and witnessed men under the stress of battle, made a percipient comment which could have been tailor-made for Calvert. Describing the Border Battalion he wrote, "They belonged to a culture in which 'windy' is the ultimate insult, and in which the synonym for 'brave' is 'mad', and that is all there is to be said about it."

## White City

The first priority of Operation Thursday had always been to block the main road and railway system which went through Indaw and Mawlu and up to Mogaung and Myitkyina, and which was the main supply route for the Japanese 18 Division and 56 Division facing Stilwell. While 77 Brigade had the chief rôle, the second part of the plan involved 111 Brigade which had flown in to Chowringhee and had the task of blocking the road and railway south of Indaw.

After the fly-in, Lentaigne, following Wingate's plan, sent off two independent Columns made up of 4/9th Gurkhas, known as Morris Force, to move eastwards towards Bhamo, and then march north and block the main Japanese supply road from Bhamo to Myitkyina. These columns achieved considerable success due largely to the inspiring leadership of Major Peter Cane who commanded 94 Column, and the road was blocked for several months. Morris Force was supported by another small unit called Dah Force which operated in roughly the same area and tried without much success to encourage the brave Kachin people to rise up against the Japanese. After Wingate's death Dah Force was withdrawn and the Kachins were left to the mercy of the Japanese.

The Stronghold at Broadway was quickly established, with 3/ 9th Gurkhas as the garrison battalion and with all the defensive and co-ordinating arrangements under Calvert's second-in-command, Colonel Claud Rome. By 8 March, with the airstrips in constant use, and with floater Columns operating successfully around the base, Calvert was ready to undertake the next aggressive part of the plan.

Under his personal command, he led a substantial force, made up of the South Staffords, 3/6 Gurkhas and the Lancashire Fusiliers, and moved westwards from Broadway to set up a block on the road and railway in the area of Mawlu. This force, which operated as classic Chindit Columns but under the control of Calvert's HQ, set off on 8 March. Two Columns attacked roads, bridges and the railway north of Mawlu, notably at Kadu, while another attacked Pinwe south of Mawlu. Calvert and the main force moved closer to Mawlu and, having seen the ground, he decided to establish the block at the small village of Henu, about one mile north of Mawlu, where the road and railway ran close together. This block, which had a different tactical role from the Stronghold, was intended to be fairly permanent and to be strong enough to prevent Japanese forces from moving northwards until such time as Stilwell had defeated 18 Division.

It took eight days of hard slogging through difficult jungle, and over a range of hills which rose to 4000 feet, for the main force to reach the Mawlu area. It has never been fully explained why the Broadway site was chosen when it lay at such a great distance from the main action at Mawlu. Surely there must have been a possible site in the hills immediately to the east of Mawlu, which would have cut out the exhausting week-long slog through the jungle, while meeting all the criteria of the Stronghold.

As Calvert approached Mawlu he appreciated the opportunity he had had some weeks before, when he had been able to recce the area in a Mitchell bomber of the Air Commando. The pilot had flown over the site of Broadway, had flown up the railway past Mawlu, and he had even allowed Calvert to bomb a few targets and handle the 75mm guns. Calvert thought that the real value of such a recce was to enable the commander on the ground to appreciate what was feasible in the air and not to make absurd requests.

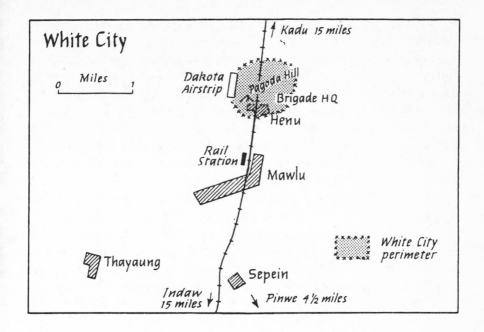

White City

Kadu 15 miles

Miles
0      1

Dakota
Airstrip

Pagoda Hill

Brigade HQ

Henu

Rail
Station

Mawlu

White City
perimeter

Thayaung

Sepein

Indaw
15 miles

Pinwe 4½ miles

He chose the site for the "block" immediately to the north of Henu village where, to the east of the railway, lay a ridge of low hills, and to the west fairly flat paddy fields. The South Staffords and Gurkha Columns reached the railway first and signalled for a drop of barbed wire, ammunition and food, but when it came it landed too far away to be used. They started to dig in, but before they were ready the Japanese attacked and infiltrated between the two Columns. Calvert, with his HQ Company, led by Ian Macpherson, whom he admired tremendously, heard the noise of this early skirmish and approached as rapidly as possible. He called the Columns by wireless and reached them quickly. They had had a fierce fight and sustained casualties. The Japanese held Pagoda Hill immediately west of the railway. Calvert rapidly assessed the situation and saw that urgent action was needed. After issuing brief orders, he shouted "Charge!" Some charged, but some hung back until a second mighty bellow got them moving and the whole body rushed towards Pagoda Hill. There, in Calvert's words, "At the top of the hill, about 50 yards square, an extraordinary mêlée took place. Everyone shouting, bayoneting, kicking at everyone else, rather like an officers' guest night!" The Japanese were driven off the top of the hill and kept at bay by a hail of grenades. After a brief lull the Chindits charged again and drove the Japanese off the hill and back into the village. Following up as quickly as possible, the South Staffords and Gurkhas, using kukris, Bren guns, rifles, bayonets and portable flame throwers, drove out the remaining Japanese. The Gurkhas took over Pagoda Hill while the wounded were tended and the dead counted. The cost was heavy. The Chindits sustained twenty-three killed including three officers. Lieutenant Cairns of the South Staffords had his arm cut off by a Japanese officer during the mêlée, but continued fighting. He killed his opponent and led his men on. Later, he received a posthumous VC. Others won MCs and DCMs. This first real fight, ending with victory over the Japanese no longer the fabled supermen, set a fine example for the Brigade in the many actions which followed.

After the fight on Pagoda Hill, more wire and entrenching tools were dropped and the base was soon secure. It lay across low hills and had water at each end. One slightly higher hill was used as an observation post. By 19 March the defences were complete, the HQ was established inside the block and Calvert called for Mustang attacks on the Japanese in Mawlu. At the same time Columns of the Lancashire Fusiliers had established blocks on the Irrawaddy and at Pinwe further down just to the east of the railway line. During the next few days, while the block defences were strengthened, stores of water, food and ammunition put in place and fire plans completed, the Japanese made a number of probing attacks. These were easily repulsed and, by 21 March, strips for light planes and for Dakotas had been cleared and the wounded flown out. However, there were still signs of a probable major Japanese attack. To counter this the block had eight 3-inch mortars and eleven Vickers machine guns; they were also able to call up Air Commando Mustangs and RAF Vengeances at short notice. The block received such excellent support and such massive supplies, much of it by parachute, that it was soon named "White City", because of the parachutes festooning the trees.

The Japanese attacked on 21 March. Their techniques included shouting in English: "OK Johnnie", "Cease Fire", "Stand down now", or on other occasions crude abuse: "We'll kill you, you hairy bastards". This had little effect. The attack fell on the perimeter held by the South Staffords and did make some headway. The Chindits counterattacked at dawn and drove out the intruders, killing or capturing them all. The enemy was driven across the barbed-wire defences and finished off by the floater company from outside. The Chindits suffered from Japanese lying doggo, so the Gurkhas were sent in to clear the area, largely by using their kukris. They killed eleven. One Japanese officer was captured and the Japanese-speaking Intelligence Officer gained valuable information from interrogation. This Intelligence Officer also went forward during the night and discovered from Japanese chatter that they had lost all their officers and were unsure whether to continue their attack.

In this action the Chindits lost thirty-four killed, including six officers and forty-five wounded, including seven officers. The enemy had sustained even higher casualties and these were identified as coming from five companies, mostly from 18 Division. The Japanese officer gave the valuable information that their unit had been resting in Mandalay and had been rushed up to deal with what they thought were a few hundred intruders. Valuable documents were sent back to Force HQ, but Calvert suspected that many were kept as souvenirs by the pilots.

He was well pleased with the Chindit performance. The 3-inch mortars, the flamethrowers and the booby traps had all been excellent. As he said, they could not afford to be genteel. The co-ordinated fire plans and the telephone links had worked well, though the barbed-wire fences had proved inadequate and were quickly improved. All of these issues were addressed in lulls in the fighting over the next three days, 23 to 27 March. At the same time the Chindits kept the initiative by active patrolling, by attacking roads, railways and bridges in and around Mawlu, and by calling down air-strikes by Mustangs and Vengeances on enemy positions that could easily be identified.

On 24 March, 1944, Wingate flew into White City. He commended them all for their outstanding achievements and passed on a request from Stilwell that they should not destroy too much of the railway as he would like to use it later! Wingate also gave Calvert details of the attack which three Japanese divisions were currently making on Imphal and Kohima. The Chindits were now being criticized for being too far away from 4th Corps positions at Imphal, a view which failed to understand that the first priority of the Chindit operation had always been to assist Stilwell, not 4th Corps. While Mutaguchi was attacking with three divisions, Slim had three and a half divisions, including armour, with five more divisions coming to help, making almost nine in all. Both Wingate and Calvert felt that one of those divisions might have been better employed by flying into Indaw to exploit the success of the Chindit attack and to destroy the retreating Japanese divisions. Calvert still argued that they should not be diverted to help 4th Corps, which heavily outnumbered the Japanese attackers, but keep to their original plan and purpose. Wingate, as usual, visited every part of their position giving people a pat on the back and making helpful suggestions. When he left Calvert to fly on to Broadway, he said, "I will see you lack for nothing." He flew off. Later that night, 24 March 1944, he was killed when his aircraft crashed into the hills near Imphal. This dire news did not reach the Chindits until they had attacked and captured Mawlu.

Feeling confident that Broadway and White City were well-established and well-defended, and that he had completed his mission to block the road and rail link going up to Mogaung, Calvert decided to go on the offensive and clear the Japanese from Mawlu. He planned to send two strong patrols of Lancashire Fusiliers to skirt round the town and to prepare an ambush south of the town, while the 3/6th Gurkhas attacked the town from the north and drove the enemy into the ambush. On the evening of 26 March the Lancashire Fusiliers moved off to set up their ambush and at dawn the following morning the Gurkhas put in a spirited attack. Calvert, with his HQ Company closely followed the Gurkhas who through chaotic noise and smoke stormed into Mawlu firing their weapons, hurling grenades, wielding their kukris and using their flame throwers with deadly effect. A visiting staff officer witnessed the attack and wrote, "The Japanese broke ... they ran ... they abandoned everything – dead, documents, equipment, weapons." Unfortunately the two Lancashire Fusilier patrols had encountered difficulties and did not reach their ambush positions in time to inflict further casualties on the fleeing enemy. Even so, the defeat was decisive and the Japanese fighting troops of 113 and 114 Regiments (the equivalent of two brigades) and all the administrative staff from a large Records

Centre fled from the town. Their panic was so great that in their flight they took with them the units from Sepein and fled south as far as Indaw, 25 miles away. The records and other booty captured at Mawlu were valuable and were sent off to Force HQ. This admirable attack on the first town to be won back from the Japanese was achieved with relatively few casualties, seven killed and forty injured, and it gave a great boost to the confidence of the Brigade.

Clearly the Japanese could not accept the situation the Chindits had created and an attack on Broadway or White City was expected, but in the meantime Calvert worked hard to establish good relations with the local people. He rode round a wide area on his white pony Jean to give an impression of calm and security and to back up the good work of the intelligence gathering by the Burma Rifle units. He even called on the Headman of Mawlu and paid him 1500 rupees for the damage that had been caused in the attack.

While Calvert had established control over the area around White City, the Stronghold at Broadway had been further strengthened. It had suffered attacks by Japanese Zeros but these had been effectively defeated by the Bofors anti-aircraft guns of the garrison, and at one stage by a flight of Spitfires, though these were later withdrawn. On 27 March Colonel Rome received warning of the approach of a Japanese battalion which had been withdrawn from 56 Division in Yunnan. He received accurate information about the enemy from the King's Regiment floater Columns patrolling outside Broadway, and he confidently awaited the attack. It came at midnight on 27 March and initially involved a company of 3/9th Gurkhas holding the area around the airstrip. This turned into a fierce fight in which the Gurkhas sustained over fifty casualties, and the Japanese even more. During the next three days the Japanese mounted a series of attacks in which 3/9th Gurkhas, as well as the King's Regiment, were heavily involved, but at no time was the Stronghold in danger of being overwhelmed. Sometimes there was poor co-ordination between the perimeter defences and the floater Columns outside, and Calvert, who was loath to criticize his commanders, did comment that the Commander of one Column had tried to control his Column from behind, which "was quite hopeless". He then added a dictum which could apply to every commander in action and which he certainly carried out himself: "A commander must place himself where he himself can influence the battle at short notice; otherwise he is nothing but a military commentator." By 31 March the Chindit forces, with air support, had driven off the Japanese attackers and the concept of the Stronghold had been successfully proven.

## Death of Wingate

Calvert heard the news of Wingate's death on 27 March, and made his well-known comment, "Who will look after us now?" This has been widely misinterpreted as a cry for help, which it was not. Calvert knew the vicious in-fighting carried on by the military establishment against Wingate and the Chindits and he realized that only Wingate with his powerful personality and high-level contacts could continue to fight their corner successfully. So, with dread and apprehension, this fell news spread among the Chindits.

The appointment of Wingate's successor was a highly complex matter, involving many different characters, and it was to have a dire effect on Calvert's future. At Force Headquarters near Imphal, Derek Tulloch, the Brigadier General Staff, who controlled the day-to-day running of Operation Thursday, was Wingate's loyal and trusted friend. When Wingate was killed, Slim, who was facing the major Japanese attack on Imphal and Kohima, asked his advice about a successor. Tulloch, whom Wingate had appointed immediately after the Quebec Conference, had never commanded a Chindit unit in action, and he therefore ruled himself out. Who was he to recommend to Slim?

To the surprise of most of the Chindits, he chose Brigadier Joe Lentaigne who was then commanding 111 Brigade in the area of Chowringhee. Lentaigne had led a Gurkha unit in the 1942 retreat with bravery and distinction, but later, in 1943, 111 Brigade had been part of 70 Division which had been broken up to become Chindit units. Lentaigne and his staff, including John Masters, the novelist, did not accept Wingate's ideas or his methods, and there was deep antipathy between them. Tulloch must have known this when he recommended Lentaigne. He did not know that, after about a week behind the Japanese lines after landing at Chowringhee, although Lentaigne had only a small fraction of his brigade under his direct command, and although he had not been in contact with the Japanese at all, his nerve had completely broken. Masters, his Brigade Major, was in the extraordinary position of trying to get a signal out to Wingate that Lentaigne should be taken out and relieved of his command when he received the signal appointing Lentaigne to command the whole Chindit operation.

Tulloch's decision, which he deeply regretted for the rest of his life, is quite inexplicable. One possible reason is that he knew Slim liked former Gurkha officers to command his major units. In recommending Lentaigne, Tulloch also made another blunder. General Symes had commanded the 70th Division before it was transferred to Chindit training and he had shown admirable restraint and leadership as Deputy Commander to Wingate, who was his junior in every way. When Wingate was killed, Symes naturally concluded that he would succeed him, and when he heard that Lentaigne had been appointed, he was naturally furious and asked to be relieved of his post.

To most of the Chindits there was one person who was fitted in every way to be Wingate's successor, who was totally imbued with every aspect of Wingate's philosophy and who in both campaigns had proved himself to be the outstanding commander in action. This was Brigadier Michael Calvert. The Chindits knew him as the tough fighting commander. But his reputation as "Mad Mike" probably did not help at that moment and, as a newly appointed brigadier aged only thirty-one, he was possibly considered far too young to take command. On the other hand, he was a Cambridge graduate and had very wide experience of warfare within the parameters of Chindit operations.

Instead of commanding the Chindits, Calvert now had the unenviable task of commanding 77 Brigade under the direction of Lentaigne, whom he knew did not accept Wingate's principles of warfare, which were a matter of life and death in Chindit operations.

While Calvert and 77 Brigade had been establishing Broadway and White City, Fergusson and 16 Brigade, after their long march, had failed in their attack on Indaw, but had established the Stronghold "Aberdeen" to the north. Aberdeen was then chosen as the venue for a conference of all Chindit Brigade Commanders which the newly appointed Lentaigne called for 3 April, 1944. In addition to Calvert and Fergusson, who acted as host, the conference included Brigadier Brodie commanding 14 Brigade, Brigadier Gilmour commanding 3rd West Africa Brigade as well as Peter Fleming and Squadron Leader Bobbie Thompson.

At this time, in addition to 77 Brigade at Broadway and White City, 111 Brigade at Chowringhee and 16 Brigade at Aberdeen, 14 Brigade had flown in on 24 March. It had carried out classic Chindit attacks on Japanese stores and lines of communication over a wide area both south and west of Aberdeen. The 3rd West African Brigade was also about to fly in while the conference was taking place.

At the conference the difference in the atmosphere was immediate and obvious. No longer the sharp, confident and inspiring tones of Wingate, but the tentative and diffident approach of Lentaigne who must have realized that some conference members knew of his breakdown at Chowringhee. He also had to tread warily because he was known to have rejected many of Wingate's principles, and Fergusson and Calvert at least would be alert to this. Lentaigne explained the critical situation at Kohima where the Japanese had nearly broken through and he added that he was under great pressure to divert Chindit forces to assist in that area. He stressed that he had called this conference to hear the views of the Chindit leaders and to formulate a plan to present to Slim. Calvert argued strongly that Broadway and White City, which had been set up at such high cost in lives and materials, should be held. It should be garrisoned by the 3rd West African Brigade which was just arriving, while 77 Brigade drove north up the axis of the railway to meet up with Stilwell before the monsoon arrived in the middle of May. His views were in accordance with the priorities of the original Quebec Plan, and were certainly in line with what Stilwell was demanding.

Any tentative plans made at Aberdeen were immediately changed when, on the day after the conference, 4 April, patrols from White City made contact with a new and formidable Japanese force near Sepein. This was 24 Independent Mixed Brigade, a powerful force of six infantry battalions supported by medium and heavy artillery and heavy mortars which had been withdrawn from other areas. They had been ordered by Mutaguchi to annihilate the Chindit forces.

By 5 April enemy forces were approaching White City in strength and Calvert had a tricky situation to handle. A Dakota strip was just being completed and Bofors guns and 25-pounder guns were being flown in. He was desperate to get these guns into the block before the main enemy attack took place, but the pilots were alarmed at the volume of firing over and around the strip. Calvert had to stand nonchalantly by, trying to assure them that this was quite normal and nothing to worry about, while twenty-five Dakotas flew in and were hurriedly unloaded. He was amused at how frightened the pilots were when they were on the ground, but admitted that, when he was in an aircraft, "his bowels turned to water".

This was the start of a prolonged assault on White City, and was unique because it was taking place over 100 miles behind enemy lines. Within the Chindits, Calvert was notorious for insisting on the constant digging of trenches and the provision and renewal of overhead cover. This now paid off, for most of the defensive positions were strongly and effectively protected against anything except a direct hit. The Japanese had 77mm and 105mm guns, but their most dangerous and unnerving weapon was the 6-inch mortar which fired a projectile 6 inches in diameter, 60 inches long, and took 32 seconds to arrive.

The first major attack on White City happened on 6 April and was repeated with little variation every day until 17 April. After a preliminary bombardment, the attack usually started at dusk with wild cries, shrieks and clamour. The defences were well prepared, and most nights put down a barrage of about 500 3-inch mortar bombs as the Japanese assembled for the attack. As soon as the attackers reached the edge of the barbed-wire defences they were lit up and illuminated by flares from 2-inch mortars and then they were slaughtered by Vickers and Bren machine-gun fire, and by rifles and 36 grenades. By midnight the attacks would die down, but the bombardment would resume after a couple of hours while the enemy tried to take out their dead and wounded. Calvert found that the telephone lines, carefully laid well underground, were crucial to the defence of the whole perimeter. Even with the Japanese attacks going on through the night, supply drops continued and light planes landed and took out the wounded. At dawn the Chindit defenders went out to retrieve documents from the enemy dead who often had been killed by mines and booby traps as they approached the wire. Each day mines were relaid and booby traps reset. Calvert soon noticed that the pattern of attack hardly varied, and he also had the advantage that his Japanese-speaking Intelligence Officer had been wired in to the enemy telephone system, and they knew when and where an attack was planned. Very occasionally the Japanese attempted a daytime attack, but these were usually countered by the ever-vigilant Mustangs. On one occasion a couple of tanks approached, but they were badly handled and caused no serious difficulty.

Calvert described the White City siege in almost casual terms, but clearly the prolonged bombardment wore down the defenders' nerves, and even such a robust warrior as he admitted that during brief periods of rest he would lie in his trench and give way to uncontrollable fits of shivering. He hated being cooped up, feeling he could not retaliate, but, with the constant supply drops, the defences gradually reduced the Japanese bombardment.

As the enemy attack dragged on, the conditions around the perimeter became appalling. Over 1000 Japanese bodies were decomposing in the damp heat and lying just outside the wire, others were hanging, grisly and macabre, on the wire itself. Everywhere and everything was permeated by the stench of decomposing bodies and dead animals, and putrefaction began to threaten the water supply. The ever-resourceful supply planes flew in quicklime but this achieved little. Even the use of flame throwers did not solve the problem. Within the perimeter, despite the carnage, Calvert was proud that all Chindit casualties were buried in ground consecrated by their own padres. One Sentinel pilot said that he was able to navigate by smell for he could always smell when he was close to White City!

While the siege of White City continued, the floating Columns of the King's, the Lancashire Fusiliers, the Leicesters (briefly detached from 16 Brigade at Aberdeen) and the Nigerian Regiment carried out attacks on Mawlu, on the Indaw Road, and along the railway both north and south of the town. By 12 April the White City defences had shown that they could withstand any attack the Japanese put in and orders came from Lentaigne at Force HQ that Calvert should fly out and lead an assault on Sepein. This was the base of the

Japanese HQ which controlled the entire operation against White City. On that day Calvert flew out to conduct an aerial recce and then made his plan. For the attack on Sepein he had available Columns from 3/6th Gurkhas, the South Staffords, the Lancashire Fusiliers, 45 Reconnaissance Regiment (also detached from 16 Brigade), and 7th Nigerian Regiment under Lieutenant-Colonel Vaughan: a total of 2,500 men.

The operation started on 17 April with a dawn attack on Sepein by 3/6th Gurkhas assisted by 25-pounder guns from inside White City. Initially the Gurkhas advanced steadily through Sepein, but then discovered that the main Japanese position lay outside the village and was located in particularly thick scrub. This thick jungle growth was almost impenetrable and it was impossible to charge through it. The Gurkhas were completely bogged down and Calvert had to change his plan. He consolidated his forces at Thayaung. There had been confused fighting by all the Chindit units throughout the area. For example, the Nigerians, in a spirited attack, had taken Mawlu and were able to send back their wounded to White City by rail. By the end of the first day the main Chindit force had sustained fifty casualties, including sixteen killed.

At this critical stage of the battle Calvert received an urgent signal from Gilmour who had been left in charge at White City. It said that the Japanese had forced the perimeter in their night attack and that he could not hold out much longer. Later it was discovered that other senior officers in the garrison knew nothing of this message and it appeared to be an example of a local commander losing his nerve. In fact the Nigerian battalion in the garrison had put in a strong counter-attack and had completely destroyed the Japanese intruders. Calvert did not know all this at that time and he decided that he would have to advance as quickly as possible towards White City with the major part of his force in order to relieve the pressure. He therefore made a new plan that, when the Japanese next attacked White City, he would attack them from the rear with all his force, while, from within, the Nigerians would make an aggressive foray and the enemy would be squeezed from both directions.

The Japanese force numbered about 2,000 and, when the Chindits attacked, there was a costly and confused fight, involving hand-to-hand combat using bayonets, kukris and grenades. The two sides were grappling so closely in the jungle that artillery and mortars were of little use. The Japanese were well- disciplined and well-led, and they turned on Calvert's force and put up such a determined attack that his HQ was nearly overwhelmed.

He had the unnerving experience, as he huddled in a shallow trench, of watching a stream of bullets hit an unfortunate mule which was standing up. Little spurts of blood came from its side before it collapsed beside him. In the middle of the battle a slight gap emerged between the rival forces and Calvert was able to call up a squadron of Mustangs. He asked them for particularly accurate bombing and cannon fire because the Japanese were only about 100 yards away. The Mustangs responded and, by diving almost vertically, were able to bomb the enemy position. Confusion and vicious close-quarter fighting still continued, but the Mustang attack did finally break the will of the Japanese. The momentum of the battle changed and slowly the Japanese began to pull out. Sadly, the Chindits had lost so many men and were so exhausted by the prolonged fighting that they were unable to follow up this advantage.

As the fighting had neared its climax, Calvert was told that Ian MacPherson, who commanded the Defence Platoon, had been killed. Calvert considered him to be the finest soldier and the finest human being he had ever met. Throughout the campaign, wherever there was trouble, Ian MacPherson had dealt with it. Under the intense stress of battle, with carnage and death all round him, the news of Ian's death nearly broke Calvert. He could not believe it. He said that he must go back into the battle area and check for himself. His Brigade Major, Francis Stuart, realizing the mental and emotional turmoil Calvert was suffering and realizing the intensely close relationship Calvert had had with Macpherson, took out his revolver and said, "If you go back, then I will shoot you". This stark warning was sufficient and Calvert regained his self-control.

For some considerable time the Chindits did not realize that the Mustang attack had finally broken the Japanese advance and, after weighing up their heavy casualties and their exhausted state, Calvert gave the order that they should rendezvous at Thayaung where the Nigerians were waiting. They made pitifully slow progress because so many wounded had to be carried on make-shift bamboo stretchers. The Nigerian Battalion was superb. It sent out men to carry in the wounded, it provided guides to each group as it arrived, and, best of all, provided a mug of hot tea for each survivor. The Nigerians

1. Calvert (*left*) with his parents and three elder brothers, Seaton, 1939 (see p.6).

2. A portrait drawn in 1944 for the Belgian SAS.

3. Calvert bids farewell to Wingate at White City.

4. Calvert (*left*) at Mogaung after his remarkable victory, July, 1944.

5. The Burma Road.

6&7. Chindit reunions: *above*, Calvert with (*centre*) Sir Robert Thompson and Earl Mountbatten; *below* with Matron MacGeary, who was revered by all the Chindits.

had even cleared a light plane strip with their machetes, and so the wounded were speedily flown out.

At Thayaung the Chindits slowly regrouped and sent out fighting patrols. Although these ranged over a wide area and eliminated several pockets of Japanese survivors, the main momentum had gone because the troops were so totally exhausted. They had sustained over 200 casualties, including 100 dead, but the Japanese had sustained 3,000 casualties. Also 24 Mixed Brigade, which had been ordered to wipe out the Chindit intruders, had itself been destroyed, never again to operate as a fighting formation.

During the battle several units from 16 Brigade had come under Calvert's command. These included two Columns of the Leicestershire Regiment, but, just as they could have destroyed a retreating Japanese unit, they were ordered away. This difficulty was really caused by a breakdown in communications, nevertheless Calvert sent an insurbordinate message to Lentaigne saying that if units were taken away in the middle of a battle, he could not be blamed for failing to destroy the Japanese completely. Later he wrote, "We had shot our last bolt. I was tired, sick and irritable." He also made a very honest assessment of the battle and listed his mistakes, such as, for example, using his reserve unit too soon, choosing the wrong objective and not carrying out a detailed recce of Sepein. He could have added that by 25 April the concept of the Stronghold had been brilliantly vindicated at Broadway. At White City the blocks on routes going north had been total and, under Calvert's leadership, it had absorbed the assault of Japanese forces, approximately a division, and then totally destroyed it. The Chindits had won an outstanding victory, but there was no joy nor elation, because the price had been too high and too many close friends and fine soldiers had been killed. Many years later, when Calvert was commanding the SAS in Malaya, he spoke openly to a brother officer and said that in wartime one should not make close friendships because it made the death of a friend harder to bear. There is little doubt that he was thinking of Ian MacPherson.

Operation Thursday had been launched on 5 March when Calvert made the brave decision to take his entire brigade to Broadway, and it was on that very same day that Mutaguchi launched his attack on Kohima and Imphal with three divisions. Many years later, when critics maintained that the Chindits had achieved nothing, Sir Robert

Thompson (the Bobbie Thompson who had been on both expeditions with Calvert) in his book *Make for the Hills* made the apt comment that the Chindit landings just behind the Japanese lines on the day they attacked, would be like two German divisions landing in southern England on D Day.

# The Chindits Move North

By the beginning of May, 1944, the strategic situation in Burma had changed and new plans had to be made. The Japanese attack on Imphal and Kohima had been contained and their three divisions were starting the long and costly retreat which would end in their complete destruction. Around Indaw and Mawlu the Chindits had destroyed 24 Independent Mixed Brigade, and the Indaw valley with the railway running up to Mogaung was now virtually clear of Japanese troops. On the eastern extremity of the Burma theatre, Morris Force, consisting of Columns which were detached from 111 Brigade after landing at Chowringhee, were still blocking the road up to Myitkyina and were advancing towards it. In this situation, Slim initially had grounds for expecting the Chindit forces to move westwards and to assist in the defeat of Mutaguchi's three divisions. In contrast, Stilwell demanded that the Chindits should keep up the pressure on 18 and 56 Divisions facing him, the plan agreed at Quebec. This was in order to clear the Japanese from Burma north of latitude 24 and to open the Burma road to China, always the American's highest priority.

In this context Wingate would have argued – indeed he did argue before he died – that the Chindits were specialist troops highly trained for Long Range Penetration. After the battles at Broadway and White City they should be withdrawn, restored, re-equipped and used again as Long Range Penetration groups to destroy the Japanese as they retreated. Wingate had even given Slim a plan to drop a Chindit brigade at Pakokku near Meiktila to cut off the main Japanese withdrawal. He had constantly to argue that, because Chindits were trained for a specialist rôle, they lacked the back-up of normal infantry units, and, above all, they had no armour nor artillery support. It needed a leap of the imagination to envisage the correct rôle for the Chindits and it has to be said that Slim never made that leap; he never fully supported the idea of Long Range Penetration. After the death of Wingate, when his powerful advocacy was removed, there was scant chance of the Chindits being used in their LRP role, and the wider strategic issues decided their fate. However, when the actual decision about the use of the Chindits was made, the most dangerous pressure on Slim and the 14th Army was past, and he therefore agreed that the Chindit brigades should move north and assist Stilwell. He made yet another fateful decision and agreed, for the sake of administrative tidiness, to put all Chindit units under Stilwell's command. For many of 77 Brigade and 111 Brigade this proved to be a death warrant.

Vinegar Joe Stilwell had a reputation as a tough no-nonsense commander in the field, and he had had a frustrating experience trying to control several divisions of Chinese troops when, as it was discovered later, Chiang Kai-shek secretly countermanded his orders. Stilwell's anti-British sentiments, which came close to paranoia, were well-known as an amusing eccentricity, but when the lives of thousands of Chindits were put in his charge this prejudice became a dangerous threat. An example of his milder criticism was that "Limeys were lily-livered cowards," and he openly said to Slim in May, 1944, that the British units were cowardly and would not obey his orders. He had shown a grudging respect for Wingate, but it is doubtful if he ever considered or understood the concept of Long Range Penetration. From the middle of May, 1944, the destiny of the Chindit Brigades lay in his hands.

These strategic ramifications reached the Chindits as instructions from Lentaigne. After their valiant battles around White City, he ordered 77 Brigade to move north into the Gangaw Hills. They set off almost immediately after their final clash with the Japanese at Thayaung, and for a few days, away from the tension and the stench of White City, they enjoyed some relaxation. They could order supply drops at leisure and build up their strength for their next assignment. Their move to the Gangaw Hills was part of a major redevelopment of all Chindit brigades. 111 Brigade, now under the command of Masters, moved north to establish a Stronghold code-named "Blackpool". 14 Brigade and 3 West African Brigade were to close down Broadway, White City and Aberdeen, and then move north to support 111 Brigade at Blackpool. 16 Brigade, after their long march, were flown out.

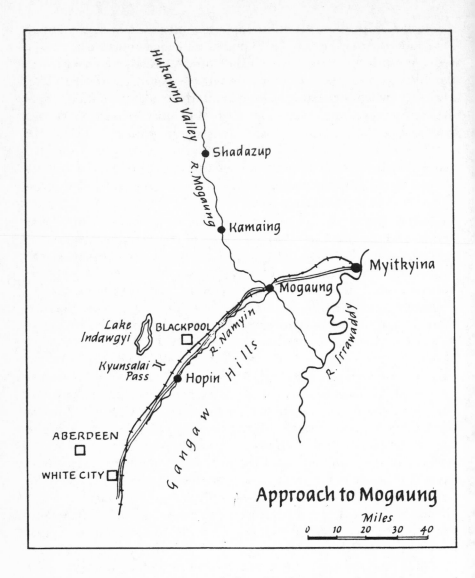

Approach to Mogaung

Calvert vehemently opposed the abandonment of Broadway and White City. Also, during the few days' rest in the hills, he suffered a severe attack of malaria and, due to his psychological reaction to the stress and trauma of battle, he had a serious bout of depression. During this he sent off increasingly insubordinate signals to Lentaigne, though his loyal Brigade Major, Francis Stuart, tried to intercept them. After several of these Lentaigne flew in to reprimand

Calvert. In contrast to Wingate who frequently flew in to support the Chindits, this was the only occasion Lentaigne visited one of his units behind the lines. Lentaigne asked the Chindits for one final effort to prove their theory was correct, but Calvert went to him in a mood of grim determination and suppressed rage. He totally opposed giving up all their gains and walking in to the death trap of Mogaung in the monsoon rains. Then Lentaigne said, "I have not seen you like this before, Michael. If you really feel like that I will have to relieve you, which I do not want to do." "That brought me to my senses and the mental storm passed," wrote Calvert many years later. Lentaigne's appeal to the loyalty of the Chindits and Calvert's loyalty to his own brigade was wise. In moments of high drama and passion, it must be remembered that arguments are rarely logical. Lentaigne did not intend to "prove their theory correct". He had rejected Wingate's principles and this was a main cause of the slaughter of 77 Brigade and 111 Brigade in the weeks to come.

Having accepted that his Brigade would have to move north to Mogaung, Calvert had some modest satisfaction in watching the admirable evacuation of Broadway under the command of Brigadier Abdy Ricketts and the West African Brigade. They managed to have all the guns, equipment and stores flown out by Dakota, and then to plaster the area with booby traps. Then they saw a major bombing attack by Japanese planes and a full-scale attack by 53 Japanese Division on a completely empty base. Calvert felt that it always improved the morale of troops to see their own HQ get a pasting, and he pondered over whether it would be worth arranging a bombing attack on his HQ just to improve the morale of his men.

# Mogaung

Most of the Chindits realized that Lentaigne was not strong enough to stand up to Slim and Stilwell, as Wingate would have done. In his book *Chindits* Calvert criticized Slim's decision to hand the Chindits over to Stilwell. "Slim's total misunderstanding of the Chindit rôle influenced Lentaigne, who later said that he would have preferred the Chindits to remain in the Indaw area, rather than to be caught on the hop near 18 Division rear echelon. Slim's misinterpretation of the Special Forces rôle was a blind spot in one whom many believe to be the greatest general, bar Wavell, that Britain produced in the war." (*Chindits*, p. 115).

When the Chindits moved north they entered a totally different strategic situation. Stilwell with two Chinese divisions, 22 and 38, had been making slow progress southwards up the Hukawng valley. He also had under his command an American unit nicknamed "Merrill's Marauders" after its commander, Brigadier Merrill, Stilwell's son-in-law. The Marauders had been trained on Chindit lines and were a tough fighting force about the size of a Chindit Brigade. Stilwell's aim had always been to drive the Japanese southwards past Mogaung and Myitkyina, and then further south to Bhamo, so that the Burma road could be opened up. This remained the Americans' absolute priority and the Chindits now became part of this plan.

111 Brigade under Masters led the move north and set up a Stronghold near Hopin, codename Blackpool, in order to put a permanent block on the railway to Mogaung. At the same time Morris Force was blocking the road further east which ran up to Myitkyina. 14 Brigade and 3 West African Brigade, after they had closed down Broadway and White City, moved north to help 111 Brigade at Blackpool. 77 Brigade, under Calvert, was given the task of capturing Mogaung.

As the brigade approached the site of Blackpool the monsoon started in earnest and the whole area was lashed by torrential rain. The Lancashire Fusiliers, the South Staffords and 3/6th Gurkhas, in appalling conditions, sent out fighting patrols to eliminate enemy units and to prevent the Japanese using the railway. All battalions had received reinforcements and the new officers were keen to prove themselves. This gave a new impetus to many companies and platoons which were worn out by so many weeks behind the lines. As they got closer to Blackpool, Calvert commented, "The exhilarating sound of gunfire swept away all our doubts and cares and we were ready for action."

At this stage several units were changed. 3/9th Gurkhas joined 111 Brigade in the Blackpool perimeter and Calvert asked for the King's battalion to be returned to him from 14 Brigade. The prolonged heavy rain made all such moves difficult, but, more important, turned the small Namyin River into a torrent which was impossible to cross. Day after day 77 Brigade made desperate efforts to cross the river and come to the help of 111 Brigade, but it proved impossible. Further away, 14 Brigade and the Nigerians had captured the Kyunsalai Pass, but were held up and they, too, failed to reach Blackpool.

111 Brigade had set up the Stronghold at Blackpool, but it lasted only seventeen days, days of carnage and slaughter inflicted by the immediate Japanese attack. Masters certainly rejected all Wingate's principles about establishing Strongholds. Also, he could have placed Blackpool nearer to Hopin, which would have been remote from Japanese artillery and would have enabled the other brigades to come to its help. Masters grumbled violently at the failure of those brigades to reach him. He asserted, "Forty flaming Columns of Chindit bullshit sat on their arses," but the real cause of the disaster at Blackpool was due to Masters' own decision. Blackpool had come under Japanese fire from the start and, although a glider strip and a Dakota strip were established, they were of little value because the enemy brought up anti-aircraft guns which prevented the Dakotas flying in.

While 77 Brigade was trying urgently to cross the Namyin River and come to the help of Blackpool, Calvert, on 18 May, received the surprising news that Merrill's Marauders had captured Myitkyina. This was not true. The Marauders had in fact captured Myitkyina airfield a couple of miles to the west of the town, which at that time was weakly defended by only about 700 troops. Colonel Hunter, the admirable leader of the Marauders – Merrill had been flown out after a heart attack – signalled for another infantry unit to fly in at once in order to seize the town. This appeal was ignored and from that moment a series of grave blunders and wrong decisions meant that Myitkyina was not captured until 3 August. Stilwell's failure to capture the town was to cost Calvert dear.

Lentaigne had ordered 77 Brigade to assist 111 Brigade at Blackpool and at the same time to carry out a detailed reconnaissance of Mogaung which was said to be "weakly held". On 21 May Calvert's recce patrols reported that there were roughly 4,000 Japanese in Mogaung in well-prepared defensive positions. This was confirmed by intelligence from 14th Army. Calvert faced a dilemma – he anticipated that his brigade was going to be ordered to capture Mogaung, yet he still wanted to relieve the battered Chindit forces in Blackpool. There, the Japanese bombardment continued relentlessly, accompanied by determined infantry attacks. Meanwhile the Chindits hung on grimly, suffering very severe casualties and waiting desperately for help from the other Chindit brigades. Facing complete disaster, Masters signalled urgently to Lentaigne and Slim for permission to withdraw his Brigade, but this permission never came. Finally, on 25 May he took the decision himself and ordered the emaciated and shattered remains of his brigade to retreat to Mokso Sakan from where they had set out seventeen days before. The dire condition of the Brigade is illustrated by the fact that, as they retreated, they had to shoot their own grievously wounded men to prevent them from falling into the hands of the Japanese. 111 Brigade had inflicted heavy casualties on the Japanese too, but when Blackpool had to be abandoned it meant that units of the Japanese 53 Division could hurry off towards Mogaung.

By 25 May Lentaigne had moved Special Force HQ to Shadazup to be close to Stilwell's HQ, and here he suffered Stilwell's vitriolic fury when the news came that, without permission, Masters had abandoned Blackpool. This reinforced all Stilwell's neurotic prejudices about cowardly Limeys who did not obey orders. It also prompted the weak Lentaigne to try to appear decisive. On 27 May he issued a peremptory order to Calvert, "You will take Mogaung."

The original plan had been that, while 111 Brigade held Blackpool, 77 Brigade, together with 14 Brigade and 3rd West African, and assisted by one of Stilwell's Chinese regiments, would attack Mogaung. In practice things were very different and a potentially disastrous situation was exacerbated by the inadequacy of Lentaigne. Although at Shadazup his HQ was then quite close to where all his brigades were operating, Lentaigne did not once go in to visit them to see for himself the condition they were in, or to observe the sort of ground they had to cover. As a result he continued to issue orders which bore little relation to the reality of the situation, and which his commanders increasingly ignored. As a result of this grave inadequacy and his complete lack of control of the battle, although 14 and 3rd West African Brigades were in fairly close proximity, they were not involved in any way in the attack on Mogaung. Instead, it fell once again to 77 Brigade, which had borne the brunt of the fighting around Broadway and White City, to carry out the attack by themselves.

Having received Lentaigne's orders to take Mogaung 77 Brigade moved as swiftly as possible towards their target under a constant monsoon downpour and through deep mud and slime. To add to

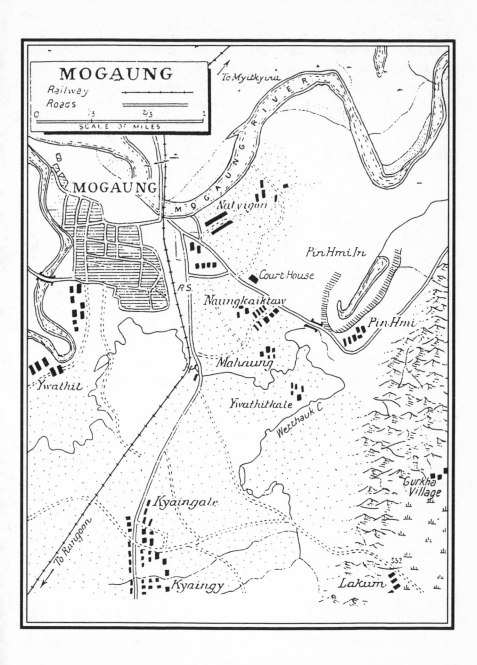

their discomfort, the area was plagued by leeches and these were so bad that several men needed blood transfusions. On 2 June the South Staffords advanced and, after a fierce battle with the Japanese defenders, captured Lakum which lay about two miles south-west of Mogaung. The Chindit advance through the hilly country around Lakum involved them in many brisk skirmishes in which both sides sustained casualties. The conditions were dreadful. Men and mules slipped and slithered down precipitous slopes with the added burden of having to carry all the wounded on makeshift stretchers. In one day the Chindits lost over thirty killed and wounded, but, because of the superiority of their weapons (especially the 3-inch mortar) they inflicted heavier casualties on the enemy.

Lakum lay on a low hill overlooking the plain, and from the HQ it was possible to see Mogaung. The RAF liaison section was soon installed and, after a hastily constructed strip had been laid, they arranged for supplies to be flown in and for the wounded to be flown out. Realizing the threat to supplies by the constant rain, Calvert was determined to build up an adequate store of food and ammunition before the attack started. While the build-up continued, small units of local Kachin people, led by Burma Regiment officers, established control over the area and provided accurate intelligence about Japanese movements.

As the position at Lakum was consolidated, Calvert and his second-in-command, Colonel Rome, studied the ground in detail. Mogaung, which had been reinforced by the Japanese units formerly investing Blackpool, lay on a bend of the wide and swiftly flowing Mogaung River. The railway, which they had blocked at White City, crossed the river at the north-east edge of the town on a substantial bridge, and continued eastwards to Myitkyina. From his HQ, when it was clear enough, Calvert could see all of this and was able to call down Mustangs to bomb and shoot up the Japanese defenders in and around the town. Unfortunately Mogaung was out of range of 3-inch mortars, but Calvert had heard that in India there were some 4.2-inch mortars with a longer range. He sent a signal and soon had the only two 4.2 mortars in India, together with all the available ammunition. As soon as they arrived they went straight into action and with the Mustangs of the Air Commando, did their best to silence the enemy artillery in Mogaung which had been causing the Chindits about twenty casualties a day.

Before the final attack on Mogaung, the hilly area around Lakum had to be completely cleared of the enemy. This was done by the South Staffords and the Gurkhas. The Lancashire Fusiliers then made a carefully prepared attack on Pinhmi village. They took the village fairly quickly and to their surprise and delight discovered twenty ammunition dumps, fifteen lorries and a large well-concealed hospital with supplies of medical equipment and drugs. Most of the patients tried to escape across the flooded Wetthauk Chaung (river), but many drowned and many more committed suicide. This great success boosted the morale of the entire force. Although the village fell fairly easily, the Lancashire Fusiliers were repulsed by well-prepared defences on the bridge where the road from Pinhmi to Mogaung crossed the Wetthauk Chaung. In the following attacks along the Chaung the Lancashire Fusiliers suffered heavy casualties and Calvert blamed himself for not having made a personal recce of the ground. He wrote, "There can be no exceptions". Later, a recce patrol found a ford through the Chaung and on 9 June, after a brilliant attack, the Gurkhas captured Mahaung. Slowly the attacks progressed and on 10 June the Gurkhas after one bloody repulse, attacked again and captured the vital Pinhmi bridge. The struggle for the bridge cost 130 casualties. Calvert had been urging the battalions forward in the hope of capturing Mogaung before further reinforcements reached the enemy garrison, but between 10 and 12 June two more Japanese battalions arrived.

On 13 June the situation had to be reassessed and Calvert called a meeting of all the battalion commanders. In every case, their battalion strength had been reduced to the strength of a company, i.e. one quarter, and the total number of all the available men in the Brigade was now 550. Of these, the majority had been wounded at least once and nearly all were suffering from malaria, jungle sores or trench feet. At Brigade HQ 250 wounded, many of them stretcher cases, awaited evacuation. Applications for air supply and evacuation now had to go through Stilwell's notoriously chaotic HQ. Air supply became unreliable too because of the heavy losses of light planes. Calvert paid tribute to one American pilot who just flew in and out, not even turning off his engine, until all the wounded had been taken out.

Even in those circumstances Calvert had to endure yet another threat from Lentaigne, from the safe distance of Force HQ. In one of the South Staffords attacks, Archie John Wavell, the son of the Viceroy, had been badly wounded in the wrist. This information had gone to his parents and there was some concern that if the Japanese captured him they could blackmail Wavell. Lentaigne, ever one to give in to pressure from more senior ranks, sent a signal threatening to dismiss Calvert from command of the Brigade unless young Wavell was flown out that day. Calvert was unaware that he had been wounded. When he investigated the matter he discovered that, although badly wounded at his wrist, Archie saw that there were more seriously wounded men already awaiting evacuation, and he refused to fly out until they had gone. He was a brave young officer who was later killed in Africa in the Mau Mau campaign.

The prolonged suffering of the wounded caused Calvert great concern; he visited them as often as possible, as he said, to remind him of the true cost of any victory. A wounded man would be treated first in his Regimental Aid Post, then sent or carried back to Pinhmi where a surgical team operated. If he needed further treatment he was flown out by light plane to Myitkyina and thence by Dakota to hospital in Assam. Such was the determination of the Chindits that often seriously wounded men would return to their unit to help out in an attack.

Before the final attack on Mogaung all the battalions sent out active fighting patrols to cover all the approaches to Mogaung and even to penetrate in to the town where they were able to identify targets to be bombed the next day. The leadership of this type of patrol fell to the platoon commanders and Calvert described the situation in the South Staffords. They had had forty officers killed; only two of their original platoon commanders survived and they had been wounded four and three times respectively. At this stage a group of platoon sergeants came to Calvert and said that they were sorry to see so many keen, inexperienced young officers being killed, and they offered to command the platoons themselves. Calvert agreed.

The battalions were suffering many casualties from accurate Japanese artillery fire because the ground was so waterlogged that they could not dig adequate slit trenches. The men spent days standing in mud or water in an incessant downpour, and frequently had to fling themselves down in the mud for shelter. To help with the cases of trench foot caused by the constant damp, Calvert signalled for 1,000 pairs of wellington boots. He received a reply saying that the best answer to foot problems was to keep the feet dry!

On 14 June a Burma Rifles officer was sent north over the Mogaung River to find the long-promised Chinese regiment, and boats were prepared to bring them over the river, should they appear. At the same time Rome went out to try to see Stilwell and Lentaigne, and to hasten reinforcements. Next day, because of the increasing casualties, Calvert started to pull back from some of the most forward positions, but when the Gurkhas told him that the Japanese were pulling back towards Mogaung, he countermanded the order.

Many Chindit casualties were caused by accurate enemy fire coming from Naungkaiktaw, and so the next attack was planned to remove them from that area. On 18 June, just before dawn, Mustangs attacked and all the 4.2 and 3-inch mortars laid down over 400 bombs. Then the Lancashire Fusiliers and the King's attacked and overran most of the village, and when they were held up, a newly acquired flame thrower unit went into action. Almost immediately a large number of the enemy broke away and ran back to Mogaung. Chindit guns from the Court House areas and from the other flank inflicted more casualties as they fled. Calvert and his Brigade Major, a little overconfident, decided to take a short cut across the paddy to the village and were fired on by the Japanese, so they had to run and fling themselves down in the mud. Calvert, in considerable danger, started laughing hilariously. He wrote, "By the time we reached safety I was completely exhausted by the laughing, running and flinging myself down," thus reinforcing the "Mad Mike" legend. Over 100 Japanese had been driven out of the village and over seventy killed. The Chindits sustained fifty casualties. The mortars on which they relied so much were not always accurate, and later in this mêlée about half their casualties were caused by their own mortar bombs. This, unlike today or during the Gulf War, was accepted as a normal hazard of war.

The Chindits rapidly consolidated their position in the village and at dusk, as they prepared a hurried meal, a weary group of soldiers staggered in and started to take off their equipment. It was a Japanese patrol who had not realized their position had been captured. They were quickly despatched. The same evening, to everyone's surprise, the Burma Rifles officer reported that the Chinese 114 Regiment had reached the north bank of the river. The first battalion started crossing immediately. Within 77 Brigade Calvert had a number of Hong Kong Chinese whom he had first known when he served in Hong Kong, and who had eagerly joined his brigade from a transit camp in India. They now proved extremely useful, acting as interpreters and liaising with the newly-arrived units.

There were three Chinese battalions and an artillery battery, which more than doubled the strength of the Chindit force, and they were led by competent and highly professional officers. They did not come directly under Calvert's command, and he had enough experience to understand that, having fought the Japanese since 1931, they had a very different approach to war. He showed the Chinese Colonel Li round and they established a good rapport. After a detailed recce, the Chinese 75mm guns were established at Pinhmi, and one of their companies took over in Mahaung.

The arrival of the Chinese made possible the final attack on Mogaung, though the Chindit strength had been further and dangerously depleted. The Lancashire Fusiliers and King's together could must only 110 men, the South Staffords 180 and the Gurkhas 230. Those were all that were left of a full brigade of over 2,000 men. The new arrivals did present Calvert with problems. The worst of these was a so-called American "liaison officer" who did more to cause dissension than everything else together. Calvert at first tried to be affable. In the end he was forced to comment on the American's bad manners and general odiousness and considered him an appalling person by any standards. He was to reappear later. Calvert heard that his fellow American officers were so disgusted by their colleague that they hoped to get a chance to shoot him. Another problem was the pilfering by the Chinese labour units. It was difficult for them to change the habits of a lifetime, even though the Chinese Colonel shot a few in order to deter the rest.

The most heartening factor in this worrying situation was the continuing brilliant work of the Air Commando. The Mustang close support and their daily and accurate bombing of targets in Mogaung played an important rôle in weakening the Japanese resistance. The Chindits were comforted too in the knowledge that, should they be wounded, they would be flown out by the Sentinel light planes.

Even with the air support, Calvert had to face yet another dilemma. He was continuing to lose men from battle wounds and sickness, and he realized that he would soon have too few fit men to mount an attack at all. He had long discussions with Colonel Li on this subject, but his approach was entirely different. The Chinese were always loath to make a direct attack: they preferred to try to get around or behind an objective and slowly wear down the enemy. They would rather capture a position by a subtle trick than by straightforward action. Calvert said, "It is much cheaper that way, but it does not win wars."

After this abortive discussion with the Chinese, Calvert turned to Claud Rome. He, however, declined to given an opinion on whether to attack or not. Once again Calvert felt the intense loneliness of the commander who has to make the final decision. The battalion commanders genuinely believed that their troops could not keep going much longer. Then, when he was close to despair at the loss of so many fine soldiers and good friends, Calvert learned that the Chinese had occupied the area of Mogaung railway station. This would secure the left flank of the assault. With this information, he decided to attack, and preparations were made to start at 0300 hours on 24 June.

The plan was clear: a straightforward night attack led by the Gurkhas and South Staffords; and the Lancashire Fusiliers and King's with the flame-throwing unit just behind in reserve and ready to reinforce where necessary. Just before the attack Calvert went round all the units as they made their final preparations and he was heartened by the confidence and determination of the officers and NCOs briefing their men. He had given an Order of the Day and everyone responded to it splendidly – a true example of sound leadership. He reminded them that Mogaung would be the first main town in Burma to be recaptured and that their achievement would be watched by Churchill and the whole country. He was not being sentimental but he had "a sincere belief that we must do our stuff and uphold the honour of the British Commonwealth in the field of battle." Calvert was very moved when, unseen, he overheard a corporal in the South Staffords give orders to his own section. He calmly gave clear, crisp details and added instructions about who was to take over if he was killed. The possibility of failure was not considered. This was the final appeal to the decimated, diseased, starved, exhausted, mud-soaked troops who had been fighting behind the enemy lines since 5 March. Francis Stuart, the Brigade Major, wounded and desperately ill with tuberculosis, was carried forward, determined at last to see the capture of Mogaung.

Just before 0300 hours on 24 June seventy Mustangs dived on the Japanese positions in Mogaung, then all the 4.2 and 3-inch mortars joined in and fired a barrage of over 1000 bombs. So often in battles in Burma the Japanese were subjected to a horrendous barrage, but the moment it ceased they came out of their dugouts and continued to fight. So it proved, and as soon as the barrage stopped Japanese artillery started to shell the "form-up" area. This caused casualties, so all the units hurried forward in the dark to keep as close to their own barrage as possible. The Gurkhas on the right, with Michael Almand and other young officers showing incredible bravery, rushed forward, captured the railway bridge and began to clear the remaining strongpoints. The flame throwers were used with deadly effect: in one underground strongpoint twenty Japanese were slaughtered. While the Gurkhas consolidated their gains, the South Staffords, who had to make a longer advance to their objective, were caught by heavy machine-gun fire from a strongpoint on their flank which had not been identified. Calvert was right at the front and was able to react at once to this danger. He immediately brought forward the Lancashire Fusiliers and the flame throwers. At the same time he directed 200 mortar bombs and all available machine guns and anti-tank weapons onto the strongpoint. The Chindits made a final desperate charge, the strongpoint was captured and all the Japanese were killed.

The Chindits had won the first phase of the battle, but at a terrible price. Some of their casualties had been caused by enemy fire from the left flank. The Chinese had not taken the railway station. That was a lie emanating from the odious American liaison officer which cost the lives of many brave Chindits. In the town Michael Almand lay dead: he was later awarded a posthumous VC. Calvert found the Corporal who had issued his orders the previous night lying dead on the position his section had captured. Some Japanese artillery was still firing, but was soon silenced by accurately directed Mustang attacks. The enemy had been defeated, but there were no troops available to move through the town to eliminate the last pockets of resistance. For several days rather desultory mopping-up operations continued. The reaction to four weeks of continuous fighting, death and destruction had begun to take its toll on the Chindits.

During a lull in the fighting an announcement was made on the BBC news that Chinese/American forces had captured Mogaung. The Chindits were absolutely outraged. Clearly this was the work of the despicable liaison officer whom Calvert had dubbed "Lieutenant-Colonel Bluster". When Colonel Li heard of this, he came directly to Calvert's HQ accompanied by the odious Bluster, apologized, and said, "If anyone has taken Mogaung it is your Brigade, and we all admire the bravery of your soldiers." The fury can be imagined, but Calvert alleviated it a little by sending another signal to Stilwell's HQ: "Mogaung having been taken by the Chinese, 77 Brigade is proceeding to take Umbrage." The story goes that Stilwell's son, who was his Intelligence Officer, remarked that Umbrage must be a small place because he could not find it on the map!

Bluster was clearly an appalling character, but he was typical of the seedy sycophants that Stilwell attracted to his staff, people who pandered to his anti-British paranoia and who only told him what they thought would please him. This caused suffering and anguish to 77 Brigade and also to the other Chindit unit, Morris Force, which was operating around Myitkyina.

There were a few more days of mopping up isolated pockets of resistance, and the Chinese, with the co-operation of the Lancashire Fusiliers, did carry out an attack, but the battle of Mogaung had really been fought and won by 77 Brigade under the superb leadership of Michael Calvert. After the victory he felt no elation, rather a deep anguish over the atrocious losses sustained by his Brigade. There were over 250 killed, over 500 seriously wounded, and many more men who had kept going just lay down and died now that the pressure was off. Others were so totally emaciated and exhausted that a trivial injury, such as cutting a finger, led to their death. Francis Stuart flew out to India, only to die shortly afterwards. Calvert was haunted by the thought that his loyalty to Wingate had made him ask too much of his Brigade, that he and 77 Brigade had been the willing horse whom others had relied on, with the result that over one third of his Brigade had been killed or wounded, their bones scattered along the grim trail from Broadway to Mogaung. He described the four-week battle as a mini-Passchendaele. He pondered over Wellington's remark, "The next greatest misfortune to losing a battle is to gain such a victory as this." As he pondered he received congratulations from many people and from many quarters, but none pleased him more than the message from Derek Tulloch who wrote: "Wingate would have been proud of you."

The quality of Calvert's leadership has long been recognized and revered. Fifty years afterwards General Sir Michael Rose, in recommending the re-issue of *Prisoners of Hope* and referring to Calvert, wrote that in peacetime soldiers should study those qualities in men which bring victory in battle: "Fighting is an attitude of mind, a determination to take war into the enemy camp, an acceptance of risk and the seizing of initiative." Calvert's description of Mogaung was "a stark and necessary reminder of what it takes to be a fighting soldier amidst the chaos and extreme violence of war." There were few examples even in the Second World War of a commander who was put under such stress, in such conditions behind the enemy lines, in constant contact with the enemy, and over such a long period. In the Gulf War the stress of the commanders was illustrated in the well-publicized incandescent exchanges between Schwarzkopf and Colin Powell, and their mediator Calvin Waller. Their stress, however, lasted a matter of days and cannot be compared to the five months behind the enemy lines in which all those stresses fell on Calvert.

In leading 77 Brigade from Broadway to Mogaung, Calvert gave a unique example of distinguished leadership in war, not from a comfortable, well-supported HQ safely behind the lines but from the thick of the fighting. At Pagoda Hill he led a bayonet charge which won the Chindits their first crucial success. At Mogaung his presence in the South Staffords' front line enabled him to deploy his reserve decisively and turn the tide of battle. The quality of his leadership has rarely been equalled and is still revered today by all those who study the art of war, especially by the Chindits whose Old Comrades Association elected him their President in 1996.

Such fame lay in the future, and in Mogaung on 27 June, 1944, he had to face more mundane issues. He received an order that his Brigade had to march to Hopin. He immediately refused because his men were in no state to march anywhere, let alone to fight. Asked how many fit men he had, he replied, "Three hundred". When told to send them to Hopin, he refused again. He signalled again: "I have 300 men all told. Do you want me to form The King's Royal Staffordshire Gurkha Fusiliers?" He emphasized that he would stand by his decision and his signals in front of Stilwell or Slim or anyone.

Next, the Brigade was informed that 36 British Division was coming forward to take over. The Brigade Medical Officers advised that they should move away from the battle area as soon as possible because the men were collapsing with malaria, dysentery, scrub-typhus and other diseases against which they now had no resistence. Another dispute with HQ centred on the Brigade's mules. The mules were highly trained and Calvert wanted to keep them, ready for the next Chindit expedition. There was no way the RAF were going to fly his mules out and another lot in – a point he regretfully had to concede. He kept up his excellent relationship with Colonel Li and, when 77 Brigade finally left, a Chinese regiment took over from them. Colonel Li wrote a moving letter praising the fortitude and bravery of Calvert and 77 Brigade, and the entire brigade was pleased that Colonel Li was awarded the OBE and two of his officers the MC.

The disagreements between Stilwell, who became quite irrational about the Chindits, and Lentaigne, who was not strong enough to stand up to him, became so serious that on 30 June Mountbatten came personally to intervene. As Commander-in-Chief SEAC he was not so completely involved in the great 14th Army battles as Slim was at the time. Also, as Supreme Commander he was the only person in a position to give orders to Stilwell. When Mountbatten arrived he was horrified at the physical condition of the Chindits, both in 77 and 111 Brigades. He ordered an immediate medical inspection of all ranks, and shrewdly included Merrill in the inspection team. Merrill knew that Stilwell had driven the Marauders to such lengths that, in the end, they just refused to fight, so he had some sympathy for the Chindit position. The medical report was decisive. It considered that all the survivors of 77 Brigade were physically and mentally exhausted. Every day men were dying from dysentery, from malaria and from total exhaustion. Mountbatten ordered the Brigade to be flown out at once.

The decision took a little time to reach Calvert. Meanwhile tense and angry signals flashed between Brigade HQ and Shadazup. In one, the Brigade was ordered to leave the mules at Mogaung and march to Myitkyina, from where they would be flown out. Calvert later agreed that he and his Brigade had a phobia about Myitkyina which Stilwell had not yet captured. Were they, the exhausted remnants of 77 Brigade, expected to capture that too, when over

10,000 Chinese troops were in the area? They felt that this was more than flesh and blood could bear. Calvert therefore shut down his wireless and sent a signal that 77 Brigade were moving to Kamaing to be airlifted out. He later agreed that this act of disobedience was unwise, because it left a free hand to Colonel Bluster. Bluster sent messages to Stilwell saying 77 Brigade were "cowards, yellow, deserters, they walked off the field of battle, they should all be arrested." (*Prisoners of Hope*).

The march to Kamaing had two other drawbacks: it meant that the Chindits never met 36 Division which received only Stilwell's biased views about them. Also the route to Kamaing was very difficult through waist-deep mud and mile after mile of flood water. One man who had survived the whole campaign just dropped dead from sheer exhaustion. Calvert had to rescue his batman and pull him a great distance to the safety of dry land. Even when the nightmare journey was over and they had reached Force HQ, a veterinary officer was drowned while trying to rescue a mule from the flooded river.

Calvert has recalled the pleasure of sleeping in a hut with a roof for the first time in four months. The following day he had to report to Stilwell and quite expected to be court-martialled for disobedience. Lentaigne, who had had to suffer Stilwell's endless criticism of the Chindits, nervously accompanied Calvert to Stilwell's HQ.

They were shown in to a room where Stilwell sat with his son and with Boatner, his 2i/c. Stilwell told them to sit down and started aggressively. Their first exchanges can be told in Calvert's own words:

"Well, Calvert, I have been wanting to meet you for some time."

"I have been wanting to meet you too, Sir."

"You send some very strong signals, Calvert."

"You should see the ones my Brigade Major wouldn't let me send." This was a moment of high tension when Calvert's career and possibly the future of the Chindits was at stake, but, to everyones' relief, Stilwell roared with laughter. He agreed he had had the same problem over sending signals to Washington. Calvert had hit exactly the right note, and Stilwell showed that he respected a man of his own mettle. Calvert was then able to outline the achievements of 77 Brigade: the establishment of Broadway, the battles at White City to block Japanese supplies to *his* front, how they had hoped for *his* advance down the railway, the struggle for Mogaung, how tough commanders had wept at the casualties, the effect of the erroneous BBC bulletin about the capture of Mogaung, and Colonel Li's message. He concluded, "I am sorry, Sir, if I disobeyed orders but I think that you will realize the strain we were under."

Throughout this conversation Stilwell sat, amazed, saying, "Is that true?" or "Why wasn't I told that?" He then, began to realize how far his staff had concealed all the Chindit achievements and successes. Then he said, "You and your boys have done a great job." He awarded the American Silver Star to Calvert and four more to officers in the Brigade.

It is not easy to assess the magnitude of Calvert's contribution to the success of the Chindit operations, but one question should be asked. If Stilwell could award Calvert an immediate Silver Star, if Calvert's brigade won three VCs and numerous other awards, if Colonel Li received an OBE for his tentative co-operation at Mogaung, how should Calvert have been adequately decorated? There is evidence in the Rylands Library in Manchester in the Tulloch Papers that consideration was given to whether he should receive the VC or CBE. There was at that time a precedent for the award of the VC not for a single act of bravery but for prolonged and outstanding leadership in the face of the enemy. Group Captain Cheshire won the award in this way. Many people believe that if there was ever prolonged leadership from the front and in constant contact with the enemy, there was no better example than Calvert. There were actions, notably at Pagoda Hill, where he could have received an MC, but it is not customary for brigadiers to receive the MC, largely because they are rarely quite close enough to the action. So the question still remains, how should Calvert's outstanding bravery have been recognized, and why was it not? One possible reason could be that Lentaigne, a weak man and out of his depth, stopped an award or at least did not back it strongly. He had suffered from Calvert's insubordination and it was no comfort for him to know that most of the Chindits would have backed Calvert against him. Because of the nature of Chindit operations, if Lentaigne did not back an award for Calvert, few other people in authority would know of his achievement. On the other hand, if Lentaigne did propose a suitable award, where and why was it stopped? The most likely reason was the hostility in both the Indian Army and the British Army establishment to Wingate and to everyone associated with him. That there was a vendetta against Wingate, led by Kirby the editor of *The Official History of the War against Japan*, has now been clearly proved.* Unfortunately, this prejudice has flourished for over fifty years since Wingate's death in 1944.

It is an unfortunate aspect of this matter that for generations, while no one has attempted to detract from the magnificent achievements of Slim and the 14th Army, many of Slim's supporters have gone out of their way to denigrate Wingate and to belittle the effect of the Chindit campaign. As one example, the clear Japanese evidence about the achievements of the Chindits has been deliberately suppressed or ignored. Calvert was certainly a victim of this prejudice in a situation where a greater generosity of spirit could have been shown. Many years later, in correspondence with Major General Tulloch, Calvert pondered on the reason why he did not receive an award for Mogaung. He was aware that he had been considered for a CBE and wondered if he lost that chance because he might have been awarded the VC. He concluded, "Was it spite and envy by Lentaigne?" (Letter Calvert – Tulloch, 30 July, 1970. (Tulloch Papers, Rylands Library.)

The interview with Stilwell and the immediate award of the Silver Star, which highlighted the British failure to recognize his bravery and leadership, at least removed some of the cloud of anger and mistrust over the way Stilwell and his staff had treated the Chindits. This, in itself, was a considerable achievement. Calvert then flew out with the remains of his Brigade for medical treatment and recuperation in Assam and northern India. In one hospital he visited, a Chindit was just coming round from an anaesthetic when he saw Calvert. He gripped his hand and said, "Thank you for everything". It was an embarrassing, but gratifying moment.

As soon as possible he went down to Calcutta to see Francis Stuart, whom he now discovered had advanced tuberculosis. He could not believe that, after all they had been through together, Francis would now die. He arranged for the latest drug to be flown from America but, sadly, it proved ineffective. Calvert described his last visit to the hospital: "After which I was ushered out. I went and got drunk, and joined in quite a nice fight in a Chinese restaurant.

* *Wingate and the Chindits – Redressing the Balance*, David Rooney, Arms & Armour Press, 1994.

Francis died a week later." Calvert then went on leave to Ceylon where he heard of his mother's sudden death.

By September, 1944, all the Chindit brigades had been flown out and, after a spell for recuperation, had started training for their next expedition. During this build-up Calvert suffered an almost absurd anti-climax. He was playing football in an inter-unit match and injured his Achilles tendon. The injury was so severe that he had to be flown back to London to Millbank Hospital for treatment. Here – languishing, frustrated and anxious to get back to the Chindits – he heard, to his utter dismay and amazement, that the Chindits were to be disbanded. It fell to Mountbatten to give this order to the Chindits and he was gracious enough to say that it was the hardest duty of his life. He tried to soften the blow by saying that the whole army was "Chindit-minded" now and there was no need for the Chindits. This, though kindly meant, was not true. The Chindits were disbanded because Slim and the High Command never believed in Long Range Penetration, and there was no Wingate to fight for it at that level.

Mountbatten also wrote personally to Calvert, a gesture which Calvert appreciated. Then he was left to wonder where his future lay.

# CHAPTER SEVEN

# THE SAS, EUROPE, 1945

Calvert had a miserable and depressing time in Millbank Hospital. He still suffered from the exhaustion of the Mogaung campaign, and the disbandment of the Chindits caused him fury and frustration, because from his sickbed he could do nothing to fight it. Despite this, the treatment of his Achilles tendon succeeded, and after some rest and recuperation at Seaton, he waited and wondered where his next posting would take him.

His reputation for the aggressive leadership of 77 Brigade behind the enemy lines was clearly a major factor in the decision to offer him the command of the SAS Brigade when, early in 1945, he was once again fit for duty. His appointment was not universally welcomed in the SAS, since it had been operating successfully all over Europe and there were many outstanding and frequently decorated leaders among its members, though none had had the experience of commanding a brigade in action.

In 1944, as a result of the success of the Long Range Desert Group, the Chindits, the Commandos and other irregular forces, it was decided to place the SAS on a more regular footing under the overall command of General Browning's 1st Airborne Division. This decision proved controversial since the SAS argued that their rôle was strategic, and essentially different from that of the regular airborne forces. Lieutenant-Colonel Bill Stirling, brother of David Stirling who founded the Long Range Desert Group and who was then a prisoner in Colditz, resigned over the issue of how the SAS should be used in the final campaign against Germany. This caused serious consternation in such a tight-knit group in which the Stirlings had played such a distinguished part, but Lieutenant-Colonel Brian Franks stayed on and loyally supported the Brigade Commander, Brigadier McLeod. Together they contributed to the continuing success of the SAS operations. In the brigade were 1 and 2 SAS, a Belgian unit and two battalions of French SAS, who were frequently at loggerheads, but in action fought with bravery and panache.

In the run up to D-Day, the SAS ably and loyally supported by 33 Group and 46 Group RAF, mounted major operations to disrupt the main rail and road routes around Dijon, Tours, Orléans, Limoges and St Malo. These excellent operations, working from bases established behind the enemy lines, though sustaining heavy casualties, caused major disruption to the defending German forces in the summer of 1944. Some of the most effective SAS attacks took place in the Vosges mountain area of eastern France, where, supported by Phantom – the key signals and intelligence element – the SAS caused widespread disruption by sudden attacks on strategic targets and by the laying of mines and booby traps. At one time a crack German SS division of the front-line troops had to be withdrawn from the coastal defence area to deal with them. The SAS units in occupied territory always faced a dilemma. They certainly gave a great boost to the morale of local resistance fighters, but they were conscious of the ever-present threat by the German forces of the most savage reprisals against the local population in areas where the SAS were active. The SAS have a moving and enduring link with the village of Moussey in the Vosges. The people remained loyal to 2nd SAS, commanded by Colonel Franks, and denied all information to the Germans even though 200 men from the village were taken off to concentration camps from where only seventy men ever returned.

After the Allied forces were established in Normandy, the rôle of the SAS changed and they attacked targets all over France. Most operations took place with about thirty men heavily armed and liberally provided with explosives and grenades, but sometimes bigger attacks were needed. In one of those Major Roy Farran DSO MC led a group of SAS sixty strong, with armoured four-wheel-drive jeeps which had been dropped by parachute. They destroyed crucial targets in the Nantes area. In addition to their campaign in France, the SAS successfully operated in northern Italy where, with active support from partisans and deserters, they were strong enough to attack a German Corps Headquarters. With such a wealth of experience and leadership among its members, it can be understood that the SAS initially had some reservations about a new commander whose whole recent experience had been in Burma, but when Brigadier McLeod was posted to GHQ Delhi early in 1945, Calvert took over and soon gained their respect and support.

The village of Earls Colne and the neighbouring small airfield at Halstead, lying just to the west of Colchester, formed the bases for the Special Air Service Brigade, which Calvert visited for the first time in January, 1945. Soon after this, 1 and 2 SAS were detached for operations under 2nd Army Headquarters. Therefore Calvert, with an administrative HQ in Essex, and an advanced tactical HQ in Holland, retained under his direct command a Belgian SAS unit and two battalions of Chasseurs Alpin Parachutistes. Many of these men had served in the French Foreign Legion and the Maquis and were a tough and wild crowd. Soon after he arrived, Calvert received a serious complaint from the local landowner, Lord Ullswater, that the French soldiers were shooting his hares and pheasants with .303 ammunition. Ullswater had powerful government connections and Calvert addressed his unit severely. Then he received another more furious complaint. The French pleaded their innocence and assured Calvert that all their ammunition was accounted for. He then went into a store and saw piles of ammunition lying everywhere in heaps. He was so angry he brought the CO, Colonel Bollardière, the Quartermaster and other officers and locked them in the store for the whole day until the ammunition was checked. After he released them in the evening he expected an adverse reaction, but found that by taking a really tough line he had won their respect. In the short time available, he put the whole brigade through an extremely severe training programme.

At this time the 2nd Canadian Corps, supported by a Polish division, were the forward Allied troops pushing fairly swiftly through Holland. While the training programme was carried through, Calvert made several recce flights to his tactical HQ in Holland and also over the Dutch country lying to the west of Zwolle and Groningen, and out as far as the Zuider Zee (now the Ijsselmeer). He then swiftly planned an operation codenamed, "Operation Amherst". He divided the French and Belgians into groups of about fifteen men and planned to drop them in twenty different places in north-east Holland, particularly along the road from Groningen to Leeuwarden, in order to secure the road and rail bridges, and to hold them while the Canadians advanced northwards from Apeldoorn and Deventer.

From secure bases on the bridges they aimed to disrupt German communications, destroy equipment and transport and liaise with local resistance groups in order to send intelligence reports back to the Canadian HQ.

Calvert's French and Belgian troops, who had seen their countries overrun and who had families living under German occupation, had an intense hatred for the Nazis and were eager to get to grips with the enemy. Their enthusiasm was reassuring to Calvert as they prepared for their first action under his command.

On 6 April he gave a final detailed briefing at Halstead airfield before they left. At the end of the briefing he described the type of country around the dropping zones and added, "There will be plenty of game like hares and pheasants". They gasped for a moment, then, roaring with laughter, they gave a great cheer. They flew off that night in Stirlings of 38 Group RAF.

The meticulous planning work of the admirable Brigade HQ resulted in trouble-free and accurate drops for all the different groups, and as reports began to come back it appeared that they had achieved total surprise. Of course Calvert could not resist the temptation to indulge his macabre sense of humour by dropping heavily booby-trapped dummy parachutists, which he hoped would confuse and delay any German troops in the area. The drops took place in an area away from the main fighting and they did not expect to meet any highly trained front-line units, but they were surprised by the feeble opposition they encountered. One corporal with eight men had captured 100 prisoners and needed barbed wire to build a compound.

A swift allied advance through northern Holland would quickly pose a threat to the German North Sea ports at Emden, Bremen and Hamburg, so Calvert, anticipating a strong German reaction, kept some of the Belgian SAS in reserve at his advance HQ. They were well-prepared and had the latest version of the armoured jeep, with bullet-proof screens, Vickers machine guns front and rear, self-sealing petrol tanks and equipment to lay smoke screens. In spite of these advantages, when the Belgians went into action with their jeeps they suffered very heavy casualties, partly because of the flat Dutch landscape and its waterways which forced vehicles to keep to roads along the dykes. These excellent vehicles were most successful in open country and proved their worth when Lieutenant-Colonel

Brian Franks with seventy-five jeeps from 1 and 2 SAS drove ahead of the main forces and reached Kiel in early May.

As had happened at Arnhem, the Allied advance was delayed, but there appeared to be little German response to the SAS operation, and this prompted Calvert to embark on a dangerous but ultimately successful enterprise. Reports coming back from the dropping zones suggested that there were few active German units in the area, so, taking a calculated risk, he drove off in his large staff car, with a Union Jack flying, towards Groningen, accompanied by a detachment of self-propelled 25-pounder guns manned by Poles. Feeling distinctly nervous, they drove into the first village. They received a rapturous welcome while the local resistance group dealt with any Germans in the area. Their triumphal progress continued with few hitches. At one village a French NCO ran up to Calvert saying, *"Attendez, mon Général, attendez"*. He rushed into a house and, to the delight of his comrades, came out and presented Calvert with a pheasant.

The toughest opposition came just south of Groningen where a German parachute unit had dug itself in on a road leading directly to the German border only twenty miles away. Then the well-tried techniques which the SAS had developed came into play. Calvert called up a squadron of fighter-bombers, which flew in, and with bombs, cannon shells and bullets devastated the German position. The Polish guns fired over 100 shells, and then, under cover of smoke, the Belgian SAS went in with rifle and bayonet. They took the position, killed or took prisoner all the Germans and suffered only one casualty.

At this stage it was difficult to know exactly where the front line lay and Calvert, trying to maintain contact with his widespread SAS groups, had one final adventure. In his staff car, with the French Commanding Officer, Colonel Bollardière, he drove down a minor road and came to a large barbed-wire compound, guarded by a few elderly German soldiers who immediately surrendered. It turned out to be a camp for 6,000 Polish women who had been taken away after the Warsaw uprising of 1944. As soon as the two officers entered the camp they were mobbed by excited and hysterical women who hugged and kissed them and grabbed their hats, their badges and their buttons as souvenirs. The women only released them when Calvert promised to send the nearby Polish division to see them. The

Polish division arrived very soon. The women took charge and pointed out the guards who had been decent, and the remainder were taken out and shot. Driving away, Calvert said to Bollardière that he would prefer to face a group of German parachutists rather than face those women again. The Frenchman did not concur. Later Calvert wrote in his non-commital way, "For some time after that there was something of a dent in the Allied lines while the Poles and girls had a tremendous reunion beano. Having seen the Poles in action, it must have been quite a party."

Operation Amherst had cleared a large area of northern Holland, had cornered a substantial number of German troops who had hoped to escape along the coast to Emden, and had also captured von Ribbentrop. The SAS received warm praise from the GOC, General Gale, later echoed by Browning and Montgomery.

Calvert himself received the French Croix de Guerre avec Palme, and the Legion of Honour (Officer), together with the Belgian Croix de Guerre and the Order of Leopold. He considered these to be a tribute to his units rather than to him personally. He remained steadfastly loyal to them, feeling that they did not receive the recognition they deserved. Later he argued strongly with the editors of the Official History, who treated Operation Amherst in a most cavalier fashion. Calvert remained a respected and honoured member of the Veterans' Associations of both the French and Belgian SAS, and he crowned fifty years of close and affectionate contact by appearing as Guest of Honour at the 1995 celebrations in Paris and Brussels.

The SAS operations in Holland in April, 1945, in which they lost thirty killed, coincided with the final offensives of the Canadian, British and American armies across the Rhine and deep into Germany. The Canadian Army reached Groningen on 16 April, in the same week as the British and American Armies drove across the North German Plain and reached the Elbe. On 4 May, on Luneburg Heath, Montgomery accepted the unconditional surrender of the German forces in N. W. Europe. At this stage the Germans made strenuous efforts to divide the Allies, but they held firm and further unconditional surrenders took place at Rheims on 7 May, and in Berlin on 8 May, which became VE Day. While the western countries started to celebrate, serious problems still remained. In Norway over 250,000 German troops under General Boehme did not at once accept the surrender. Along the Norwegian coast lay the bases of much of the German U-Boat pack and, although Admiral Doenitz had ordered all U-Boats to return to harbour and surrender, many initially failed to respond. This was the background to the urgent demand for the 1st Airborn Division to be flown to Norway.

The SAS Brigade, because of available air transport, had been among the earliest units to return to England. At Earls Colne the French and Belgian units began to leave for home, but 1st and 2nd SAS under Calvert had to leave the day after VE Day with the advance guard of the 1st Airborne Division. Calvert and his advance party landed at Stavanger (See map p. 15) and when the weather closed in, preventing the main force from arriving, Calvert and 36 men set off for Kristiansand to enforce the surrender. At the same time a mission from Supreme Headquarters Allied Expeditionary Force (SHAEF) flew in to force Boehme to sign the surrender document, but Calvert was not certain that news of this would have reached Kristiansand.

In the area lay 3000 German troops commanded by a Lieutenant General, 40,000 Russian prisoners of war, a huge naval base with twenty-six U-Boats and other German warships and a Luftwaffe base. The General was punctilious and surrendered as instructed. Calvert took a very strong line about saluting and respectful conduct towards all his staff, and he demanded that German officers enforce this. With only thirty-six men this was pure bluff, but it worked well. Initially, the Luftwaffe pilots were truculent but did not attempt any violence. The naval base claimed the right to surrender to a naval officer, but in the end accepted Calvert's authority. The U-Boat pens illustrated the absurdity of the situation. In the harbour lay twenty-six of the world's most advanced submarines, all fitted with the latest Schnorkel apparatus which enabled each craft to travel under water for lengthy periods, but Calvert could only spare one man to guard them. He could do little more than count them morning and evening. In fact one got away and is believed to have reached Argentina.

The Russian prisoners chose to stay in their camp, where Calvert did his best to provide them with adequate food and clothing. He even obtained an air drop especially for them. This established a sound rapport which was helpful when, a few weeks later, relations became much more difficult.

Calvert kept up his bluff for five days, after which major units of the Airborne Division, together with civil affairs officers, arrived.

Calvert then had to take his two units further north along the coast to Bergen. Here problems became more complex, though he was supported by the two complete SAS Regiments. These included some of the legendary characters of the Regiment, among them Lieutenant-Colonel Paddy Mayne who, among other honours, won four DSOs and several rugby caps for Ireland; and Major Roy Farran DSO MC who distinguished himself in many SAS operations. The British were not particularly popular in the area. Many residents of the town rememebered that during the war an RAF raid on the naval base had scored a direct hit on a school and had killed 300 children. Similarly, feelings were ruffled when, in an attempt to include local people in some celebrations, they were invited to a Sergeants' Mess dance in a building which, unbeknown to the British, had been the Gestapo headquarters where many loyal Norwegians had been tortured to death.

The harbour and the beaches had been heavily mined and the most urgent task was to clear the mines so that food and supplies could be brought in. Calvert ordered the Germans to organize the clearing of the mines, and added one refinement, that, when an area had been cleared, German soldiers were made to walk back over it to prove they had done their work properly.

Generally the German forces co-operated adequately, but one incident had an amusing sequel. During an over-boisterous dinner night in the Mess, Calvert had been heaved over the shoulder of Paddy Mayne and had sustained two black eyes. The following morning he had to interview the German general and his ADC. This youth, in an arrogant and supercilious way, sniggered at Calvert with his black eyes. Calvert hardly noticed, but Mayne and Farran were furious. The next day another interview was arranged, and, beaming, Farran ushered in the General and his ADC, who had two black eyes!

For the remainder of the time in Norway the greatest problems centred on the 60,000 Russian POWs. Calvert had gone out of his way to provide the Russians with food and clothing, and amicable co-operation continued. The Russians, with their fine bass voices, always sang "God Save the King" when Calvert visited them, but then a group of Political Commissars arrived and everything changed. Calvert met them and felt that they exuded "an air of evil", and soon his anger turned to revulsion. A few days after their arrival they charged Calvert with ill-treating the Russian soldiers and with subjecting them to western propaganda. The commissars caused constant trouble, especially with the Poles among the prisoners who strongly objected to the communist indoctrination. There was further trouble with the fairly substantial number of Russians who wanted to defect to the west or stay in Norway. These incidents, within a few weeks of VE Day, proved a grim and accurate forecast of the Cold War.

The Russians caused one final crisis. The Norwegian authorities decided to have an Allied Forces Day to celebrate the victory over Germany, and it fell to Calvert to organize the event in Bergen. Once again the Russians, under the influence of the Political Commissars, refused to co-operate, so that the march past of all the Allied units – the Royal Navy, the Royal Norwegian Navy, the Army, the RAF, and resistance groups – had to be planned without them. Calvert, as the Area Commander, together with a British Admiral, took the salute. Just as the marching columns reached the dais, Russian columns appeared, marching in the opposite direction. To save an embarrassing incident Calvert and the Admiral stood back to back saluting the different columns as they passed.

Soon afterwards Calvert received a stiff reprimand from GHQ in Oslo for this "disgraceful incident". This revived some of his wartime thoughts about staff officers. One saying current at the time was "Bread is the staff of life, and a staff officer's life is one long loaf". Calvert fumed, but instead of replying in detail he merely signalled, "East is East and West is West ...".

Early in August, 1945, 1 and 2 SAS returned to Earls Colne. On 21 September Calvert presided at the ceremony to hand over the Belgian SAS to the Belgian authorities, who kept that excellent unit in being. In a similar farewell ceremony on 1 October he presented Colours and medals to the two French SAS Regiments before they were absorbed back into the French forces. All of these units which had taken on so much of the esprit de corps of the SAS were fully involved in the post-war upheavals faced by their countries in North Africa, Indo-China and the Congo.

The farewells to the Belgians and the French was but a prelude to the final ceremony for the SAS Brigade, and on 8 October, 1945, Calvert presided at the formal disbandment of 1 and 2 SAS. This came as a savage blow to those who thought that, because of the

8. Cambodia, 1972: talking to the Airborne Divisional Commander.

9. Vietnam, 1972; with the Chief of Staff.

10. Prince Charles, Patron of the Chindit Old Comrades Association, talking to
Calvert. On his right is Brigadier Scott, who commanded the 1st Bn the
King's Liverpool Regiment (see p.71).

11. On holiday with one of his nieces, 1980s.

12. VJ Parade, London, August, 1995. Pushing the chair is Tony Harris, Calvert's friend and confidant for the past twenty-five years (see p.171).

13. The Grunen Jaeger in 1996. The owner, Herr Voss, together with Herr Jacob, tried to put right the injustice of Calvert's court martial (see Ch.14).

14. 'I never thought I'd come back.' Calvert on Pagoda Hill, March, 1997. (*Picture courtesy of Piers Storie-Pugh*)

development of airpower, there would be an increasing demand for Special Forces, but all was not lost. Calvert, with all the other SAS leaders, was involved in a serious and detailed War Office enquiry into the achievements of the SAS during the War and its possible rôle in the future. Calvert, as commander of the SAS Brigade, wrote a significant letter to his erstwhile colleagues.

Dated 12 October, 1945, and addressed to many of the great names in the Regiment – Stirling, Mayne, Franks, Lloyd-Owen, Jellicoe, Farran and others – his letter illustrated one important technique which has remained part of the SAS ethos, namely "the discussion" in which every member has both a right and a responsibility to put forward their views. Addressing men who had taken part in SAS operations world-wide, Calvert asked them to consider the principles on which they operated, and from that point to consider how to train and maintain units for a future rôle. Bearing in mind the negative attitude of some of the military establishment towards irregular operations, he proposed that once the operations of special units behind the enemy lines was accepted, this concept should become an integral part of training at Staff College and at all military training establishments. He also proposed that there should be a specialist officer at divisional headquarters level, similar to CRE and CRA. He stressed that the SAS would have an equally important future rôle whether the army was advancing or retreating, and he saw the SAS as being complementary to the SOE and other clandestine and intelligence-gathering organizations. He refuted the suggestions that such forces took away the best officers and NCOs from normal units, or that they were expensive, or that any good battalion could do their job. Other more specific requests which had come from the Director of Tactical Investigation included recruitment, the provision of specialist equipment and weapons, signals communication, liaison with the Royal Navy and the Royal Air Force and, finally, the command structure.

In the very positive replies to this enquiry, the majority argued strongly that in an age of nuclear warfare there was a rôle for SAS operations because air power and the development of helicopters had created a totally new scenario. David Stirling, not unexpectedly, made a significant contribution and brilliantly summed up the central theme of "discipline": Discipline in the testing and selection of all SAS members, discipline in every aspect of service, and the power of the CO to RTU (Return to Unit) anyone who does not measure up to the exacting standards of the Regiment.

This substantial enquiry resulted in a War Office Report which suggested that the role of the SAS should never be confused with that of the normal infantry, since it should be highly specialized and manned by men of individuality who might not always fit into a normal infantry unit. The report concluded that in a future war small parties of well-trained and highly disciplined troops operating behind the enemy lines could achieve results out of all proportion to the numbers involved, and that there was considerable scope for development. These were encouraging words but they did not prevent the disbandment of this unique regiment which had such brilliant achievements to its credit. Fortunately, there were sufficient determined characters among its members, and sufficient support at a high level in the military establishment, to ensure that its demise was only temporary.

# CHAPTER EIGHT

# THE POST-WAR YEARS, 1945–1949

At the end of the war many officers enjoyed lengthy periods on leave or waiting for their next posting, but Calvert was less fortunate. After a brief leave in Devon, he reported to Department AG7 at the War Office to discuss his next posting. He was offered the appointment of Zone Commander in Austria with the rank of Brigadier. He turned this down – a decision he later regretted – and accepted the posting as CRE (Commander Royal Engineers) as a Lieutenant-Colonel in the 1st Indian Armoured Division at Secunderabad in central India. He made this decision because he thought that after years of action with the Chindits and the SAS he ought to return to a Royal Engineers unit and refresh his engineering skills.

He flew out to India and reported to Divisional HQ at Secunderabad. He found the atmosphere in "A" Mess, the Mess for senior officers, to be very stuffy, and he moved out to the Mess of the Sappers and Miners with whom he was to work. Later, in Hong Kong he again moved out of a Senior Officers' Mess, and this gained him the reputation of being rather a bolshie character. His main responsibility at Secunderabad was to plan and carry out suitable post-war training for a number of units of the Bombay Sappers and Miners, and the Madras Sappers and Miners, regiments which had done excellent work in the Burma campaign. This met his criteria of returning to the engineering field, but he found the training work frustrating and he began to drink rather heavily. There was a little light relief when, backed by most of the sappers, Calvert rode their largest horse and managed to come fourth in an inter-unit race. Soon afterwards he was delighted when he was picked out by Auchinleck to lead a small group of sappers on a serious reconnaissance through Baluchistan and up to the border of Persia (Iran). The India High Command was concerned about the danger of a Russian incursion into India through Persia and Calvert's task was to carry out a detailed recce and report back to Auchinleck. This issue, the "Great Game" which featured in Kipling's *Kim*, had preoccupied the British Raj through much of the nineteenth century and had involved Calvert's father when Lord Curzon was Viceroy. Now Calvert was to take part himself.

He was allotted two officers, twelve sappers, two three ton trucks, a jeep and the use of a Dakota aircraft. After some weeks of planning he flew up to Karachi in the Dakota where the rest of his small unit joined him. At this time, early 1947, in the turbulent months prior to Indian independence, the different peoples in the whole area of what became Pakistan were dangerously excited. The Pathans, based on Kabul, hoped to unite their peoples who were scattered across many other areas. Jinnah led the demand for a separate Muslim state of Pakistan, and the whole area where Calvert was to operate was extremely volatile. The situation became dangerously complex because of Soviet activity in the Central Asian Republics like Uzbekistan, along the northern borders of India.

From Karachi Calvert set out to reconnoitre the area due west of the city, leading along the coast towards the Persian border. The terrain here was mountainous and impenetrable, and he reckoned that Russia had not studied Long Range Penetration. He also enjoyed the thought that Alexander the Great had made the discovery that the route along the coast was impassable. Because of the difficult terrain nearly all the roads in the area led up to Quetta, a main junction and a long-standing British military garrison. After he had probed the coastal route without success, Calvert led his group up to Quetta and from there reconnoitred westwards towards the border areas. Although there were serious issues at stake, Calvert enjoyed the freedom of leading his small group into the remote areas and into the superb country of the Himalayan foothills. Here they could camp, plenty of game shooting was available, and they could swim in the clear mountain streams. In part of the border area there were extensive dry salt lakes and Calvert had to assess whether these could provide possible landing grounds if the Russians invaded. His Chindit experience with Dakotas landing on hastily improvised jungle landing strips was invaluable, but he found that his young post-war Dakota pilot was not keen to accept his assurances, or to try out his theories. Wherever he served, Calvert set out to establish

Reconnaissance

friendly relations with the local people, and he gained a lot of support from a Pathan leader to whom he had presented a goat's horn mounted on a silver base.

After this enjoyable and successful expedition, Calvert submitted his report to Auchinleck. The main gist was that a modern army would find it almost impossible to advance along the coast from Persia to Karachi, and therefore defences should be concentrated more in the Quetta area where all the roads converged.

Shortly after submitting his report to Auchinleck, Calvert flew back in August, 1947, to England to attend Staff College. Many of his fears about "The Staff" were confirmed. When he arrived as a student at Staff College, Calvert, who had been outstandingly the most successful Chindit commander after Wingate, found it slightly galling that Jack Masters, who had been largely responsible for the disaster of 111 Brigade at "Blackpool", was on the directing staff. Most of the instructors had experience of battle, but the inevitable Staff College solution to problems appeared to inhibit their thinking.

In all their schemes, the enemy, now no longer the Germans or the Japanese, was called Neuralia. In most of the operations the Directing Staff seemed to advise retreat, while Calvert usually suggested attack. He strongly advocated the development of close liaison between Army and RAF, building on the great achievements of the Chindits and the final Burma advance, but his views rarely carried the day. He became something of a rebel and, with a few like-minded colleagues formed the Trans-Neuralia Frontier Force. They even held a formal dinner to which they invited the Commandant. With his rather bolshie attitude and with the disadvantage (in the eyes of the establishment) of his Chindit background, he did not greatly enhance his prospects of promotion. However, he did make some impression on Montgomery who was trying to liven up stodgy Staff College thinking.

After Staff College he was invited on to Montgomery's planning staff, and they got on well. Calvert recalls one dinner night when, with a large gathering of very senior officers, Montgomery turned to him and said, "Calvert, why are you the only one to give me a straight answer to a question?" He replied that everyone present had high acting ranks which they could lose, but he was substantive major and he could not be reduced below that rank. In pondering over the most important influences in his life, Calvert did not rate Staff College very highly. In first place he put his old friend Peter Fleming, because of his clear and objective point of view about every problem, whether military or civilian.

During his time on Montgomery's planning staff Calvert saw some paintings of the Siam death railway by an ex-prisoner of war. He got permission to bring some of the paintings to HQ, and added a caption: "This is what happens if you lose". The paintings had been displayed on Brighton pier, and the pier authorities subsequently sent in a huge bill. Montgomery reluctantly ordered that the bill should be paid, but he and Calvert were both furious when they learned that the artist did not receive a penny of the money.

Carrying out research for Montgomery, Calvert came across the notes of a high-level policy meeting at which the official attitude towards the Chindits was discussed. It was decided that the rôle and achievements of Long Range Penetration and the Chindits should be played down because Wingate was a divisive influence, and the Army did not want every company commander thinking he was a "Wingate".

During his time on Montgomery's planning staff Calvert had to work out the logistics for a proposed landing on the coast of Malaya, followed by an advance up to Siam. After this he was next posted, in 1948, as a Lieutenant-Colonel, to the Staff of the Allied Military Government in Trieste, one of the first places to experience real clashes between communism and the west.

After a successful campaign in the Balkans, Marshal Tito had attempted in 1945 to grab Trieste for Yugoslavia. General Sir Harold Alexander, as Commander-in-Chief Mediterranean, had resolutely prevented this. Prolonged negotiations took place between Britain and Yugoslavia and a settlement was agreed in 1947 which divided Trieste into two zones. Tito controlled the hinterland and the southern Zone B, while Zone A was administered and controlled by the Anglo-American Military Government. Alexander had been correct to hold on to Trieste because it was essentially an Italian town, and when a permanent treaty was signed in 1954 it reverted to Italy. Thus in 1948 the Allied Military Government was popular with the local inhabitants since it protected them from communist aggression. Most of the problems facing the Allied Forces in Trieste centred on the lengthy frontier with Yugoslavia, but Calvert was fairly heavily involved in what he considered fruitless bureaucracy. As Director of Parastatal Property he had to spend tedious days deciding what property belonged to the state, and indeed to which state. He had to make decisions on the supply and price of food and he had to monitor Allied intelligence about Yugoslavia. Against the tedium of such tasks he had the more interesting and enjoyable responsibility of commanding the Boundary Commission. This involved him in an incident which illustrates many of the tensions of that time and the ideological clashes which were soon to divide Europe along the line of the Iron Curtain.

In one of the British units there was a private soldier who was in constant trouble and who spent much of his time confined to barracks for drunkenness and other misbehaviour. He finally decided that he had no future in Britain nor in the British Army and he tried to desert to Tito's forces. Unfortunately, in trying to cross the no-man's-land along the border he was shot by the Yugoslav forces and killed. They were quick to realize that here was the chance of an ideological coup. The Yugoslavs took the body and, claiming that the man had been shot by "The Imperialist Monarchic Fascist forces", gave him a state funeral with considerable publicity. This was a challenge to the Western powers which could not be tolerated. Calvert, as head of the Boundary Commission, was fully involved in the difficult and prolonged negotiations for the return of the body. In the end agreement was reached. The body was exhumed and formally transferred to a waiting Allied guard at the border. Then it was escorted through Trieste by two military bands and reburied with full military honours. Thus a sad private soldier achieved posthumous fame as one of the early victims of the Cold War.

In spite of such occasional excitement, and the chance to keep fit by captaining the British garrison water polo team, Calvert was ill at ease in his staff posting and he looked with a severely critical eye at the peacetime army. Recalling the small, fit and efficient staff of 77 Brigade behind the lines in Burma, he looked askance at the bloated, inefficient and top-heavy administration of the British garrison. He produced a remarkable document which illustrated his wide grasp of military affairs and his sound and critical approach. He painted an interesting picture of the post-war army and entitled his paper "Kicking against the Pricks".

He started by considering the problem of the huge number of HQ staff at every level. This he blamed on the deluge of orders and requests from the War Office and the Government. He reasoned that increasing bureaucracy in an empire was always the first sign of decadence and he quoted examples from Persian, Greek, Roman, Moghul and other empires "where unnecessary parasites batten on the nobler tree".

Because officers were badly paid, the Army had used the subterfuge of raising the number of higher ranks and increasing the number of staff appointments. Calvert referred to the pre-war Shanghai garrison with a staff of twenty, as opposed to the staff of the British garrison in Trieste of one hundred and twenty. There was a shortage of good clerks in the army with the result that captains and majors were employed to do what corporals did before the war. Such officers had to attend courses learning to do clerical work, then return to their units and stay in their offices, "after which they cease to be good soldiers and finish up with petty, pernickety clerk-like minds – unable evermore to command soldiers in battle".

Reverting to his long-held theory that the best is the enemy of the good, Calvert argued against the "Financial Sinbads" at every commander's elbow, saving a penny here and a penny there. He grieved that every CO was enmeshed with pettyfogging regulations and at the mercy of more and more staff officers and officials being driven in more and more staff cars. "The British army is like a beautiful, glossy, over-bodied, under-engined limousine, filled with all sorts of patent gadgets, but with little power and no cross-country performance." He clinched his argument by quoting part of the Order of Battle of the Rhine Army: "the Sausage Manufacturers Supervisory Increment (Germany)", and he added "Sausage Stuffers of the world, unite. You have nothing to lose but your skins".

He suggested, as the first remedy for his situation, to remove every trivial parliamentary question, such as "Why Tommy cannot buy toothpaste?" and to refer parents of National Service soldiers to their son's CO. Next he proposed a very substantial reduction in the number of high-ranking officers. He quoted Marshal Saxe and added, "It is not high-ranking officers who win battles. It is good ones". Considering the rôle of the British army in policing trouble spots around the world, he observed that it took a brigade to achieve what a seasoned battalion would formerly have done, and he referred again to the Romans who preferred a small disciplined force to large numbers.

Next, in order to curb the time that military officers, all potential commanders in battle, had to spend sitting in offices, he proposed a well-trained and efficient Corps of Clerks as the Indian Army had. This corps should have a career structure and be open to women. As a rather lonely bachelor, he had often considered that married personnel were much better treated than bachelors, and he argued that a Corps of Clerks could end the system of employing wives to carry out confidential work in overseas commands.

Concluding his diatribe, he pointed out that, because of the overloaded and inefficient British staff system, with its insatiable demand for accurate returns and statistics, the American unit in Trieste with the same manpower as the British, could muster four more fighting units of company strength. He demanded a return to the time when a commander was trusted and was not beholden to a mass of supervisory officers and pettyfogging regulations.

He wrote that, having commanded, in action, British, French, Belgian, Australian, New Zealand, Nigerian, Gurkha, Indian and Chinese troops, he strongly agreed with Lord Wavell that the British Army was the most over-administered army in the world. Finally, a delightful ambiguous comment: "I suppose it is of little use kicking against the pricks. There are too many pricks."

Calvert clearly wrote this paper in a disgruntled mood, but it did contain some useful and critical thought. In spite of his disillusionment, he had performed well in Trieste. After roughly two years he was posted back to the Far East as a Lieutenant-Colonel General Staff Officer Grade 1 (Air) at HQ Hong Kong. The authorities in Hong Kong had watched with interest and some alarm as Mao Tse-tung and his communist forces rapidly overcame Chiang Kai-shek in the Chinese Civil War, 1947–49. With the communist victory in 1949, the Hong Kong authorities anticipated trouble and decided to bring their available forces up to a higher state of readiness.

Calvert's renown as a successful Chindit leader and his experience in developing close air support for the Chindit columns on the ground had led to this appointment. As GI Air he was responsible for training both RAF and Fleet Air Arm pilots in close-support air bombing. The RAF and Fleet Air Arm each had two squadrons involved in the training which was entirely devised by Calvert and based on his Chindit experience. He received high-level support for this training project and he was able to use a remote part of the Colony as a practice bombing range. The training was made more effective by the relay to the assembled trainees of the conversation and orders given in the aircraft's cockpit during their bombing runs. Each training session was discussed in detail afterwards.

The climax of the training was a formal bombing competition between the four squadrons. This was attended by the Governor, the GOC and senior officers from the three Services. Calvert devised a trophy for the best squadron. This was a figure of a naked woman and was called the Bhang Ohn Prize. Calvert had been amused at the attitude of the naval commanders, who, before the competition, announced confidently that they were bound to win because all their pilots were officers. They lost. Calvert was gratified that his close-support bombing training schedule was adopted by the Services and was used to good effect in the Korean War which followed soon afterwards.

After the communist victory in China their forces, both overt and covert, stepped up their activities in countries all over the Far East. Once again Calvert, because of his experience and reputation as a Chindit leader was soon called to help elsewhere.

# CHAPTER NINE

# MALAYA 1950–51

Calvert had played a major part in driving the Japanese out of Burma, but in 1948 the aftermath of the Japanese withdrawal created a situation in Malaya which was once again to bring him to the Far East.

In the early years of the war the Malay Communist Party was fairly active, but the British civil and military establishment, with their attitude of superiority, stood aloof from any suggestion of co-operation. A slight change came when Hitler attacked Russia in June, 1941, with 145 divisions in Operation Barbarossa. This dramatic end to the Nazi-Soviet Pact meant that Russia became an ally of Britain in the fight against the Fascists, and so the Russian Communist Party ordered its satellites in Malaya to co-operate with the British. Little was achieved in practice before the Japanese attack in December, 1941, but the British administration, far too late, did set up the 101 Training School under Captain Freddie Spencer Chapman to train guerrilla fighters and to co-ordinate intelligence gathering.

As a part of their attack in the Pacific, the Japanese landed at Kota Bharu in north-east Malaya on 8 December, 1941, the day after Pearl Harbor, and rapidly swept aside the resistance of British and Indian troops. In a few disastrous weeks Malaya was overrun and on 15 February, 1942, Singapore surrendered. In spite of the abject surrender – nearly 100,000 troops at Singapore – a number of groups which had been trained at the 101 Training School, including Spencer Chapman, did stay behind in the jungle to harass the Japanese forces. These were supported by Force 136, an intelligence-gathering unit based on the SOE which had its headquarters in Ceylon. However, few groups survived and few took any effective action against the Japanese. By 1945 the only real opposition to the Japanese came from the Malayan People's Anti-Japanese Army which numbered nearly

7000, and was composed substantially of Chinese communist supporters.

The sudden and unexpected end to the war against Japan in August, 1945, took all the opposition forces by surprise, and as the British colonial authorities began to return, the Chinese, who had provided most of the opposition to Japan, decided that they were no longer going to accept their pre-war subservience and went into immediate opposition. While keeping intact their military structure and operating as the Malayan Communist Party, they infiltrated many organizations, particularly the trade unions and teachers' associations.

In the years after the war Russia took control of Eastern Europe and struck the first blows in the Cold War. In China, Mao Tse-tung gradually drove out the corrupt and inefficient Chiang Kai-shek. Neither were able to give much support to the Malayan communists. The British administration in Malaya failed to capitalize on this advantage and proved to be hopelessly inept.

In the civilian and police organizations fierce antagonisms raged between those who had been prisoners of the Japanese and those who had got away, illustrated by the case of a man who got away and returned in 1945 as a plump colonel to greet his emaciated former colleague who weighed five stone as he emerged from prison camp. Antagonism also raged between the pre-war Malayan police and the newly arrived officers from the Palestine Police when the British mandate there ended in 1948; there was also antagonism between the civilian and military forces. Thus little was done to prepare for the growing emergency.

In 1948 the Chinese communists in Malaya, under their young leader Chin Peng, felt strong enough to take the initiative. As part of a wider plan to cause disruption across the whole south Pacific, they set out to disrupt and destroy the Malayan economy which depended heavily on the export of rubber and tin. In June, 1948, they attacked and killed two British mining officials and three rubber planters in Perak. The British colonial administration belatedly declared a state of emergency and the long and difficult struggle against the communist terrorists began. Several factors favoured the terrorists. In 1945 they had grabbed some of the surrendered Japanese weapons, and they had also received large supplies of British weapons which were dropped for them in June, 1945, prior to Operation Zipper. This was the proposed plan to retake Malaya, which, because of the sudden end to the war, never took place. The terrorists had retained their command structure from the struggle against the Japanese and many of their 4000 operators were veterans of that campaign. Their main active support came from the aboriginal people who lived in communities scattered through the jungle, and secondly from the groups of Chinese squatters who lived on the fringes of the developed areas of the country. Perhaps the most important help for them came from the Min Yuen, Chinese people who, while not being particularly active, formed cells throughout the whole of Malayan society, and provided the terrorists with information and food. They worked in post offices, on the railways, in military messes and many other places where they could obtain and pass on information about the movements of the security services. Later, when Sir Henry Gurney, the Malayan High Commissioner, was assassinated in 1952 it was discovered that his butler was in the Min Yuen.

There were many different terrorist organizations with different names and, to eliminate confusion, they are referred to as "communist terrorists" or CTs. The weakness of the CTs was their alienation from the Malay people who felt a strong loyalty to their traditional rulers, the Sultans. The CTs also failed to gain the support of the bulk of the Chinese population who were the industrious backbone of the Malayan economy, and who, after Mao Tse-tung won power in China in 1949, did not wish to come under a Communist régime. The CTs, in attempting to take control of the rural areas, were thwarted by the tough determination of the rubber planters on the estates who armed themselves, and, under the control of the Malayan Police, organized the defence of their estates and refused to be daunted. Their brave stand encouraged a similar stand in the tin mines. In the tin mines and on the rubber planatations the workers, following the example of their managers, refused to give up their livelihood. The resolute attitude of the planters and the miners slowed the advance of the terrorists, but the army and the Malayan Police then had to face the problem of how to destroy a shrewd and experienced enemy in its jungle hideouts. This is where Calvert reappeared.

In 1950 he had been posted to Hong Kong as part of the build-up during the Korean crisis. He had never taken kindly to a staff appointment and was delighted when General Harding, the Commander-in-Chief Far East (later Lord Harding) called him for interview in Singapore. Harding, dissatisfied with the lumbering and ineffective military response to the communist insurgents in the Malayan jungle, needed someone with experience of jungle fighting. Slim, then CIGS, who knew all about Calvert's brilliance as a Chindit leader, strongly recommended him. Harding, who followed Slim as CIGS and crowned an outstanding military career with a distinguished record of public service, endeared himself to generations of officers by his shrewd dictum that the main problem facing young officers was slow horses and fast women. Now, faced with a different type of problem he was glad to call on Mike Calvert's experience, though he had some reservations about the rôle of the irregular forces.

Calvert has given an interesting description of his ideas when Harding invited him to spend six months investigating the situation in Malaya. Harding told him, "Things are not going nearly as well as we had hoped. General Slim says you know all about guerrilla warfare. I give you carte-blanche: go where you like, see who you like, and discover what is wrong. The police are not working well with the army: the civil government is not doing this and that: there's the problem of the Sultans: the Chinese versus Malays: the commercial interests of the rubber planatations: the tin mines and the like." (Letter – Calvert Papers) Harding told him to investigate all these aspects and to report back. By this time 1300 police, civilians and soldiers had been killed by the CTs.

Calvert, who later became a world-renowned expert on the wider issues of guerrilla warfare, was already maturing his ideas. Looking at the Malayan situation, he reasoned that the insurgents would try to gain their ends by disrupting the economy until the government, facing the increasing financial demands of security forces and the destruction of the economy, gave in to their demands. He compared the terrorists to the malaria germ in the blood stream and saw the rôle of the special forces going in to the jungle as the quinine which would destroy the germ.

He had an energetic six months during which he travelled all over Malaya and also accompanied innumerable patrols from the regular battalions which were fighting the terrorists. He quickly sensed a feeling of lethargy and futility. Many patrols, acting on inadequate or out-dated information, lumbered off into the jungle and rarely saw a terrorist, and even more rarely caught one. On one patrol which was on a promising trail to a terrorist camp, the pursuit was abandoned because the Major in charge had to return to his unit because the CO insisted that all officers had to be present at a Guest Night in the Mess. In another well-publicized part of his report, Calvert recorded how he had accompanied several patrols of the Scots Guards, but, although they were smart, keen and efficient, real aggressiveness was lacking. After further inquiry Calvert discovered that the CO thought the Scots Guards should not be in Malaya anyway and it was not their job "to chase bare-arsed niggers". Calvert tried not to be specific in his report about those problems, but Harding insisted on exact detail, then sacked the CO. The example of Ferret Force which was set up in June, 1948, to seek intelligence by penetrating the terrorist forces was not encouraging. Originally created from a nucleus of Force 136 which had been effective against the Japanese, Ferret Force was itself divided between civil and military elements, and, in spite of some successes against the terrorists, was abandoned after a few months. Calvert criticized the military operations for being too cumbersome and too slow, rather as Wingate had done in Palestine in 1938. That did not make him popular either.

In the most significant part of his report, Calvert made clear and specific recommendations. He proposed a highly trained force to carry out long-range penetration into the jungle in order to attack the terrorist bases and destroy them. At the same time he addressed the wider problem of denying support to the terrorists by winning the "hearts and minds" of the aboriginal population who were often brutally coerced to supply information and food for the terrorists. Calvert has never been given sufficient credit for this report, both parts of which were accepted by the Malayan administration, and one of which, "the winning of hearts and minds", later became a major plank of the Briggs Plan, which during the 1950s led to victory over the terrorists.

After presenting his thesis to Harding, who clearly approved of it, Calvert had to go to London to argue his case in Whitehall. He also suggested that one man should be given absolute control over operations against the terrorists. The speed with which Calvert's proposals had been accepted meant that they had never been thought through in adequate detail. Although he had been given direct access to Harding, Calvert's whole enterprise was bedevilled by the lack of good quality administrative support, and this caused many of the major problems which came later.

He was pleased to have the opportunity to decide the title and rôle of the new unit. He had had the melancholy experience of witnessing the disbandment of the Chindits in 1944 and of the SAS at their final parade in October, 1945. With this in mind, he grasped the opportunity to suggest that the SAS should be re-established, and when this was initially refused he proposed a compromise – to use the SAS title with another designation. One proposal, made in the light of the growing menace of communist activity in many territories in south east Asia, was "South Pacific Rangers". This had too much of an American ring for the British military establishment, but a compromise was finally accepted. It was "The Malayan Scouts (SAS Regiment)". A clear and impressive badge depicted the title "The Malayan Scouts" centred on a Malayan kris or dagger, with SAS forming the base. The official approval of the title was a great personal achievement for Calvert: his next urgent challenge was to recruit men for his force. He threw himself into this task with eager enthusiasm, proud to have the chance to re-create the SAS, and at the same time to imbue the new force with the ethos and philosophy of the Chindits. Facing this challenge, it was a disaster that initially he lacked the back-up support which could have made the project a real success. The key positions in the establishment of a new unit – Second-in-command, Adjutant, Quartermaster, and Training Officer, where men of real calibre were needed – were just not provided. This inadequacy put far to much pressure on Calvert himself, with unfortunate consequences. Soon afterwards some excellent men joined the unit, but by then certain hand-to-mouth methods seem to have been established. He interviewed all officers personally, and several have described his unusual and eccentric methods. Colonel Winter from the Scots Guards volunteered for the Malayan Scouts "because my opinion of the Brigade of Guards was almost as low as their opinion of me". Calvert took him to a coffee shop, the sort of place a Guards Officer would never have patronized. After a long discussion they found that they hardly had enough money to pay for the coffee. On the basis of that interview, Winter was accepted.

Most of the officers Calvert interviewed were impressed by his remarkable grasp of the whole Malayan situation, and the clarity and enthusiasm with which he outlined his main policy for beating the communist terrorists. This, with more detailed ideas than in his initial report to Harding, included several plans, based on long-range penetration into the jungle, in order to deny the CTs their safe bases and to remove their traditional support. He was determined to win over the Aborigines with a "hearts and minds" approach in order to cut off the CTs from their food supply. The Chinese squatters on the edge of the cultivated areas and the jungle had been a fertile source of recruitment and support to the CTs. Calvert, with a remarkable grasp of detail, aimed to remove them from their illegal squats into fortified villages where they would be given a house, granted land, given the opportunity of paid employment and, above all, be protected against the terrorists from the jungle. This key element of the Briggs Plan in fact originated in Calvert's fertile brain.

During his recruiting drive he approached Hugh Bailey, a Police Superintendent in Perak. They discussed Calvert's ideas of three-man patrols penetrating deep into the jungle and preparing ambushes on paths used by terrorists. Bailey had wide experience of police operations against CTs, including raids on jungle camps, and he commented, "From this experience I was convinced that Brigadier Calvert's excellently aggressive programmes would fail."

Bailey and Bill Hillier, who both served in the Malayan Police throughout the emergency, reject Harding's statement, repeated by Calvert, that the police and army did not co-operate. They maintain that police and army units fighting in the jungle had the closest and most successful co-operation. For example, one police unit working with 42 Royal Marine Commando took over guard duties at the Commando camp over Christmas, while the Commandos recipro-cated for Muslim festivals like the end of Ramadan. Tony Crocket, in *Green Beret Red Star* (London, 1954), expressed great admiration for the Malayan Police who were "overworked, understaffed, under-armed, and insufficiently protected yet, always ready to tackle anything that happened, and give advice and support in every situation." Bailey took part in joint police and military operations where some, at least, of Calvert's tactical ideas eventually brought success.

Colonel John Woodhouse, who had a most distinguished career in the SAS, became the Squadron Intelligence Officer, and in a detailed document at the time, vividly described the impact Calvert had on everyone. In briefing Woodhouse, who was to play an important rôle in their operations, Calvert emphasized the need to win over the Aborigines, known disparagingly as the Sakai, and who had been dominated by the CTs for years. Under great pressure to get on with training and to get units out into the jungle, Calvert nonetheless warned of the danger of officers with stereotyped ideas who could not adapt to new challenges. The squadron faced a new situation where there were no manuals nor battle drills, and they had to produce something new. Woodhouse writes, "Mike Calvert dominated all of us. None of us in experience, prestige, or personality came anywhere near him. In consequence he was a lonely man.... His faith and enthusiasm were exhilarating."

The first camp for the Squadron lay near Johore Bahru just over the strait from Singapore, but by September, 1950, it had moved to Dusan Tua nine miles from Kuala Lumpur. This was to be the HQ and base camp combined. Both of these were run-down, depressing camps with totally inadequate training facilities. Volunteers varied from national service conscripts whose military skills were minimal to veterans of the Chindits and the SAS. Calvert's appeal for volunteers caused resentment among commanding officers who faced the prospect of war in Korea and did not want to lose their best officers and NCOs. Naturally though, they used the opportunity to get rid of their real trouble makers, who, almost unscreened, ended up in the Malayan Scouts. Because of the urgent haste to set up this unit, Calvert clearly accepted many unsuitable volunteers, including a group of the French Foreign Legion who had deserted from a ship going to Vietnam and who were to damage the image of their new regiment.

The training had to start, for officers and men alike, with weapon training, fieldcraft, grenade throwing, and the skills of moving in the jungle. This task was made infinitely more difficult by the lack of adequate maps. Calvert, then a Lieutenant-Colonel, personally led the PT parades at 6am with rifle and Bren gun exercises, assault courses, marksmanship and grenade throwing. Accurate shooting was encouraged by a stalking exercise in which two men were issued with fencing masks and air guns which fired pellets. They had to stalk each other, and the extremely painful pellets led to a swift improvement in fieldcraft.

Calvert encouraged the closest co-operation with the police and sent his officers to study the most effective police units. Some of

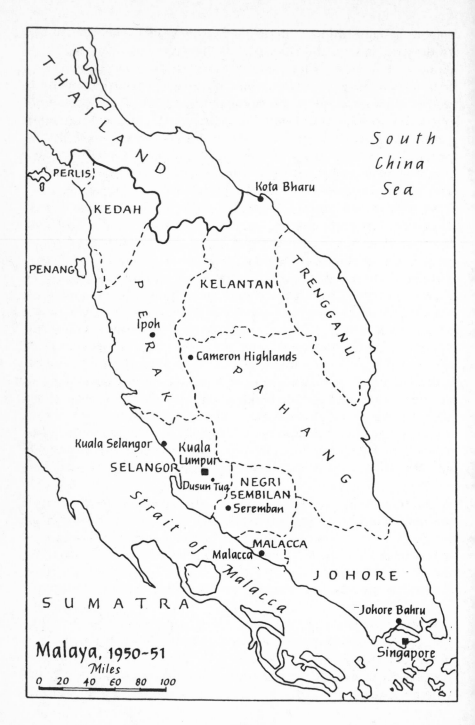

South
China
Sea

THAILAND

PERLIS

KEDAH

PENANG

Kota Bharu

KELANTAN

TRENGGANU

Ipoh

P
E
R
A
K

Cameron Highlands

P
A
H
A
N
G

Kuala Selangor

Kuala
Lumpur

SELANGOR

Dusun Tua

NEGRI
SEMBILAN

Seremban

Strait of Malacca

MALACCA

Malacca

JOHORE

SUMATRA

Johore Bahru

Singapore

Malaya, 1950–51
Miles
0   20   40   60   80   100

these had established bases in the jungle where they obtained valuable information about the CT's activities. After one particular visit when Woodhouse went patrolling with the police guides, collecting information from every available source, he began to envisage the pattern the Squadron could adopt. He planned for the Squadron to establish a base in the jungle and from there each of the four Troops to probe outwards from the base. Each Troop would then sub-divide into four patrols of three men. Each Troop would have a signaller and wireless to keep contact with Squadron HQ – a valuable lesson Calvert had learned in the Chindits. Woodhouse aimed also to have a police lieutenant with each troop to help with language and with Aboriginal liaison. Such a programme anticipated, to the horror of the military medical advisers, that the Troops would stay in the jungle for up to three months.

Against this background, "A" Squadron The Malayan Scouts (SAS Regiment) under its commander, Major Rex Beatty, prepared in October, 1950, to complete its training by spending up to eight weeks in the jungle north of Ipoh, where it was known that there were active terrorists. Calvert, supported by other HQ staff, went in to direct the training. Setting off in the inevitable three ton trucks, they were deposited near the camp of the Royal Marine Commandos, and then, using their newly acquired skills, entered the jungle. They faced a long march carrying very heavy packs which got heavier trudging through tropical rain and plunging through swamps. They stopped at 1600 hours to make their bashas (shelters) and to try out the feeding and sentry arrangements. As the Chindit columns had discovered, the signallers had the hardest task in this type of operation. They shared all the physical effort and the hardship, they had to be as efficient soldiers as the rest, they had to carry the same weapons, but, when the others could relax, the signallers had to start their urgent and demanding work. On the first night Calvert angrily demanded that a message be sent to HQ. After three hours the Intelligence Officer, with a signaller working the pedal generator, got through.

In his preliminary six months' reconnaissance with other units, Calvert had covered much of the country. His reputation did not always help. One patrol had clashed briefly with a terrorist group, and as he took cover a grenade landed beside him. To it was attached a note: "How do you do, Mr Calvert?" This, he presumed, came from someone he had trained in the war years and who must have remembered him with at least a modicum of affection. His recces certainly paid off in the choice of the Squadron's first jungle camp. An old terrorist site, it had been well chosen on a hilly spur with very steep sides, with a handy supply of clean water and with very difficult access for any attacker. As Wingate had done before him, Calvert personally supervised the erection of bashas and fields of fire.

Policy on sentries was a serious issue for every unit in a theatre of terrorist attacks and Calvert had his own clear-cut views, which did not always accord with normal army policy. He maintained that a strong camp, like his first operational camp, would be an unlikely target for a terrorist group. Similarly, the three-man patrols which carried out most of the probing actions were far safer lying up overnight in thick jungle where their chances of discovery were minimal, whereas a three-man patrol trying to cover full-time sentry duty would have been an absurd waste of effort. Calvert constantly and confidently repeated his theme that everything – weapon training, field craft and tactics – must have one aim: to destroy terrorists.

After the rigours of jungle training and patrolling, the evenings in the security of the camp, helped by the daily active-service rum ration, were a time of relaxation and camaraderie. In that atmosphere – helping them to "get into his mind" – Calvert's enthusiasm and leadership qualities made a terrific impact on his young officers. They admired his faith and his idealism. He always welcomed the contributions of the Australians and Rhodesians and saw them as exemplifying those great qualities of confidence and initiative which had created the Commonwealth, and he looked to the younger countries to give a lead as Britain appeared to falter. Woodhouse, who shared some of these evenings, when he was not pedalling the signals generator, said, "People who saw Mike Calvert as just a professional soldier, happy in any war, were absolutely wrong. He fought for an ideal, a patriotic ideal, and he believed in showing chivalry to an enemy, however evil that enemy might be."

This lengthy operational training exercise gave Calvert the chance to mould his unit and to imbue its members with his ethos. Much of the time this went smoothly, but the stress of the previous months and the ravages of tropical diseases, of which he carried an alarming cocktail, were beginning to tell on him. From time to time he had volcanic eruptions of temper which many came to fear. These were sometimes in support of positive policy – for example, when he castigated a young officer for suggesting that a prisoner should be tortured. Sometimes a trivial incident would cause an outburst. Some officers were surprised that, while certain aspects of discipline were fiercely upheld, Calvert seemed not to be aware or not to bother about others which they felt were important. Although the period of training had been absurdly short, many newly joined officers, who had some jungle experience, were surprised at the lax discipline on the march and in movement through the jungle. When the patrol was advancing there was often far too much noise, and the amount of litter – including equipment, food, sweet papers and even weapons which could be used by terrorists – had serious consequences from the security angle. Other units, too, failed to establish good jungle discipline and lost weapons to the terrorists. The 4th Hussars were ambushed in December, 1948. They sustained heavy casualties and lost many weapons as did the 2/7th Gurkhas.

Poor jungle discipline persisted throughout the Scouts' exercise and deteriorated further as the operation drew to a close. As they came out, having in all the time not made one contact with the terrorists, they became increasingly disillusioned. They were exhausted and, as a result, they were careless, ill-disciplined, noisy and left a trail of litter behind them. The soldiers thought increasingly that there was no point in going deep into the jungle when the CTs were mostly near the fringes and near the towns.

After the exercise the unit went on leave, having accumulated a considerable amount of back pay. Soon reports started to come back of incidents of drunken ill-discipline involving the Scouts. Even in those early days, the press, both local and international, showed a keen interest in this Special Force Unit. The publicity often caused resentment from local regular units upon whose good-will the Scouts often had to depend, and it also meant that, when members of the Scouts caused trouble, their bad behaviour was greatly magnified.

This is where things began to go seriously wrong. Woodhouse, who felt an intense loyalty to Calvert, nonetheless became increasingly worried about the breakdown of discipline in the unit and could not understand why Calvert failed to crack the whip. On one occasion, when they were alone together in the mess, Calvert challenged him and became abusive, asserting that he had no loyalty, no faith in the Regiment and was afraid. White with anger, Woodhouse walked out. But, in a friendly voice Calvert called him back and they spoke of their feelings. Calvert, who dwelt on his lonely isolation, explained that since his experiences in the war he had never made close friends. He added, "Anyway, a soldier should not make close friends because it is so much worse when they get killed." Despite being deeply involved in all the troubles of the unit, soon after this incident Woodhouse, who had thought of returning to his Regiment, said, "I could never leave this Regiment or desert the man who made it".

Perhaps to curb the discipline problems, but also to curb press criticism and to impress local units which were increasingly critical, Calvert decided to mount an exercise over Christmas, 1950. Reports had come in of terrorist activity in the mountainous country along the border of Selangor and Pahang, so the Squadron set out to intercept traffic along the mountain paths, and to booby-trap them. The exercise went fairly well, but once again they made no contact with the CTs. The unit returned increasingly disillusioned.

Calvert now made a major blunder. He decided to throw a party for all ranks in the unit and for representatives of all the local support units – "a party which they would never forget". He certainly succeeded, but failed to realize that the increasing number of his critics would never forget the party either. There is little doubt that this party sealed the reputation of Calvert and the Malayan Scouts which he had created for drunken ill-discipline.

Details of the party vividly illustrate the atmosphere of the unit, the rôle and personality of Calvert and the reactions of his critics. He invited officers and other ranks of the air-support units, including Australian and New Zealand air crew, to come to lunch. In the Officers' Mess, as the guests sat down in the circle of chairs provided there were several yelps and the smell of singed cloth, because most of the chairs had been booby-trapped. The cook house was liberally provided with Tiger and Anchor beer and, soon after lunch, the men were demanding the start of the football match between SAS and the visitors. This started well, but the visiting team were put off their stride when detonators started exploding under their feet. Then, as the SAS attacked, clouds of smoke enveloped the pitch, and when it cleared the ball was seen lashed inside the visitors' goal. The spectators then joined in, generously supplied with thunder flashes.

Several visiting officers clearly thought things had gone far enough and began to walk away. They had to pass a deep sulphur pool fed by a spring where some of the soldiers were already pushing each other in. The cry went up: "All officers into the pool". Calvert roared with laughter and leaped in. A spirited battle, violent but fairly good-natured, followed, as soldiers and officers struggled on the edge of the pool. Woodhouse shrewdly swam through the pool and went to the mess to be ready to help rig out his guests. He wrote: "They did not know how to take this party. They had heard that we were a mad lot, and now waited in fascinated resignation, rather like rabbits hypnotised by a snake."

At this stage Calvert ordered a boat race in their inflatables down the swiftly flowing river beside the camp. Woodhouse tried to stall this suggestion but was over-ruled and Calvert dragooned everyone into the inflatables, with one or two SAS soldiers in each boat, ostensibily to help with the paddles. Calvert started the race, but warned that he would command an ambush party somewhere along the one-and-a-half-mile course. As the boats approached a corner, carbine fire swept over the boats and a shower of thunder flashes landed inside them. The SAS paddlers then leapt out to counter-attack the ambush party. In the mêlée, rifles, carbines and other equipment were lost, but this did not seem to worry the QM who was alleged to drink twelve bottles of Carlsberg every lunchtime.

Just as, fifty years after his death, Wingate's critics believe that he was a crude showman because he walked around with an alarm clock on his wrist, though no Chindit ever saw him with an alarm clock, so Calvert's party, which certainly did take place, passed into legend.

Early in 1951 the wider issues of Far East history once more impinged on Calvert's career. During the turbulent and uncertain post-war years, the Army had slowly begun to realize the continuing need for Special Forces, and in September, 1947, the SAS rose again, reappearing as SAS (Artists) TA. This happy reunion with a proud TA Regiment, the Artists Rifles, proved effective and long-lasting. In 1950 General Douglas MacArthur, facing the crisis caused by the aggression of communist North Korea, called for SAS units to bolster the United Nations forces under his command. Soon 21 SAS, made up of many wartime SAS veterans and some TA volunteers, under the command of Major Tony Greville-Bell DSO, were ready for action. To their great disappointment, MacArthur changed his mind and used American marines. Instead, the unit was given the option of volunteering to serve in Malaya under Calvert with the newly formed Malayan Scouts (SAS), and nearly forty did so. Thus, in January, 1951, Greville-Bell and M Independent Squadron, soon to be named B Squadron, arrived at the Scouts base at Dusun Tua. Almost from the start problems arose.

The new B Squadron, accustomed to traditional military discipline, backed up by the proud SAS ethos that the only major punishment was RTU, were horrified and disgusted when they arrived and saw what appeared to them to be a crowd of scruffy, bearded, drunken layabouts. In the weeks after the Christmas exercise and the party, this was probably not far from the truth. Although troops on operations in the jungle, for sound tactical reasons, were allowed to grow beards, most of A Squadron officers believed that beards should have been shaved off when they came out, because this incensed other units and damaged their reputation more than anything else.

The newcomers fiercely criticized A Squadron and especially Calvert. Some, formerly in 2 SAS, recalled the unpopularity of his appointment to command the SAS in 1944 and feared the worst. Within A Squadron, which showed him intense loyalty, were many officers who were equally concerned about the discipline. Woodhouse, who was more fully involved with this problem than anyone, said, "We were aware that the discipline was not right, but Calvert dominated us in a way that is hard to explain." He added that with any other CO he would have made more forceful objections, but concluded that "Calvert's weakness was that he did not seem to appreciate the importance of good discipline".

Soon after the arrival of B Squadron, Calvert went off to Rhodesia, where, with the encouragement of the Prime Minister, Sir Godfrey Huggins, a force of volunteers was called for to help Britain fight against the communist threat in the Far East. The volunteers responded enthusiastically to Calvert's challenging address and, in March, 1951, under Captain Peter Walls, who later commanded the Rhodesian Army, the Squadron arrived in Malaya, to become C Squadron of the Malayan Scouts.

While Calvert was away in Rhodesia, Woodhouse ran the Headquarters and carried out the necessary operational administration for A Squadron which was then in the jungle. He described his eighteen-hour day as he tried to keep things going. He stressed his four essentials: to keep up the level of discipline, to ensure the soldiers received their pay, to give maximum support to the squadron on operations in the jungle, and to guard the more valuable stores. In this situation he realized again that the unit was desperately short of experienced administration staff, a problem Calvert had never been able to solve. Administrative problems became more acute during that particular operation because Malaya was hit by the heaviest rains for a decade, with floods destroying main roads and railways and completely flooding the areas where A Squadron was operating. Helped by Royal Navy launches and police units with motor launches, the Squadron survived these very difficult conditions and came out of the jungle with improved tactical discipline and with growing confidence to offset their poor reputation.

Early in February, 1951, Calvert returned from Rhodesia full of enthusiasm about the Volunteer Rhodesian Squadron which arrived soon afterwards. Having a close rapport with Woodhouse, in spite of some awesome outbreaks of anger, Calvert now discussed with him the idea of establishing a Chinese squadron. He argued that two-fifths of the Malayan population were Chinese, contributing success-fully to the Malayan economy, and, if there was a successful squadron, young Chinese could be encouraged to join instead of going off to the CTs.

During the early part of 1951 A Squadron had improved consider-ably because of its lengthy operations in the jungle and in spite of the frustration of rarely achieving contact with the terrorists. It did have one success. It found a camp, made a dawn attack, wounded a terrorist, but failed to kill or capture any more, though some useful information did result. During the action Trooper O'Leary lost contact with his section, illustrating the very serious problems of movement in jungle warfare. The Squadron spent a long time searching for him but without success. Much later, it was discovered that, after losing contact, he had walked for miles and eventually found a group of Aborigines. They looked after him well until a squad of CTs arrived and forced the Aborigines to kill him. This incident was handled insensitively by the Army and was raised in the House of Commons in November, 1951. It did not help the unit's reputation.

Discipline problems still remained in A Squadron in spite of their lengthy operational experience. Towards the end of their February operation HQ officers traced one troop by following a trail of sweet papers, food cartons, equipment, and even live ammunition dumped along the track. Challenged about the role of discipline in the Malayan Scouts, Calvert reiterated his view that he thought the army had too much restrictive discipline, and that he was always trying to establish a different type of discipline which made his troops use their brains all the time to think positively and to use their initiative. This is confirmed by his officers who found, whether in the Mess or on operations, Calvert was constantly making them think about tactics, strategy and every aspect of the fight against the terrorists. When the situation in the Malayan Scouts was contrasted with the Chindits, Calvert admitted he had made mistakes, but suggested that when he commanded 77 Brigade he already had these ideas on discipline, and that within 77 Brigade the COs of the three battalions established their own discipline.

The operation of A Squadron under the direction of Woodhouse continued through March, 1951, and the Squadron became a fit, tough and highly efficient unit. Much of the criticism of drunken layabouts at camp never took into consideration the grinding physical effort of having spent days and weeks in the jungle on an exercise which the unit had successfully completed. This laid the foundation of the SAS successes later in the 1950s in Malaya, in Borneo and elsewhere. Their rough resilience under harsh conditions became a byword. The Squadron's success completely vindicated Calvert's view that troops can operate in the jungle for several weeks and confounded his medical critics who had argued that it was impossible. Towards the end of the operation, which had ranged over much of the State of Johore, Calvert marched in to join the unit.

Woodhouse went out to meet him, but, having searched in vain, returned to his HQ to find Calvert waiting for him. "Just being unpredictable," he chuckled. Later Woodhouse commented, "My admiration for Calvert's tactical doctrine was now higher than ever. I still had reservations over his system of command and discipline in camp, but I had seen enough of jungle operations to be certain that Calvert's tactical theories were right. Calvert told me that opposition to him was growing. He knew that there were weaknesses in the administration, but he hated to get rid of men who had tried. It was curious to me, that Calvert, so ruthless on operations, was so reluctant to throw out men. He was very loyal to his subordinates."

Calvert clearly enjoyed his visit to A Squadron in the jungle, delighted that his planning and tactics for the operation had been vindicated. He had created a system which was to form the basis for much future success and was to be developed and built upon by John Woodhouse, who in the following months was to command both the newly arrived Rhodesian Squadron and B Squadron after Greville-Bell left. The contemporary comments of Woodhouse are interesting in view of the crisis then about to hit the Malayan Scouts. He considered that the Rhodesians were a particularly fine group of men, physically bigger and stronger than the British, well educated and full of idealism, with a fine sense of discipline of their own, but, perhaps because of their higher standard of living at home, more prone to the sicknesses found in the jungle. B Squadron, which came out from England with several experienced veterans, had stronger overall discipline, but never achieved such a high level of performance in the jungle and did not match the operational achievements of A Squadron. Woodhouse concluded his comparison by stating: "A Squadron had experience and the immense unshakeable physical endurance and determination of young British soldiers at their best."

From the Squadron's jungle camp Calvert was brought back by helicopter to see General Urquhart, the GOC, in Kuala Lumpur. Calvert left for the trip with light-hearted and facetious remarks about whether he should go to GHQ in his jungle greens so that the staff officers could experience both the look and smell of the jungle. Whether this interview was caused by the growing opposition he had mentioned to Woodhouse is not known, but it was followed fairly soon with a visit to the unit by General Sir Harold Briggs, the Director of Operations in Malaya.

Recommended by Slim, Briggs had come out of retirement to take on this difficult post. He had done an excellent job in cutting through all the rivalry and divisions between the civil, police and military authorities, and in the Briggs Plan, he had implemented many of the ideas, like resettling the Aborigines, which had first been suggested by Calvert. On 8 June, 1951, Briggs came to the Malayan Scouts HQ at Dusun Tua and spent many hours listening to the reports of the operations, and having discussions with the officers, and with Calvert alone. These serious discussions were followed by another memorable cocktail party with a fair number of guests. Noticing one guest about to leave, an officer said, "Don't go yet. Once the old General has gone it will really get going." "I am the General" was the withering reply. The party did continue for hours, with Calvert strangely quiet. Then, suddenly, he insisted on some singing. The traditional mess songs were sung, and the evening ended with Calvert's favourite. This song, which had been sung with particular poignancy by the Chindits of 77 Brigade before the Battle of Mogaung, was sung with all present holding a full glass on the back of their hands:

> Betrayed by the country that bore us,
> Betrayed by the country we're in,
> All the best men have gone before us
> And only the dull left behind.
> Stand to your glasses steady.
> Here's a toast to the dead already,
> And here's to the next man to die.

No one knew until the next day what a distressing moment that had been for Calvert, for then he announced that he had to go into hospital at once, and would be flown to Millbank.

Speculation and controversy have continued about the events surrounding Calvert's departure. Certainly the reputation of the Malayan Scouts in 1951 was deplorable, and there were many critics both in Malaya and Whitehall who wished to disband the unit. Even Woodhouse, the best-informed and most balanced observer, had said, "The reputation of the Regiment was rapidly sinking, until contempt for us was shown quite openly." Yet the criticism centred largely on the discipline problems in the camp at Dusun Tua when the troops had come off operations, and not on the increasingly effective work carried out in the jungle.

B Squadron, which arrived early in 1951 with its own clear-cut standards, was, from the start, highly critical of everything at Dusan Tua – the camp, the accommodation, the training facilities and, above all, the discipline. It was unfortunate that, when they arrived, A Squadron was already heavily involved in operations, and the training available for B Squadron was haphazard and completely inadequate for men who may have had experience of war in Europe, but had no knowledge of jungle fighting. Thus everything conspired to create bad feeling between the two units, with Calvert seen as the man responsible for most of the problems. The discipline issue can be seen as a positive experiment which went disastrously wrong, but the heavy drinking and ill-disciplined truculence which went with it cannot be explained away. Calvert himself was drinking very heavily at the time and there were many, including the ex-Chindits, who followed his example. Stories of drunkenness can easily be exaggerated but one incident does ring true. A young doctor, on his first day in the Mess, went into breakfast. The mess waiter asked if he wanted a regular breakfast, and when he said "yes", he received a double brandy.

Greville-Bell, a distinguished SAS officer who had won the DSO in the war and who brought "B" Squadron out to Malaya, became increasingly concerned about the whole set-up of the Malayan Scouts and did not wish to see his fine unit besmirched. He agonized over what he should do, because Calvert appeared to pooh-pooh any criticism. The NCOs of B Squadron had an increasingly difficult time trying to uphold normal discipline in the face of drunken disorder which they often came across in the other Squadron. Tension mounted dangerously when men who had committed court-martial offences – for example when a soldier had assaulted the MO, or when drunken men put out of the canteen assaulted the Orderly Officer with a loaded rifle – were merely ticked off by Calvert. The anger and the tension can easily be imagined and, in the face of this growing crisis, Greville-Bell, for very proper reasons, complained to General Harding. Harding came to Kuala Lumpur and, following the time-honoured army tradition, interviewed Greville-Bell who received, as he said, "the biggest bollocking I have ever had in my life". He felt he was treated as a criminal. In complaining over the head of his CO he had committed what the army considered the unforgivable sin, and in doing so he wrecked what had been a very promising military career. After the interview he was taken away from the unit and held incommunicado until he was posted to another area. After this he had a few remote staff postings, but by the mid 1950s he realized that he had no future in the regular SAS or the Army and he resigned his commission.

The Army has admirable and well-proven ways of solving difficult problems and protecting the good name of the service against scandal or sensationalism. In this case there were many who connected Greville-Bell's sudden departure with the equally sudden departure of Calvert soon afterwards. Certainly Briggs would hardly have come for a long conference with Calvert in June, 1951, just to tell him he was to be invalided home on medical grounds, even though he was ill enough to go immediately into hospital with amoebic dysentery, malaria, leptospirosis and fairly substantial damage to the liver. Whatever the truth of this situation, the most valuable comment came from John Woodhouse. He was there at the time. He recorded in detail the feelings of the Regiment and he came back to Malaya several years later as the most outstanding commander of the Malayan Scouts (SAS). Then he put into practice those tactical precepts he had learnt from Calvert and which in the meantime had been forgotten.

Referring to that final cocktail party, Woodhouse wrote, "Next day Calvert said to me that he was going to hospital and would be sent home. I was very shaken. 'But you can't go Sir. Who will command?' 'I must go, they'll make me go'. It seemed no one knew who would command. Calvert showed no bitterness when he spoke. 'You chaps must carry on. It's up to you now.' His words were casual, almost jocular.

"At times I had bitterly resented his criticism; but always I knew he had that spark of genius in military affairs which a soldier is lucky to see at close quarters once in his career. Almost anything was bearable from him, but much less would have been insufferable from a mediocrity. Calvert seldom gave us the answers but made us think for ourselves. He taught us to calculate the effect of our actions on our men. Most leaders have a little of the actor in them but sincerity is essential, for soldiers have an unerring eye and a rude word for the impostor.

"Calvert was always sincere. He admired his former commander, Wingate, above all other soldiers. Perhaps he was much like Wingate himself, but never, I am sure did he try to model himself on Wingate in any narrow sense. Living in his Regiment with him was to be incessantly under instruction. At meals, in the bar, in the office, in a jeep, even wallowing in the sulphur spring, he bubbled with ideas himself and probed our brains to make us think as well. It was exhausting, sometimes monotonous, but surely effective. The old military formula of dealing with terrorists, cordon and search, a line of ambushes and lines of 'beaters' to drive the terrorists into the ambushes, was by no means the best or only method of doing so. It was Calvert who thought of alternatives, Calvert who formed a unit to demonstrate them. He had the moral courage and tactical sense to match three-men patrols against gangs much bigger. He knew the core of the problem was to get the terrorist to fight instead of evading us. He was not afraid of risking casualties.

"He had made the Regiment, and it reflected his faults as well as his virtues. It was not his lack of ability at administrative detail, but his lack of time to supervise it which caused such chaos. He should have found more time, but it would have been better still had he found a bigger job soon after the Regiment was formed. Had he been given the appointment of Deputy Director of Operations, or even command of a Brigade and the SAS, his tactical brilliance would have had full scope. Others more suited than he could have worried over stores accounting and ration indents.

"I could not imagine anyone who could take over from him, and put our house in order, while maintaining and improving our tactics in the field. Our disbandment was being gleefully prophesied by our numerous detractors. With Calvert out of the way, their malicious hopes looked as though they would soon be realized.

"On 12 June, 1951, in a mood of despair, I went to the military hospital to say goodbye. The nursing staff to their great credit and considerable inconvenience were prepared to accept visitors at almost any hour and Calvert's room was soon the centre of activity. He was very ill with amoebic dysentery, but showed no sign of it when talking to visitors.

"When I saw him I could find nothing to say. He knew my thoughts at once, laughed and cheered me up. I got up to go.

'Remember, I expect a lot from you John.'

'We will *always* do our best. Goodbye, Sir, and good luck.' "Very quickly I walked out. For the last time Calvert's force of personality strengthened my own determination. We *must* succeed. We shall."

Forty years and many campaigns later Colonel Woodhouse confirmed his views. He agreed that it took years to produce a really efficient SAS Regiment. From 1951 it took many years to effect real improvements because bad habits are hard to eradicate. Patrols still moved too fast, often to show off their physical prowess; they were slow to adopt the virtues of modesty and cool calculation; too many men were below standard until selection became effective in 1953. Slack battle discipline persisted, but "What was right was Calvert's tactical theories". Others like Sloane and Brooke improved the administration but they were not innovators on the tactical side. "All of this shows what a tremendous personality Calvert was."

Calvert's own views of these last days in Malaya appear in a personal letter, dated 3 July, 1951. He wrote: "I have been extremely busy in and out of the jungle and eventually cracked. I am now in hospital on my way home.... My insides went finally and I am being flown home to Millbank.

"It has been a long grind raising, training, administering, operating and planning without much help, especially on the administration. However, successes are now coming through and at last we are paying a dividend.

"I may say that I also broke down mentally due to overstrain. I am alright now, but I just had too much to do and think about.

"Apart from one or two horrors who came in from civil life and who had records and very nearly ruined the show I have got an excellent lot of chaps who are very loyal, keen and good."

After Calvert left, Colonel Sloane (later Major General Sloane CBE), an outstanding and formidable leader from the Argyll and Sutherland Highlanders, tackled the problems which beset the Scouts and during the 1950s the Regiment built up its reputation. They developed new techniques for parachuting into the jungle, they swiftly developed the use of helicopters as they became available and they made effective use of the increasingly accurate intelligence which came to the unit as the battle against the terrorists was slowly won. All of this helped to establish a fine reputation for efficient and formidable anti-terrorist jungle fighting, but, as Woodhouse said, many of the soundest ideas on jungle fighting had come from Calvert. By 1957, when a major re-organization of the army took place, and many regiments were reduced, amalgamated or disbanded, the SAS proudly survived.

For some time Calvert had been using his brief periods of leisure between postings to write his brilliant account of the Burma Campaign, *Prisoners of Hope*, which, as mentioned earlier, is now regarded as one of the classic works to come out of the Second World War. It was published early in 1952, just before the tragic events covered in the next chapter.

# CHAPTER TEN

# COURT MARTIAL

On 13 July, 1952, Major Michael Calvert DSO, after a court martial lasting seven days, was convicted of committing or attempting to commit acts of gross indecency with male persons and was dismissed the service. From that day onwards Calvert has protested his complete innocence.

This incident, which inflicted far more damage on Calvert than all the Japanese armies in Burma, took place in Soltau in north Germany. Since October, 1951, Calvert had been serving there as a Royal Engineers Staff Officer with responsibility for buildings and families. After the excitement and challenge of the War and his more recent activities in Malaya commanding the Malayan Scouts SAS, this was a humdrum and depressing post. His Malayan campaign, from which he was invalided home in July, 1951, had stirred up many of the tropical diseases which had lain dormant since 1945 and in 1952 his health was dangerously undermined. At Soltau he had a flat in the area of the officers' quarters. He had no previous experience of serving in Germany, he could speak no German and, after his years in the tropics, he found the bleak north German plain during a severe winter an unpleasant prospect.

Mess life with immature National Service officers was extremely tedious and Calvert began drinking heavily. To escape from the tedium of the barracks and mess life he would occasionally visit a German gasthaus or pub in Soltau called the "Gruener Jaeger".

(NB *All quotations in this section are from the Summary of Evidence of the court martial in Brigadier Calvert's file in Army Records.*)

At the court martial it was alleged that in April, 1952, Calvert committed an act of gross indecency with Lothar Gebien, and on 10 May, 1952, he attempted to procure an act of gross indecency with Horst Bartels and Heinz Fuhrop.

The first prosecution witness, Jürgen Jacob, a German youth of 17, alleged that in April Calvert had asked him the way to the cinema. They met by accident the next day and Calvert invited him to walk to his flat. Calvert invited him in, gave him a beer, and "asked him to bring along more boys". Jacob said that he left the flat, went to the cinema, and some time later returned to the flat with Lothar Gebien and Egon Schneider. The boys, aged 17 and 18, arrived at the flat and Calvert, who was naked, asked them in. He gave them beer and schnapps, and then asked them to undress, which they did. "He then committed acts of gross indecency with all three." Calvert then saw them downstairs, gave them some English money and a yellow pullover, and they left.

Speaking in his defence at the court martial, Calvert completely refuted this allegation. He agreed that he had spoken to Jacob when asking the way to the cinema and had bumped into him the next day. Then Jacob came to his flat when he was changing for dinner in the Mess and Calvert got the impression that he wanted a job as a batman. Then Jacob offered to fetch the other chaps. Calvert considered that Jacob would be unsuitable as a batman and therefore agreed to him fetching the other boys who might be more suitable. He had dinner in the Mess, returned to his flat and, after reading, went to bed. He normally slept naked. He was awoken by a noisy knocking on the door and Jacob was there with Gebien and Schneider. Calvert had merely intended to ask other officers what the system was for employing German youths as batmen, and was amazed to see Jacob and the other two at his door. He was unable to communicate with them at all and, after some playing-acting as to how they would work as batmen, he got them to leave. He agreed they could keep some English money and an old yellow pullover. He completely denied any act of indecency with the youths.

The court-martial evidence showed that Jacob was "the ring-leader of a gang of youths proved to be of infamous character". Between the time of the alleged incident and the trial – April and July, 1952 – they were involved in burglaries at Calvert's flat, and thus able to produce plausible evidence. No case against Jacob was brought to the Court and, during the trial Schneider became truculent and refused to give evidence. Thus the only charge against Calvert from the incident in April involved Lothar Gebien.

A second alleged incident took place on 10 May. The prosecution witness Horst Bartels, aged 17, charged that at the Gruener Jaeger on 10 May Calvert had approached him to ask about the address of a local guide. Calvert "asked if he would go with him". Bartels refused, and Calvert asked if he would go with him the next day, and he again refused. "He then went to the lavatory and the accused touched him in an improper manner." Calvert admitted that, having had quite a lot to drink, he may have given Bartels a friendly slap in the sense of saying, "Well, cheerio old chap," but there was nothing indecent at all.

The final prosecution witness, Heinz Fuhrop, aged 20, alleged that about 10pm on 10 May, 1952, after several people had been drinking together, Calvert invited them home for a drink. He went off with Calvert in an army Volkswagen with a military driver and they went to his flat. Fuhrop then alleged that Calvert "showed him indecent photographs and began fondling his private parts and kissed him on the lips". He made an excuse to go to the lavatory, having managed to pick up Calvert's identity card, and was able to slip out of the flat and run back to the Gruener Jaeger. Calvert's version of this incident is that, having been drinking in the pub, he invited several Germans back to his flat and gave a lift to Fuhrop. Back at the flat while he was getting some beer he found Fuhrop looking at his collection of photographs. When the other people did not arrive, he asked Fuhrop to leave. He denied kissing Fuhrop or acting in any way improperly.

Bartels and Fuhrop reported the alleged incidents to the German police within a few days. All the incidents referred to at the trial were connected with the pub, the Gruener Jaeger, considered by the authorities as the centre of a gang of criminals, and frequented by the group of youths who made the allegations against Calvert. In the postwar situation, when there were still strict rules about fraternizing with the Germans, it must have been unusual for a British officer as senior as Calvert to frequent such a place, and he must have been an object of considerable interest.

Significantly, the youths involved in the incident, which took place in April, did nothing, and made no complaint until after they heard of the case involving Fuhrop and Bartels on 10 May. Also, within weeks of the trial, Bartels signed a statement "that his evidence at the trial had been misinterpreted and nothing improper had occurred".

Some weeks after the court martial, in a Post-Trial Investigation, further evidence was produced. The Military Intelligence Officer at

Hanover District HQ, at the request of the British Field Security Force, investigated the situation and repeated that the Gruener Jaeger pub was "the centre of a gang of criminals". In addition, a German investigator taken on by Calvert's old friend Peter Fleming, who had supported him throughout the trial, interviewed the prosecution witness. "He obtained signed confessions from Gebien and Jacob that their evidence had been false." The summary of evidence provided further detail, with a reference to Jacob who was the leader of the gang. It stated: "Jacob said a similar incident occurred a few days later, but his statement is not supported by the other youths. It is not clear whether he is lying to blacken Major Calvert's character or has made a genuine mistake." Unfortunately for Calvert, the Deputy Judge Advocate General refused to accept any of this evidence because it had not been presented to the police. Since this would have demolished the prosecution case, it seems remarkable that Calvert's defence counsel did not pursue this matter further.

Immediately after the verdict, 13 July, 1952, defence lawyers submitted a lengthy petition against the guilty verdict, arguing that the findings were against the weight of evidence, that the evidence of the German witnesses was unsatisfactory and should not have been accepted, and that the admitted facts were capable of an innocent explanation. The defence argued further that the four principal German witnesses, after questioning by a German investigator, had retracted their evidence. Another key witness (Bartels) said that he had been misinterpreted. In conclusion it was stated, "Most or all of the German prosecution witnesses are connected with a criminal gang and through this with communist organizations."

The final summing-up of the trial by the judge recorded that the defence had denied that any indecency had occurred or was intended, and that acts of bonhomie had been construed as acts suggestive of indecency. It had been established that the witnesses in the first incident were in a criminal group and had taken part in burglaries at Calvert's flat. While this was agreed, certain facts told against Major Calvert: "For instance the admitted possession of literature suggestive of homosexuality, the admitted fact that some of the youths had been in his quarter with him, (but he says for innocent or unexplained purposes), and that there was a degree of familiarity towards them which is really incompatible with mere bonhomie having regard to the status of the persons concerned." (Summary of evidence Army

Records). The petition of the defence was rejected by Lord Russell of Liverpool, one of the Nuremberg trial judges, on 17 October, 1952.

That such flimsy and insubstantial evidence – possessing pictures suggestive of homosexuality, or familiarity and bonhomie with people of lower status – should have been used to destroy the career of a distinguished officer merely illustrates the level of homophobic prejudice at the time.

The verdict of the court martial was a total calamity for Calvert. From when he left school and after Woolwich and Cambridge, he had devoted his life to being a highly professional officer in the Royal Engineers, in the Chindits and in the SAS. He had a Cambridge degree, the wartime rank of Brigadier, together with two DSOs and four foreign decorations for bravery to his credit. At that point he could reasonably have looked forward to eventual promotion to very high command. He was well known to powerful military figures: Auchinleck, who had given valuable support to the Chindits, Montgomery, who employed Calvert on his staff in 1947, and Field Marshal Lord Slim, who did his best to help Calvert at all times. Yet all his prospects were destroyed by the court-martial verdict.

When Calvert was in Soltau in 1952, it was just at the time when Germany was emerging from the status of an occupied country and there was perhaps a measure of antagonism towards British forces, and some laws against fraternization. Calvert had always mixed easily with soldiers of all ranks, and in Malaya his initial task had been to visit every meeting place of Malays and Chinese, including many shady drinking dens, to uncover what was going on. Was this perhaps in the back of his mind in becoming a fairly regular visitor to the Gruener Jaeger? He had certainly mixed with and befriended many dubious people in Kuala Lumpur and elsewhere in 1950, only two years before. He always saw himself as someone who could disregard normal conventions and swiftly unravel a complex situation. A conceit, yes, but hardly a criminal attitude. The youths involved in the court martial were also regular visitors to the Gruener Jaeger. Did they perhaps think that they could set up and possibly profit from this lonely and rather eccentric British officer who frequently visited the pub?

Since 1952 Calvert has anguished over the question of whether he was framed. In 1945, when he commanded the French and Belgian

SAS, orders for the round-up of Nazis leaders were given under the name of Brigadier General Calvert, and since his troops caught Ribbentrop and others, he wondered if old-guard Nazis had set out to destroy him. His belief that he could have been set up by ex Nazis is not entirely fanciful. A notorious ex-Nazi, Otto Weiner, was known to operate in the Soltau area. There was another case in the 1950s when a British colonel was charged in similar circumstances to Calvert. The colonel was convicted by court martial, but, unlike Calvert, was later pardoned. Throughout the Cold War, and in many other wars, both sides have used attractive women *and* boys to compromise and blackmail their opponents.

Following another line of thought, Calvert remembered that in Malaya his report had led to the sacking of a Scots Guard Colonel and he wondered if, through the court martial, the Guards establishment were hitting back at him. Such questions haunted Calvert's thoughts for decades.

Calvert, throughout, has maintained his total innocence, but even if he was guilty, what was his crime? If the incident had happened in 1997, while Calvert is still suffering from the verdict of the court martial, it would have amounted to no more than a few visits to a pub where there might be gay contacts. The youths involved, aged 17–20, who subsequently withdrew their testimonies, even so only made fairly trivial allegations.

There is a parallel to Calvert's downfall in the case of the Scottish hero Hector Macdonald. He rose through the ranks, won fame for his bravery as the real hero of Omdurman and as a Boer War commander. In 1902, as GOC Ceylon, he was found in a railway carriage with Ceylonese boys engaging in mutual masturbation, not a criminal offence in Ceylon at that time. Macdonald was called to London and ordered to face a court martial. He then travelled to Paris and committed suicide in a lonely hotel bedroom. The Scots generally resented the way Macdonald was treated, especially because a Canon of Westminster and an Earl escaped prosecution for homosexual activity at that time. Also, a major homosexual scandal in the Brigade of Guards was hushed up. There was regret that a brave man had been sacrificed by society's prejudice when there were many who would have stood by him had they known of the trial.

The destruction of Calvert's career raises the issue of the level of homophobic prejudice at different times. In the early 1950s, when

Calvert's court martial took place, both Church and State embarked on a campaign of draconian measures against all forms of homosexual activity and this clearly affected the outcome of many trials and courts martial. Even with this campaign, the level of punishment varied considerably. In the same month as Calvert's petition was rejected, October, 1952, Sir John Gielgud was convicted of homosexual activity, given a £10 fine and told to see his doctor. (*Binkie Beaumont*, R. Hugget, p. 430, 1989). Attitudes have changed substantially between 1952 and 1997, but the issue of homosexuals in the armed forces remains a live and controversial political issue. When Calvert was growing up in the 1920s and 1930s, the British preparatory and public school system exacerbated many of the problems of men's sexuality. At prep school Calvert came across the eccentric type of schoolmaster who insisted on boys swimming in the nude. At Bradfield, like most public schools of the time, homosexual activity flourished. In the harsh and exclusively male society of the public school, it was quite normal for older boys to fall in love with the younger ones and to have some homosexual experience. In the 1930s, when Calvert went up to Cambridge, both Oxford and Cambridge were almost exclusively male societies and most undergraduates had come through the public school system. Lady Longford, interviewed in 1996, said of her time at Oxford in the 1920s "Of course every type of homosexual activity flourished". (BBC interview, June, 1996). The young men produced by this system went out into a world where the law and society in general held to an attitude of puritanical repression.

Many men and women of Calvert's generation brought up by that system had little chance of meeting members of the opposite sex and, if they had any homosexual inclination, they were condemned to lead lonely lives, fearful of stepping out of line. Most, by disciplined self-control, managed to lead dedicated professional lives subduing or sublimating their sexuality. Such people were often the stalwarts of their profession, in the boarding schools, in medicine, in the church and in other caring professions. Many found their way into the Services.

Calvert, in his philosophical way, had often pondered over the rôle of the fighting soldier and the actual experience of battle. He felt that, with his experience of action in battle, he had much more in common with a Roman centurion than with, say, a modern civil servant who had never been in action. This feeling was reinforced when, as a military historian, he built up his knowledge of the fighting forces of all the great civilizations. He did not pursue the issue of sexuality in military life, but other scholars have. They have painted vivid portraits of civilizations where homosexuality was a normal and integral part of a balanced society. Calvert's notions of a Roman centurion had more relevance than he realized.

Nearly all the early civilizations, notably ancient China, Mesopotamia, Greece and Rome, celebrated romantic love between virile warriors. Among the Greeks, homosexual love was considered superior to the love of women. Alexander the Great, though living in a society where bi-sexuality was the norm, was almost exclusively homosexual. Similarly, Julius Caesar lived a blatantly promiscuous bisexual life.

Homophobic prejudice began to flourish in the second and third centuries AD, stemming from both Christian and Hebrew teaching, particularly that of St Paul. In spite of this, homosexuality flourished among the clergy and monastic orders. St Augustine and St Anselm are two examples. The latter refused to consider sodomy a sin because it was so widespread. Homosexuality was also rife among the warrior class, including Richard the Lionheart and the Knights Templar. Leonardo da Vinci and Michelangelo were openly bisexual, as were several English kings – William Rufus, Edward II and James I. In literature many of Shakespeare's sonnets are devoted to beautiful youths, and Marlowe's famous lines "Come live with me and be my love" was addressed, not to a woman, but to a shepherd boy.

When Cromwell and the puritans came to power, they made both adultery and sodomy capital offences. They closed the theatres partly because boy prostitutes flourished in theatre society. The Restoration in 1660 brought back sexual licence. Pepys noted: "Buggery was now as common as in Italy". In more recent centuries both church and state have combined to suppress sodomy by severe penalties, including hanging, dismemberment, castration, burning at the stake and even "hanging by the virile member".

In the nineteenth century homosexuality continued and persecution became more severe. In the first half of the century over 300 men were hanged for sodomy, and the church kept up a campaign based on fear and threats. Medical experts began to warn young people that masturbation would lead to disease, consumption, curvature of the spine, insanity and suicide. Although the death penalty was removed in Britain in 1861, homosexuals continued to be prosecuted. On the day Oscar Wilde was sentenced for homosexual activity in 1895, it was noted that, instead of fifty men crossing the Channel to France, over 600 left the country.

Elsewhere in the world the same struggles continued. Homosexuality remained an accepted part of society in China and Japan, particularly among the Japanese Samurai. In this warrior society, nobles openly declared their love for their catamites (boys kept by older lovers). Among the Samurai the normal custom for a well-bred youth was to be loved by older men. When he himself grew older, he in turn, would love boys. Later he would marry and start a family. In warfare "the Samurai were always accompanied by their adolescent lovers, teaching them the skills of battle and their code of honour" (Colin Spencer, *History of Homosexuality*, p. 146). During the Second World War the Japanese were notorious for their provision of Korean "comfort-women" for their troops in Burma. At the same time they encouraged more isolated units to ease their tensions by mutual masturbation.

In America the official attitude to homosexuals varied dramatically. In the 1930s homosexuals were refused entry to the services, but many suppressed information on their sexuality in order to enlist. Their number became a serious problem to the authorities, and some military training camps, not far removed from the Nazis in their policy, insisted on homosexuals wearing a yellow D on their uniform to show they were degenerate. Some American military prisons, perhaps unwisely, kept separate wings of their prisons for homosexuals. During the Second World War there is widespread evidence of homosexual activity in the American services. Soon after the War America witnessed the great irony of Senator Joe McCarthy and J. Edgar Hoover, both of whom were gay, pursuing a vendetta against gay men. In England in the ten years after 1945 2,500 men were prosecuted for homosexuality and over 1000 were imprisoned.

The 1950s, the period of Calvert's court martial, were an unfortunate time. While no questions about their sexuality had been asked of volunteers or conscripts between 1939 and 1945, prejudice now returned. In 1996 Brian Sewell wrote: "In the early fifties a series of what can only been seen now as show trials of homosexuals was managed so disgracefully and manifested such unreasoning spite and prejudice on the part of Home Secretaries, judges and advocates that even the Church of England felt constrained to join the pleading for the reform of a harsh law". (*Sunday Telegraph*, 10 March, 1996). These trials led to a public outcry and in 1954 Lord Wolfenden was asked to investigate the state of the law relating to homosexuality and prostitution. Wolfenden's investigation uncovered strong and firmly held prejudices. The Law Society opposed any changes in the law. The BMA argued that gay men would be loyal to each other and might be a threat to the Services. The Church of England officially considered that homosexuality was a rebellion against God. In view of these strongly held prejudices, it was surprising that in 1957 the Wolfenden Report recommended that homosexual behaviour between consenting adults in private should no longer be a criminal offence. There were strong objections to the Report and the Government timidly failed to act. It took nine years and a change of government before the law was changed, after Leo Abse introduced a bill in 1967. Even this did not apply to the Services, Scotland or Northern Ireland. There Dr Ian Paisley claimed "to save Ulster from sodomy" while perhaps unaware that his great hero King William of Orange was himself homosexual.

The debate on the Wolfenden Report brought into focus another issue which is relevant to Calvert's situation. Just as recently, in 1996, the Archbishop of York admitted that his sexuality was a grey area, so, in the 1950s, there were senior military figures whose sexual orientation was at least equivocal. Field Marshal Sir Claude Auchinleck, who knew Calvert well, was thought by many to have been gay and was once reprimanded for surrounding himself with good-looking young officers. Apart from being one of the greatest of our war leaders, he was a totally honourable and discreet man who, like many of his contempoaries, led a lonely and repressed life. Field Marshal Lord Montgomery, "for reasons of sexually based moral revulsion could not get on with Auchinleck" (R. Hyam, *Empire and Sexuality*, 1990, p. 14). Montgomery gained some notoriety during the Wolfenden debate. "Of all public figures he was the most absurdly virulent and flippantly irrational. In 1965 in attacking the Wolfenden proposals in a speech to the House of Lords he even suggested an age of consent fixed at 80" (ibid). Montgomery certainly had a quixotic approach to sex. He openly expressed his love for a boy of 11, Lucien Trueb, whom he met in Switzerland in 1945. He also invited another boy to his home and encouraged him to practice drill while he was naked after his bath (T. Howarth, *Monty at Close Quarters*, 1985). Montgomery may well have taken an exaggerated stand against homosexuality because of his own rather eccentric sexual leanings – yet another figure who had to sublimate or repress his natural feelings.

In the 1950s Calvert was not alone in suffering from the prejudices of the time, and the brave and honourable achievements of many war leaders who may have been homosexual still did not overcome the homophobic attitudes of society. The Services, like the Church, are forced to take a public stand on this issue, and so the debate continues.

In 1996 the Select Committee Inquiry into homosexuals in the Forces showed a deep and continuing level of prejudice. A medical orderly who had served in the Gulf said that he would refuse first-aid to a homosexual. A naval rating warned that an accident would happen to a known homosexual on board ship. Others said that they would "smash their face in". A warrant officer, parading ignorant prejudice as original thought stated, "Men don't like taking showers with men who like taking showers with men." (*The Guardian* 5 March, 1996)

So the old prejudices have been brought out again and the House of Commons and the Government, particularly the Ministers Soames and Portillo, have taken the easy way out and have gone along with the prejudices of the day. Summing up the sorry debate, Brian Sewell wrote, "Most queers are discreet, as reliable as any man, and keep their affliction (for that is what it is, in a world of prejudice) quietly to themselves. They are not rampaging seducers exercising supernatural powers over every penis and backside within a range of half a mile. Mr Portillo may be sure that all his armed forces embrace such steadfast paragons. He and Mr Soames insult them." (*Sunday Telegraph* 10 March, 1996).

Thus the picture has changed only very slowly for homosexuals and for those men and women who for one reason or another are not attracted to the opposite sex. Such people are forced to live their lives suppressing their real feelings, often lives of loneliness and rejection, usually considered misfits and outcasts by society at large. Many have lived their lives under a cloud of suspicion and under fear of criminal prosecution and blackmail. It is no wonder that after a lifetime of repression even now they rarely feel able to discuss such matters openly.

Among the ranks of outstanding military leaders whose sexual orientation was open to doubt, there are enough examples to suggest that such men who were put under enormous pressure by the prejudices of society, carried out brave, daring and occasionally foolhardy acts to prove they were as good or better than their comrades. These pressures often resulted as well in heavy drinking, a refuge from tensions which could become intolerable.

The biography of Lieutenant-Colonel Paddy Mayne, one of the great heroes of the SAS, who won four DSOs in the Regiment, and who gave Calvert his black eye in Norway in 1945, treated the question of his sexual orientation in a sympathetic and sensitive way. There were suggestions that Mayne was drawn to those of his own sex but that he kept such inclinations under rigid control, for to admit them would have been unthinkable. "Such an inner conflict would account for the sudden explosions when, released by alcohol, the repressive lid blows off and the seething frustrations, so conscientiously contained, foam out in violence. There is ample evidence throughout the history of the armed services that many extremely gallant and honourable men shared such inclinations but suppressed them under iron discipline, subjecting themselves in the process to well-nigh intolerable strains." (Bradford and Dillon, *Rogue Warrior of the SAS*, p. 231). Paddy Mayne was deeply respected in his native Ulster in spite of explosive outbreaks of violence and wild drinking sessions. Alas, Michael Calvert, though equally brave, had a more disciplined temperament and paid a grievous price for his occasional lapses.

# CHAPTER ELEVEN

# AUSTRALIA AND THE STRUGGLE WITH DRINK

After the court martial and his dismissal from the army, Calvert returned to England. With the help of friends and service contacts he obtained a job with the Shell Petroleum Company in Australia. In a state of serious depression, and drinking heavily, he left for Australia at the end of 1952. His outstanding wartime achievements and his promising military career had been destroyed by what he believed, and still believes, was a gross miscarriage of justice.

After a miserable flight he was met by grim-faced officials from the company. They held the press reports of the court-martial verdict and immediately informed him that they could no longer offer him a job. Instead, they suggested a post in Iraq, but this he refused, believing that he had enough good friends in the Melbourne area whom he had trained for service with the Australian Commandos in 1941. He had one further advantage. Lord Slim, formerly commander of XIV Army and patron of the Burma Star Association, was then Governor General of Australia. He had exhorted the Association to help any Burma Star member who was down on his luck and, since he knew of Calvert's plight, on many occasions he did his best to help.

Thus began one of the darkest periods of Calvert's life. While he had been under house arrest awaiting court martial he had been drinking heavily, often with the active connivance of his guards. In Australia he started drinking again. He took many unskilled labouring jobs, and a pattern emerged of a period of hard and often satisfying work, followed by an angry flare-up over some dispute, and then the sack, followed by another drinking bout.

He worked as a civil engineer on a project to build a goods railway through the desert in South Australia. This tough and harsh existence, with no comforts and no drinking, initially did him some good. He gained a reputation for being tough but fair. On one occasion there was a threatened strike by a group of Italian immigrant labourers who had seized a lorry. Facing this difficult situation which more senior persons seemed unable to quell, Calvert saw a snake lying in the dust. He quickly grabbed the snake and threw it into the back of the lorry. The rebels hurled themselves out of the lorry to roars of laughter from everyone else and the situation was resolved. At this time there was considerable ill-feeling between properly qualified Australian engineers, most of whom had had experience in the Outback, and the Limey immigrants who appeared to threaten their jobs. After an incident provoked by all this ill-feeling, Calvert was suddenly dismissed – unjustly, he believes. Under these conditions, his alcoholism advanced rapidly. In December, 1953, he was admitted to hospital in Melbourne with acute gastritis, claiming that he had had to drink water from his lorry radiator while working in the South Australian desert. His main diet seemed to have been whisky. He was kept under observation for some time because initially he had been walking around the hospital in a deluded state. In February 1954 he collapsed again after a long drinking bout and was taken to hospital by ambulance. He admitted to drinking 15 pints of beer and a bottle of whisky every day. A few weeks later he was again admitted to hospital with serious face and head injuries following a brawl at a party.

He later procured a more promising position working as a safety engineer for a project building a Shell oil refinery near Geelong School. Here he was doing reasonably responsible work and, in his leisure time, he was kept busy training the boys of Geelong School in water polo. As safety officer he had to make a report on an accident when some molten metal fell into the water and injured a worker. Calvert's report blamed the Shell company. The supervisor called Calvert to his office and demanded that the report be withdrawn. He asserted that the report didn't matter because the man was only a "Balt" (a term of derision) and that he would be sacked anyway. Calvert was so angry at this injustice that he leant over, grabbed the supervisor's head and banged it on the desk. He was soon looking for another job!

His contacts with his former Commando friends did, in the end, pay off and he was employed for a time looking after a small estate in Queensland which belonged to an old friend from 1940. The area suffered from severe flooding, and on one trip into town through the floods Calvert rang the Brisbane papers to give details because he knew that federal money was available for districts suffering from severe flooding. When he proudly told his neighbours of his helpful action, they were furious because they reckoned that his report had about halved the value of their investment in the township.

This led to another bout of drinking and he eventually picked up a stevedore job humping frozen meat carcases in the Brisbane docks, but while working there he collapsed and was seriously ill in Brisbane hospital with an internal haemorrhage. Eventually, having recovered from this, he obtained a post more suited to his convalescent state, as a post office clerk. His urge to write, which had already produced *Prisoners of Hope* in 1952, now caused more trouble. He wrote for the local paper a light-hearted article entitled "Male and Female Sorting". His boss was furious and once again he was sacked. He left Brisbane and moved south to an area where he obtained a post organizing the engineers working on the Warragamba dam, part of a major water supply project.

By 1957 his alcoholism was much worse. He attended a Sydney Casualty department "intoxicated and acting very strangely". (Medical Report, Calvert Papers). He had suffered from several blackouts. He returned the next day "with unsteady gait and suffused eyes". A medical examination produced evidence of cirrhosis of the liver. During the following two years he had fairly frequent contact with the medical authorities, and also gained and lost five jobs in eighteen months.

Eventually he was given a detailed and thorough medical test. The report of 1959 paints a vivid picture of his situation. It stated that "He is physically grosser than in 1957, and his psychopathic behaviour has continued unremittingly with frequent changes of job, alcoholism, and dependency on his former military colleagues who still try to help him out with jobs. His last job was as a concrete engineer at Warragumba Dam, obtained for him by Brigadier Macarthe-Onslow, but he went on a drinking spree and ended up in Broughton Hall (a refuge for alcoholics). . . . He has no money and his plans for the future are quite unrealistic. Despite the precariousness and degradation of his present way of life he remains arrogant and full of shallow rationalizations for his behaviour.... The rehabilitation of such a grossly psychopathic personality will be a Herculean task." The report concluded with a strong recommendation for institutional treatment of his alcoholism in England.

This critical report made him realize the appalling situation he was in. He therefore resolved to keep off alcohol and get back to England, even though the Australians were kinder in their approach to alcoholics, perhaps because they had so many.

At the end of 1960, after a period of work, he managed to save £100 and took a passage on a Greek ship returning home after bringing out immigrants. He remained teetotal on the ship, but when it docked at Alexandria, he received two letters. One was from his elder brother who wrote, "We don't want you back." The second came from Peter Fleming who had stood by him during the court martial and after: he also said that people did not want him to come back to England. Those two letters came as such a shock that Calvert started drinking again, and, after the ship docked at Athens, he spent some time virtually as a down and out, but he received great kindness from the Greek people. He eventually travelled by train to Paris where his brother Denis was on the staff of NATO HQ at Versailles. Denis appeared to be terrified of Michael being seen by his HQ colleagues and bundled him on a train to England. He arrived back in England on Christmas Eve, 1960, and managed to get to his sister Eileen's home near Southampton. Here he remembers being cheered up by overhearing a conversation when, totally exasperated, his sister said – "We have forgiven him seven times already," and her daughter replied, "Doesn't it say 'Unto seventy times seven?'" "Oh God, no!" replied her mother.

His return to England did not solve his main problem. His alcoholism was in an advanced state and landed him fairly frequently in hospitals or in mental institutions. He maintained contact with the Army medical services and also spent time in institutions run by the churches. Once he had a lengthy stay in a home run by monks in Dorset. In 1962 he was admitted to the military hospital in Woolwich and they reported that on each of the previous three days he had escaped from the ward and had returned drunk. He tried hard to conquer the affliction and was also helped by Alcoholics Anonymous, and received effective support at their mental home for alcoholics near Basingstoke.

His fight against alcoholism in the end succeeded and, having recovered from being a complete alcoholic, he hopes that his experience may encourage others who are similarly afflicted. At Basingstoke he was treated by a doctor who was involved in a horrific traffic accident and lost his wife and two children. He returned to work at once and Calvert thought, if the doctor could cope with such a tragedy, surely he ought to be able to cope with his drink problem. At another time he was in a mental hospital at Hereford near the HQ of the SAS. Colonel John Woodhouse, who had worked closely with him in the Malayan Scouts, was then commanding the SAS. He arranged for a Lance Corporal to go to Calvert each morning, to salute smartly and to say, "Here is your paper, Sir." Calvert believes that this simple gesture did more than anything else to restore his self-respect and to overcome his problem. He has a life-long love of swimming and during this period he found that if his craving for a drink was getting too strong he would go and have a swim and this cured his problem temporarily.

Sometime later when he had a job and was sharing a flat with Tony Harris, who has been his friend and confidant for 25 years, he told Tony that if he started drinking again, to lock him in a room with two buckets and not let him out. During his long struggle he suffered several setbacks, particularly when people who knew of his problem, nevertheless in a totally irresponsible gesture, gave him a drink. Gradually, through months and years of anguish and disappointment, he slowly overcame his alcoholism and in 1964 he was able to give up alcohol altogether.

Having conquered his own afflication, Calvert continued to do his best to help other alcoholics. This he did, but in his turn he received admirable help from Tony Harris whom he took on initially as a historical research assistant. Calvert and Harris became close friends, and Harris, who admired Calvert and considered him his mentor, has been looking after him ever since. In the later 1970s Calvert had occasional dangerous lapses from his teetotal régime and Harris was strong enough to help him surmount the problem. Calvert also suffers from heart trouble and maintains that on at least two occasions Harris' prompt action has saved his life. Thus was formed a permanent bond of loyalty and devotion.

# CHAPTER TWELVE

# THE 1960s – REHABILITATION

During his painful effort to overcome his alcoholism, Calvert also faced the difficult prospect of obtaining work, preferably more suited to his age and qualifications than the dead-end labouring to which he had often been reduced in Australia. This was not easy, because the pattern of working for a few weeks or months and then getting the sack for a drinking binge was difficult to overcome. His jobs included work in an engineering test laboratory – lost because of a drinking bout. In 1963 he worked for several months at Marshall's airport at Cambridge, but he lost this too because of his drinking.

During this time he had re-established some valuable links, and *Fighting Mad* was published in 1964. It told in a racy, humourous and vivid way the story of his life from his first escapades in Norway to the end of the Burma campaign. 1964 was significant in another way because, in that year, with the substantial help of "The Community of Lost Souls" which he had met through Alcoholics Anonymous, he finally overcame his obsession for drink. He determined to drink no more, a resolution he has kept ever since, with very few lapses.

This great achievement soon produced a tangible result and in April, 1965, he was appointed to a fairly senior job in the Greater London Council. He was put in charge of the recruitment and training of graduate engineers for the Highways and Transport Department. This was a reasonably well-paid and pensionable post and he received, in addition, a 50% disability allowance for damage to his health arising from war service. He filled this post with distinction, and some time later received a glowing reference saying that he had carried the distinguished qualities of his wartime career into civilian life with great aplomb and could not be recommended too highly. He held this post for five years, and carried out his work conscientiously, but it is clear that his mentality was never suited to a fairly humdrum office job linked to a pension. His real interest both then and later lay in his expertise in the field of guerrilla war.

His experience, his knowledge, and his outstanding ability in this field made him a world expert. He made significant contributions to the wider debate about guerrilla war, sabotage and urban revolution in relation to the violent events which were taking place all round the world. It was tragic that he never obtained a permanent post at, say, Sandhurst, or in the war studies departments which were slowly developing in the universities, or in the Service Colleges in the Dominions or America where his positive ideas and outstanding knowledge could have been fully and gainfully employed.

Even during his time in Australia his mind had constantly been engaged in developing his ideas about guerrilla warfare and its rôle in modern society, and in December, 1976, he published an important paper entitled "The Pattern of Guerrilla Warfare". In this, which he illustrated with examples from his erudite knowledge of military history, he argued that western societies should be far more aware of the danger that, the more mechanized and technological they become, the easier it is to disrupt or destroy them. In terms of both attack and defence, Britain, now one of the weaker countries of the world, needed to use both ingenuity and cunning. He quoted Tito in 1944, who had no defences against German armour, but dressed some of his partisans as German traffic police and guided a German armoured division over a precipice. Calvert stressed that a city like New York could be paralysed by the destruction of a single part of its electricity supply system. Modern societies must identify their own weak spots in order to defend them; they must study a potential enemy's weakness in order to plan attacks. He believed that the guerrilla attack is more necessary than ever in the atomic age, since the guerrilla can penetrate the enemy area and be immune to his atomic power. He illustrated the need for far-sighted study of the enemy by the case of a British agent planted in 1938, who became controller of the Vienna marshalling yards during the Second World War. He was able to misdirect trains across the whole of Europe, and even managed to send a train-load of scrap iron to the German forces attacking Stalingrad who were desperately short of shells, and the train-load of shells was sent to the Ruhr. Calvert stressed the need for guerrilla units to have strong local support, with intelligence and medical back-up, and for the guerrilla commander to have local autonomy within a framework shaped by top-level directives. Britain had an outstanding history in insurgency and in counter-insurgency, but now needed to learn these lessons again. He quoted the case of a brilliant German agent in the Middle East in the First World War whom the British were never able to catch, but when his PO Box number was discovered a packet of gold coins was sent by His Majesty's Government with thanks for services rendered. The Germans shot him.

Calvert concluded that, in an age of ideological clashes, the anti-guerrilla must be better trained, must be better equipped, must be harder and more realistic than the guerrillas, and must win over the population by being, in the mediaeval phrase, "parfit Knights", with exemplary behaviour and dedication. "Trust the Ingeniator – the Engineer."

After all his suffering Calvert needed, above all, the restoration of his self-respect, and he was delighted by the response to the publication of this paper. He particularly treasured a letter from his former SAS colleague, David Stirling, who wrote with affectionate congratulations. Stirling thought the paper was "superbly good, and one of the best statements of the role of the SAS, – plus some good bellylaughs". (Calvert Papers)

During the 1960s Calvert increasingly developed his ideas within the context of the growing menace of communism. In Europe, the building of the Berlin Wall in 1961 had set the parameters of the Cold War. In the Far East the aggressive policy of Mao Tse-tung and his backing of North Vietnam had led to the Tonkin Gulf incident in 1964 which drew the United States into the Vietnam War. In Africa, during the decade of independence, begun by Ghana in 1957, both the United States and the Soviet Union sought urgently to swing the leaders of the emergent countries to either capitalism or communism. Many western leaders became paranoid about communist infiltration and developed the domino theory that one country after another would fall under communist influence.

In such a climate, and with the continuing repercussions of the Suez débâcle of 1956, a growing body of opinion considered Britain's rôle on the world stage to be supine and craven. Calvert was certainly one of these, and he corresponded with many, most right-wing,

Members of Parliament and leaders in other fields. Sir Hugh Fraser tried to discourage him from forming a Vietnam Fighting Force, and he received similar cautionary advice from Sir William Tilling and Philip Goodheart. Sir Basil Liddell Hart corresponded with him about tactical issues, and Field Marshal Lord Slim, then Lieutenant Governor, and later Constable of Windsor Castle, wrote him affectionate letters and invited him to visit.

In 1966, when the country was deeply divided over the crisis in Rhodesia, Calvert was approached by several right-wing groups and he also corresponded with the Rhodesian SAS which he had formed in 1950. Also in 1966, as Australia felt the menace of a communist advance in the Far East, he received a letter of appreciation from the commander of the Australian SAS thanking him for all he had taught them in both skills and attitudes. (Letter Calvert Papers)

By the end of the 1960s he was well established as a military commentator and was a full member of the Military Commentators Circle. Here he met again Sir Robert Thompson who had been his RAF Liaison Officer on both Chindit expeditions, and later an adviser on Vietnam to President Nixon. Having experienced communist subversion in Malaya in 1950, Calvert viewed communist expansion in Asia with considerable alarm and passionately criticized what he saw as the craven and pusillanimous leadership of Britain at that time.

His concern about terrorism blended with his professional interest as a senior engineer in the Greater London Council with the safety of roads, bridges and public buildings. He made a forceful speech in November, 1966, in which he argued that, when public buildings and bridges were erected, more attention should be given to their protection against sabotage, terrorism and the danger of civil unrest.

As his rehabilitation continued and he was welcomed more widely in society, he was also approached by the military establishment for his respected and trenchant views on defence matters. He was pleased when a major Staff College exercise was based on his original 1943 training notes for 77 Brigade. In 1967 he was invited to take part at a senior level in another Staff College operation. During that year he corresponded with General Sir John Hackett who congratulated him on his military articles: also with Enoch Powell and Freddie Spencer Chapman who recalled their adventures at Lochailort and with the Australian Commandos and Independent Companies. By this time he was a member of the Savage Club, which for him had the particular advantage of a swimming pool.

Although the late 1960s saw Calvert in a safe job and pursuing his many interests in the wider world, his work with the Greater London Council did not stretch him, nor did it satisfy him. At the end of 1969, therefore, he left the Council and obtained a post with the construction firm Ove Arup as a civil engineer. This offered him a considerably higher salary and brought him into contact with influential people in the construction industry. He wrote a powerful article for *The Surveyor*, the magazine of Local Government Technology, in which he argued that Britain was producing too many graduate engineers. He believed that degree courses in engineering should be more demanding and this would eventually improve the status of engineers in the country.

At Ove Arup Calvert soon discovered that he was dangerously out of touch with the modern developments in civil engineering. His rôle in recruiting graduate engineers for the Greater London Council had not tested his technical knowledge and he now found that he did not possess the up-to-date expertise to fulfil the requirements of his new post. At the same time he was kept extremely busy with those interests which really interested him, in particular the research for a book to be entitled *The Pattern of Guerrilla Warfare* which Allen & Unwin/Penguin had commissioned him to write.

Early in 1969 he received a letter from an old friend Julian Hannay, who had also been his lawyer. The letter dated 17 February (Calvert Papers) referred to Calvert's proposal to appeal once again against the sentence of his court martial. Calvert had already approached a number of senior military figures who strongly advised him against the idea. Speaking as a friend, Hannay wrote, "As you know we had the benefit of advice based on knowledge and wide experience from those whom you mention in your letter, namely, Shan Hackett, Gerry Duke, Peter Fleming as well as Bernard Fergusson. That is what I would call a pretty strong team. Their view, which I share, was that it [his application] is not a forlorn hope but a venture doomed to failure. What concerns me most is not the failure itself but the blow to your pride which rejection must entail, and the possibility which might follow, as well as the opening of old wounds.

"I know you for a man of great tenacity and determination, and I have boundless admiration for your courage in pulling yourself out of the Slough of Despond. I would hate to see you hurt again particularly when you have have won your way back to respect and esteem everywhere."

This letter admirably summed up the feelings of the many friends and colleagues who had genuinely admired Calvert's efforts to re-establish himself. He continued to correspond with Hannay, often using his letters to expound his deepest feelings.

Writing to Hannay in 1970 Calvert again brought up the court martial and its wider issues. He had discovered that there were a string of homosexual clubs across Britain and Europe, many run, he alleged, by "ex SIB officers and NCOs."' (SIB: Special Investigation Branch). He then referred to Albert Dunn, ex SIB, who had assured him that there was absolute proof that his court martial at Soltau had been a put-up job. Calvert's deep hurt and frustration over what he still considered the injustice of the court martial prompted another outburst and his letter continued, "The court martial was a nightmare, but I did not give either of you much chance with my drinking whilst under arrest. I suppose the advocate was sincere but I never liked him.... I overheard some of the remarks he made in the corridor during the trial and could willingly have beaten him to death. He was a popinjay in my opinion and never gained the confidence of the court." Calvert added that his court martial had gained a lot of sympathy from disaffected people and groups who tried to enlist his help against authority, so he tended to be suspicious of anyone who tried to show him friendship. Continuing his letter, he reverted to another fairly constant theme: the bitterness felt by the Chindits at the way the Official History had disparaged their achievements and the hostile attitude of the military establishment towards them. Finally, he referred to the help he had received from Ove Arup "to become something in my own right." Although he was earning good money with good pension rights, he decided to "chuck it all and try my hand at writing". (Letter 24 August, 1970, Calvert Papers)

He had some reason to feel confident. He had just completed a paperback *Chindit* for Ballantine Books, and was writing another book on Slim as a general. Calvert had been commissioned at £100 per month for a year to prepare a major work, *The Pattern of Guerrilla Warfare*. *Prisoners of Hope* was being republished, and he had received an advance of money for a film to be based on it.

At this time he was also in touch with Michael Elliott-Bateman and Professor M.R.D. Foot, both from Manchester University, and there was some initial discussion about him applying for a fellowship at Manchester. He took the decision to leave Ove Arup, saying that bachelors should be the ones to take risks, but this was a more grave and serious move than he realized. It was unfortunate that one of his friends in the military, academic or literary fields did not warn him of the difficulty of making a living from free-lance writing. In practice, this decision resulted in him living the rest of his life in virtual penury.

# CHAPTER THIRTEEN

# GUERRILLA EXPERT

During the summer of 1970 Calvert corresponded with Michael Elliott-Bateman, lecturer in Military Studies at Manchester University, about their shared interest in guerrilla warfare, and also about the possibility of Calvert applying for a Hallsworth Research Fellowship at the University. Calvert wrote a chapter entitled "The Philosophy of Guerrilla Warfare" for a major work, *The Fourth Dimension of War*, which Elliott-Bateman was editing. Calvert developed the theme of the difficulty of finding suitable men as guerrilla or counter-guerrilla leaders in a modern technological society. He thought that present-day governments were afraid of developing strike forces of this sort because of the difficulty of controlling them, and he quoted the frequent danger of the government disbanding the SAS, the most professional of all Special Forces. Calvert admired Elliott-Bateman's book *Defeat in the East* and they found that they agreed on many issues within the field of military history.

Their co-operation proceeded amicably and, in October, 1970, Calvert was invited to Manchester University to give a prestigious public lecture entitled "A Discourse on Guerrilla Warfare". In the lecture he referred to the rulings on guerrilla warfare in The Hague Conventions of 1899 and 1907 to show that guerrilla war was not some modern wildcat idea, but had a respectable pedigree. He produced a background display of guerrilla operations, including the Peninsular War 1803–1814, Napoleon's retreat from Moscow, Garibaldi in Italy, the American Civil War and the wars on the North West Frontier of India. In more modern times he cited Lawrence and the Arab Revolt, the Spanish Civil War, the Chindit operations, Indo-China, Cuba and Algeria, all conflicts in which guerrilla operations had played a part. These examples supported his theme that the importance of guerrilla warfare increased as both armies and countries became more technological, more sophisticated and therefore more vulnerable. Calvert developed this theme and ranged widely over modern guerrilla movements, paying special attention to the career of Che Guevara, perhaps the most successful of recent guerrilla leaders. Guevara had learnt most of his skills from Alberto Bayo, the veteran leader from the Spanish Republican Army in the Spanish Civil War. The Cuban-born Bayo in turn had learnt much from the early writing of Mao Tse-tung. Guevara provided a link through much of the turmoil of the 1960s: having assisted Castro in the overthrow of Batista in Cuba, he then took part in the Congo uprisings, and finally lost his life in an attempted coup in Bolivia in 1967.

Calvert's presentation clearly impressed his distinguished audience, and in January, 1971, he was offered the Hallsworth Research Fellowship at £4,400 per annum for one year. This appeared to give him a great opportunity and his appointment certainly fitted in with the plans and hopes of Elliott-Bateman. A former regular Army officer, he had resigned his commission when the War Office refused him permission to publish his book *Defeat in the East*. He had then accepted the post of lecturer in Military Studies at Manchester, but this put him in rather an isolated position. He envisaged the arrival of Calvert as an opportunity to establish a strong and effective school to study aspects of modern warfare, especially guerrilla warfare. He felt it was vital that the school should be untrammelled by the restricting hand of the military establishment or its associated organizations like the RUSI. In a letter welcoming Calvert to Manchester, Elliott-Bateman referred to him as one of the few torch-bearers who was still unbowed, and invited him "to come in from the cold". (Letters, December, 1970. Calvert Papers)

While this encouraging development was taking place, Calvert was developing a strongly misanthropic attitude in public affairs. He wrote a tirade to the Master of St John's College, Cambridge, where he had been as an undergraduate, demanding that he should publicly condemn the disgraceful left-wing mob riots when the Greek Colonels came to the Garden House Hotel in Cambridge. Because of this involvement in the study of guerrilla warfare and subversion, he became obsessed with the danger of left-wing plots. He wrote angrily to the Archbishop of Canterbury and received a measured reply from Lambeth Palace pointing out that the Archbishop's view on left-wing subversion was supported by the editors of *The Times* and *The Economist*, and asked if Calvert regarded these as "treasonable communists, Marxists and anarchists". (Letter, November, 1970. Calvert Papers) In the same month he wrote to his MP to demand action against "left-wing hoodlums" who had interrupted a TV programme presented by David Frost. This aggressive and slightly neurotic attitude was carried over into his correspondence with commercial firms and banks, in which he was usually at fault. He received an effective put-down from an accounts clerk at Rymans the stationers. Calvert had angrily referred to "accounts people as the bottom rung of the ladder". The accounts clerk replied, "If being at the top means writing unjust and rude letters unfairly, then I will stay where I am". (Letter, November, 1970. Calvert Papers)). His activities at that time also included joining a group called "Enoch Powell for Premier".

His most intemperate outburst was made on the subject of Labour Party policy on Nigerian oil. After several swipes at left-wing Hampstead intellectuals and pacifists, including a bevy of bishops, economists, air marshals and a left-wing admiral, he argued that the black man had "become the supreme arbiter in the affairs of the cringing english" (sic). He believed that the entire fault lay with the liberal fraternity who had done more harm to Britain than any outside enemy. He continued, "God save us from these insidious liberals, present in every party. They are out to reduce Britain to a Danish pastry pacifist nonentity. They are the real racists as they try to destroy everything good in all races in order to achieve a grey, dull, suety wodge they call atheist internationalism." (Letter, May, 1970. Calvert Papers)

He continued to give much thought to military issues arising from his wartime service, and, showing a more positive attitude, he contacted General Gale to ask for his help in obtaining more official support for the French and Belgian SAS volunteers who had been based in this country and whom he had commanded in 1945. He had received generous hospitality in Paris and Brussels as the former commander of these units and had taken part in ceremonies at the Arc de Triomphe and Les Invalides among France's leaders. He was surprised that all Britain had provided on a return French visit was tea and buns in a cheap TA drill hall in Southampton.

These outbursts clearly stemmed from a fundamentally unhappy frame of mind. Because of his insecurity, he tended to be over-sensitive and to take offence too easily. He admitted that "living alone, working hard, and often sleeping badly makes me too intro-spective and makes me harp on about things". He had reacted strongly when Mountbatten in his TV series "The World at War" had made serious criticisms of Wingate. Calvert had organized a strong protest to the press, which does not appear to have been published, supported by several former Chindit brigadiers. At the same time he attacked the committee of the Chindit Old Comrades Association for not standing up for Wingate and the Chindits whenever they were maligned. He continued, "I know of no other Old Comrades Committee or similar institution in the world that does not think that one of its main tasks is to stand up for its men and their past achievements, and remain truly loyal to their leader.... They should be unwilling to listen to slanders against their com-mander as your committee did." He went on to berate the committee for knuckling under and accepting Mountbatten's calumnies.

His insecure and over-sensitive attitude is very well illustrated in a kindly and understanding way in a letter which he received from Bernard Fergusson, to whom he had sent one of his long, rambling diatribes. The letter highlights so many aspects of Calvert's life and of his character that it is quoted at some length:-

Ballantrae, Ayrshire
17 March, 1970

Dear Michael (as Orde alone used to call you) Dear Mike comes more naturally to me!

Thank you very much for your long cri de coeur. I am touched that you should confide in me to such a degree, and even honoured that you felt like doing so. I don't quite know where to start commenting, since topics spring up in it like hares in a field and dash wildly off.

Let me begin by juggling three hares together: my books and their reference to Wingate and Slim; your relations with Slim, Peter Fleming and me; and your projected books. I rather expected that you and Derek Tulloch and others would feel that I had been disloyal to Orde in what I have written about him in my latest book, and Orde himself will certainly think so. I owe him one hell of a lot, and have said so loud and clear, but I don't feel that I owe it to him not to be objective about him, and that I have tried honestly to be. Derek is loyal to him almost beyond reason: he may sneer at "Slim's fairy tales" – a very good crack, by the way – but my admiration for Slim is almost unbounded, and has increased with the years as I have got to know him better. As for the comments on Wingate in the *Official History*, I have just reread them since getting your letter. It was not I who wrote them, as you seem to think possible. But I did see them in draft, and they were far less magnanimous at that stage than in their final form. Considering how offensive Orde had always been to Kirby, they are remarkably restrained. But I had forgotten how many inaccuracies had crept in to the *Official History*: I have spotted several in my swift re-reading this morning.

I won't defend what I have said about Orde point by point. I will only say that I weighed every word. As for what you may say about Slim in your book, I will quote his words to me: "It's a free country and you can say what you like." It is your duty to be objective if you are going to put pen to paper, it is certainly not your duty to stick up for Orde *versus* Slim or *vice versa* on any grounds of loyalty to either. But apart from that, I think you should know that you are very deep personally in Bill Slim's debt. When you were both "down and down-under", he wrote to me often about you, deeply distressed on your behalf and wondering what more he could do to help. To write, as you do, "He has been very good to me in his fashion" is less than generous on your part, and totally out of your character. (Forgive me for assuming the role of Dutch uncle, but it is an opening which you have given me!) I haven't kept his letters bar one or two on historical subjects, but I would guess that he wrote to me from Australia about you certainly not less than six times, and it was probably more like ten. I don't think that "devious" is a word applicable to Slim. He is the embodiment of integrity. You are, I repeat, deep in debt to him. I only invite you to realise that: I am not suggesting that it should colour anything you may be going to write.

Similarly, you owe one hell of a lot to Peter Fleming. I don't know if you are informed of the sequence of events before your court martial. Peter was at Merrimoles, I was at SHAPE and living at Versailles. It was Shan Hackett, whom I did not know very well, who rang me from Germany in my office in SHAPE: I think he was DQMG BAOR at the time, and he told me what was afoot. It was he who also suggested Julian Hannay as a defence lawyer. I flew over to London and met Peter and Julian, the latter for the first time. Peter and I then sent out letters asking for financial support, and got something over £2000.

I am not qualified to comment on Peter's failing to give you your due in his book *Invasion 1940*, so I won't; but he did stick by you through thick and thin, and mobilised much help. Being at SHAPE, I couldn't do much, so he did it. Actually I had a hell of a job getting leave from my (American) boss to attend the court martial. In the end he gave me 48 hours (which I over-stayed!).

No wonder that you brood from time to time, but your friends did stand by you, though you weren't easily "stood by" in your then mood. Gerry Duke was another super-loyal friend to you, despite a few rebuffs! (Dutch uncle again).

It is a major act of faith – and acts of faith are usually rewarded – to chuck up your safe but dull job with the GLC and launch out on the dubious scribble-scribble world. I am delighted to hear that the doves are returning to your Ark with something in their beaks. More power, to mix the metaphor, to your elbow.

Look, old cock, you fairly took your hair down to me, and I have answered you in the same idiom. You tell me not to praise you for hauling off the booze, but I do. Clawing off a lee shore is always a difficult feat, and this is the trickiest lee shore of all. And you've done it. I can't get to Manchester to give you a cheer or dig in the ribs, but all good luck for the occasion. I have had more than my share of good luck, for which I thank God; but I have always reminded myself of that terrible text in the Bible – "Let him that thinketh he standeth, take heed lest he fall".

This morning comes your post card, indicating that you may be having second thoughts about your wisdom in having written your three-volume letter to me. Don't. Laura and I have shared it (as you said we might), and this letter comes to you freighted with more good will and good wishes than it is reasonable to expect the Postmaster-General to carry for 5p. I wish that I could think what it was I said at our reunion dinner in 1968 that wounded you: I would have bitten off the tip of my tongue rather than do that willingly.

So there we are, with our friendship back on its usual even keel, and with extra ballast because of this frank exchange of thoughts. All the virtues of courage and determination which stood you in good stead during the war, and inspired many others including myself, are with you still, so God bless you, and all good luck. Bless you.

Yours ever,
Bernard.

On his appointment to the Hallsworth Research Fellowship at Manchester University early in 1971 Calvert decided that, in order to complete his major work on *The Pattern of Guerrilla Warfare*, he would devote his immediate efforts and most of the money from the

Fellowship to visiting those parts of the world where guerrilla activity was taking place. He hoped that this would bring his views on guerrilla warfare completely up-to-date.

He first focused his attention on the situation in Northern Ireland, then in the third year of its recent troubles, and the nearest example of urban guerrilla warfare. His actual visit to Belfast was controversial and eccentric, and could have had very serious repercussions. While appearing supremely confident, he showed an astonishing naïveté about the conditions and realities of life in Belfast. He took his car and travelled on the overnight ferry from Liverpool to Dublin. He drove up to Belfast and booked into the Europa, a hotel frequented by journalists. He gave a substantial tip to a porter, asking him to pass on any interesting information. He was soon told that there would be an interesting meeting the next morning at Flanagan's Place. Calvert allegedly passed on this information to the Army. In the morning he drove to Flanagan's and parked his car nearby. His car had an SAS badge on the front and he was wearing an SAS tie. Fortunately for him, the IRA were ignorant of the arcane niceties of club and regimental ties. As he approached the place for the meeting he met up with a German television crew and went into the meeting with them. He sat through a long meeting expecting that at any moment the army would arrive. The meeting was actually the famous press conference held by the IRA leader, Joe Cahill, the head of the Provisional IRA, to prove that his force was very far from being defeated. When the army did not arrive, Calvert decided to leave. He went through a ring of armed IRA guards, and then he did something that probably saved his life. Needing a pee, he went over to some waste ground and relieved himself. The guards probably thought that was why he had left the meeting and took no further notice of him. He drove off to the HQ of the Parachute Regiment, but it took some considerable time before he found anyone who would take him seriously. Eventually he found a brigadier who recognized him. A patrol was swiftly despatched to Flanagan's Place, but it was deserted. By this time the military realized that Calvert's actions had put his life in danger. They therefore spirited him away, kept him in total seclusion and sent him back to Liverpool in a secure, locked cabin.

Afterwards Calvert had a conceited approach to this incident, saying that the army had been there for years, yet he had only been in Ulster for 24 hours and could have rounded up the whole of the IRA leadership. He must have openly boasted about this, for, on 8 December, 1971, the *Times* Diary described the incident in some detail under the heading "How the IRA have been infiltrated". A serious and more sobering comment came soon afterwards in a letter to *The Times* (12 December, 1971) from a professional journalist, Christopher Wain. He pointed out that Calvert's action had jeopardized the life of every reporter and cameraman in Ireland. Journalists knew that their lives depended on the trust they had established with the IRA, that they would not be betrayed. Wain pointed out that Calvert's action had damaged that trust and could have had the widest repercussions in the situation of a civil dispute, the gravity of which was not then fully realized in England.

Unabashed by this gaffe, Calvert formulated some forthright views on the Northern Ireland issue. He wrote a lengthy paper, a draft of which was published in *The Spectator* on 16 October, 1971. He demanded that the security forces should form highly-trained and ruthless hunter-killer groups and should take much more vigorous action to eradicate the IRA. They should not be inhibited by some vague long-term hope of an eventual political settlement. He referred to the many half-hearted actions against guerrilla forces in Malaya, Cyprus and Aden, which had already cost the country dear, and he argued that the leaders of both sides in a guerrilla warfare situation sometimes had a vested interest in keeping the contest going. Since the IRA were making war, the security forces should go on to a total war footing.

He believed progress against insurgents depended very substantially on accurate and up-to-date intelligence. This should be sought aggressively with force, blackmail when necessary, and the widespread use of bribes to obtain information and to uncover the IRA and their supporters. Linked to this should be an active and all-embracing propaganda offensive against the IRA, instead of the current situation where the security forces merely appeared to react to initiatives taken by the IRA.

Having suggested positive ways of eliminating the IRA, he launched into even more radical proposals. Quoting the French engineer Haussmann, who cleared the worst slums in Paris in the 1850s by constructing the Champs Elysées and other boulevards, wide enough to prevent barricades and straight enough for the security forces to use heavier weapons, Calvert proposed a massive reconstruction programme. He suggested bulldozing the whole of the Ballymurphy – Falls Road area and replacing it with a new town containing attractive modern amenities, similar to Thamesmead. He reckoned that this would cost between £300m and £500m, and he saw this as a penance for all our past mistakes in Ireland. Such a scheme, he believed, would give "an aim, a goal, a star to steer by", and with labour-intensive work could submerge communal differences. "Out of evil could come forth good". Twenty-five years and billions of pounds later, £300m might appear as a good investment.

After his visit to Belfast, Calvert continued his headlong attempt to acquaint himself with the major fields of guerrilla activity and went off to Angola in October, 1971. Welcomed by the Portuguese forces, he was able to travel about the country and even to visit the area along the border with Zaire, an area which both the government forces and the MPLA (The Peoples Movement for the Liberation of Angola) claimed to control. The government policy of building roads and gathering the rural population into protected villages, as Calvert had recommended in Malaya in 1950, appeared to be working successfully. Calvert noted that since the 1960s, when America and Russia vied for the control of emergent African countries, Russia now appeared to be losing interest and its rôle was increasingly being taken over by China in both eastern and western Africa. China had obviously decided that better results could be obtained in a naïve world by propaganda in America, Europe and at the United Nations than by fighting in the African bush.

In his brief visit Calvert was heartened by the apparent success of the government in Angola, a country almost as big as the whole of Europe, yet with a population of only 5 million. It had rich natural resources, especially minerals, which were being developed for the benefit of the people in order to win them over from the MPLA and other insurgents.

Calvert's visit to Angola strongly influenced his views on guerrilla warfare in the modern world, and on wider defence issues. He criticized the western military establishment for concentrating on the vastly expensive provision of ever more powerful and sophisticated guns, tanks and aircraft for a possible war in Europe. The real wars were being fought with insurgents in the underdeveloped countries of Asia, Africa and South America. He showed that Portugal, which had few western-style armed forces, had wisely concentrated on its African commitments.

Portugal, he believed, because of her poverty of resources, had evolved more humane counter-insurgency measures. It had not used tanks, jet fighters, heavy artillery, bombers, battleships, napalm or defoliants, but faced guerrillas with counter-guerrillas. Portugal appeared to be reclaiming insurgent areas by the building of tarmac roads and the socio-economic reconstructionn of rural areas, a policy similar to that of the Romans in Britain. The success of this policy also depended on denying the guerrillas supplies of food and arms, and especially of salt.

In the 1970s the MPLA, the strongest of the insurgent groups, controlled much of south-east Angola along the border with Zambia. The MPLA was trained by Chinese and Cuban instructors and supported materially by Russia and Czechoslovakia. Calvert also discovered that the MPLA received financial assistance from Sweden, Britain and some Christian charities. He pointed out that the mines laid indiscriminately by the MPLA, which killed and maimed innocent children, could have been paid for by Christian Aid. It appeared to him that the sound policy of the Portuguese government was likely to overcome the unpopular MPLA forces, which seemed to have little purpose except the laying of mines, which had horrific consequences. He vividly portrayed the result – the one-legged farmer tending his three-legged cow. In addition to the hearts and minds policy, the government also backed strong anti-guerrilla tactics by commandos, parachute groups and other offensive units using French-built helicopters which carried small groups of highly trained anti-guerrilla fighters.

In his quest to study and understand modern guerrilla and anti-guerrilla techniques, Calvert was impressed by the Portuguese use of the *"Flesche"*. These were former guerrillas who had been captured, retrained, and then sent back into guerrilla areas in order to hunt down and kill their former commanders, which they usually succeeded in doing.

Influenced by the policies and views of the Portuguese government whose hospitality he had received, Calvert painted an encouraging picture of their sound and constructive approach to the problems of Angola. So it appeared in 1971, and Calvert could not have known then that the unfortunate country was to be torn apart for nearly another twenty years because the warring factions were supported by western capitalism, by eastern or Cuban communism, or by aggressive apartheid-based South African forces, which pursued their ideological vendettas in Angola at little cost to themselves.

During a hectic year of foreign travel and research, he continued to establish himself as a lecturer, author and commentator both in Manchester and throughout the country. In June, 1971, he addressed the Manchester Tactical Society on "The Dangers of Peace". He developed the theme that a country only made real progress under the threat and stimulation of war; too much peace inevitably led to decay. He argued that some of the seven deadly sins at least invigorated people; envy, pride and lust always stirred people to action while faith, prudence and temperance were hardly a call to arms. He quoted Glubb Pasha who said that the collapse of empires is usually attributed to the demoralizing influence of luxury and wealth, which leads to materialism, and to the decline of religion and idealism; then cynicism completes the decline.

Calvert reverted to his misanthropic views, arguing that the bureaucrats and preservationists had, since 1945, lived like parasites on the corpse of the old empire, instead of envisaging grand new schemes which could bring feelings of pride and achievement. Giving his own unfortunate situation perhaps too much prominence, he suggested, "Insurance policies, pensions and home ownership are the antithesis of progress". He concluded by saying that war develops man's attributes to the full and helps him to achieve goals beyond his dreams. Once more allowing his personal prejudices to obtrude, he argued that many men say that the war was the happiest time of their lives. "Now they are henpecked by their wives, by their bosses, by shop stewards, by income tax inspectors – the lot.... It is not the killing that is enjoyed but the thrills, the danger, the lethal competition for the highest of stakes – the pride in achievement and a comradeship unknown in peacetime.... In an imperfect world everything has its disadvantages – even peace."

During 1971 Calvert spent several months making arrangements for a trip to Vietnam, clearly the most important arena for guerrilla war. Unfortunately for him the visit ended as an anti-climax, largely because of the strongly supported decision of President Nixon to withdraw America's military commitment in Vietnam. Calvert had intended to go to Saigon in October, 1971, but all his contacts, including Sir Robert Thompson, who was one of Nixon's advisers on Vietnam, suggested that he postpone his visit until the end of the year and this he did.

He arrived in Saigon in early December and, with the help of the American forces and the South Vietnam government, he was able to travel to most of the combat areas. This was to be an important part of his overall project on *The Pattern of Guerrilla War*. His book was to include a detailed study of guerrilla movements prior to 1945 and to ascertain if a pattern emerged of the techniques of guerrilla warfare, the characters of guerrilla leaders, or the effectiveness of counter-insurgency measures. The second part of the study would test these findings on guerrilla movements in the period after 1945, concentrating not on the political issues but on the mechanics of guerrilla war. This would include the development of weapons, the use of aircraft, the increasing use of helicopters, the system of supplies, the approach to prisoners and their conversion and the effective use of propaganda, concentrating particularly on enemy atrocities. As a qualified engineer, Calvert strongly supported the idea of a large-scale reconstruction of an area in order to win the hearts and minds of the people.

In December, 1971, it was clear that the Americans were phasing out their main military effort and considering how best to support the South Vietnamese forces in their continuing struggle against the communist forces. It was unfortunate for Calvert that in Vietnam, as in Angola, he was studying war from what became the losing side but he did make some useful discoveries. He visited the South Vietnam Guerrilla School, but his most heartening find came from the enemy side.

During the 1960s Ho Chi Minh and General Giap, the brilliant military leader who defeated the French at Dien Bien Phu in 1954 and was to defeat the Americans in Vietnam, had decided that the most economical and effective use of their resources was to train combat engineers. These highly trained men would be infiltrated into enemy areas in small groups for long range penetration. Giap set up training camps and gave volunteers a long and tough training in physical fitness, endurance, unarmed combat and in the use of explosives in every aspect of sabotage. After basic training the Sappers specialized on land targets, water targets, especially American supply ships, and a third specialist group trained to attack enemy headquarters. Up to 1970 these "Sappers" had destroyed over 600 bridges and were seen as the spearhead of the North Vietnam advance. Sapper units were established in many villages and gained eager recruits by offering the chance to join an elite force with the challenge of adventure and danger. One young Sapper said that it was much more interesting and exciting to blow up a bridge than to spend day after day guarding it. The Sappers linked as closely as possible with the Vietcong, the south Vietnamese guerrillas who supported the communist cause. How disappointing for Calvert that the Sappers who epitomized almost everything he had advocated in guerrilla war were the spearhead of a cause which was anathema to him.

When he returned to England early in 1973 he took part in a BBC World Service programme. Interviewed as an expert who had recently visited Vietnam, he suggested that, with the American withdrawal, South Vietnam could no longer continue an expensive and sophisticated war, but would have to think out completely new tactics. At the same time he believed South Vietnam had created an effective militia over 4 million strong which, he thought, would be able in the end to overcome the Vietcong. America was still providing most technical war supplies and air support, and still carried out most bombing missions, but the South Vietnamese were rapidly building up their forces and already had over 300 helicopters.

As a result of these overseas visits he was writing impressive articles for quality papers and magazines including *The Spectator*, but in 1972 he was drawing to the close of his Fellowship. In spite of this he managed to make a prolonged visit to Mozambique (November, 1972). During his stay of five weeks he was able, as in Angola and Vietnam, to travel freely and meet the leaders of the government forces as well as captured guerrillas. Once again he appeared to be convinced of the success of the Portuguese government. He described the remarkable success of the socio-economic policy of reconstruction, which, he believed, was winning over the whole population. He described the good work of the 35,000 Portuguese troops in Mozambique who not only had a military rôle, but were fully involved with "social promotion and reconstruction". This aimed to provide roads, new villages, schools, medical centres, and agricultural training centres. This was intended to complement the major schemes like the

Cabora Bassa Dam and the main roads to Lourenço Marques and Beira which aimed to bring prosperity to the whole country.

While his overseas trips certainly provided material for *The Pattern of Guerrilla War*, and enabled him to write articles, in Manchester his position was less happy. His stay, which had had such a promising start, very soon turned sour. Interviewed in 1996, Elliott-Bateman was highly critical of Calvert and maintained that he had been appointed to the Hallsworth Fellowship in order to carry out serious research for a detailed study of the second Chindit campaign. He added that, when Calvert did not get down to the research and appeared to spend most of his time socializing in the University coffee bars, he and Professor Chapman considered withdrawing the Fellowship. He also reckoned that there was never any likelihood of Calvert being offered a University post, and he spoke disparagingly of Calvert always looking for the next meal ticket.

This view of Elliott-Bateman's differs substantially both from the tone and detail of the letters which passed between him and Calvert in 1970 and 1971. In October, 1970, Elliott-Bateman considered that it might not be possible for Calvert to complete *The Pattern of Guerrilla Warfare* during 1971 since it was such a large work, but the Fellowship would work wonders for it. (Letter, Elliott-Bateman to Calvert, October, 1970. Calvert Papers) It is also clear from the correspondence that from the start Calvert believed that the main purpose of the Fellowship was to enable him to travel to the world's troublespots and to complete his research for *The Pattern of Guerrilla Warefare*. Similarly, Elliott-Bateman's opinion in 1996 that there was never any likelihood of Calvert obtaining a university post appears to be contradicted by a letter he wrote in December, 1970, explaining to Calvert, in enthusiastic terms, that his appointment to the Hallsworth Fellowship would pay a large dividend in the establishment of an effective school for the study of modern guerrilla warfare, outside the military establishment. He concluded this letter, "Hence your importance to what I see developing in Manchester". (Letter, December 1970. Calvert Papers) It is also significant that in all the correspondence prior to Calvert's appointment, while there is discussion of *The Pattern of Guerrilla Warfare*, there is no mention of a new book on the Chindit campaign.

It is always unfortunate when people's memories of events are coloured or changed by subsequent disagreements. Whatever the truth of the matter, Elliott-Bateman and Calvert soon had disagreements and when the Fellowship terminated Elliott-Bateman was greatly relieved. Calvert's own memories of his time at Manchester centre on other issues. After a terrific struggle he had managed to give up alcohol, and in Manchester he found himself in a fairly hard-drinking group which was embarrassing for him in his new teetotal role. He also had the clear impression that, because of his well-known criticism of the military establishment, his colleagues assumed, wrongly, that he would be sympathetic to their strong left-wing views.

By the beginning of 1972 Calvert began to realize that, as a matter of urgency, he had to find another regular source of income. He realized too the serious consequences of having given up a secure pensionable job, albeit one he considered dull and unchallenging. His correspondence during 1972 is dominated by applications for jobs, and by letters to his many high-level contacts asking for help and advice. His applications listed his wartime achievements and decorations and then gave a long and rambling outline of his proposal for *The Pattern of Guerrilla Warfare*, and his need for a suitable post to enable him to complete it. Nearly every reply, while couched in kindly and helpful terms indicated that there was no suitable post available. Such letters came from General Sir John Hackett, Principal of London University, from Professor Michael Howard at All Souls, from several Oxford Colleges, from the Leverhulme Trust, from various institutes of Strategic Studies, and from service colleges in America. Calvert hoped that his cause would be helped by the publication in July, 1972, of his book *Slim as a General*, but this made little impact.

He received a useful and hard-hitting letter from his old friend of the Chindit campaigns, Sir Robert Thompson. He had seen Calvert's plans for *The Pattern of Guerrilla Warfare* and asked some pertinent questions: How long would the book be? When would it be ready? Was there a draft of the first chapter to show the general scope of the work? What market was it aimed at – the military history specialist or the general reader? Calvert does not appear to have found the answers to these questions. He certainly gathered together a mass of notes and information, but never got down to the task of writing realistically to a deadline. Even in the autumn of 1972, when he was facing a very uncertain future and unemployment, instead of writing his book he was stressing his need to visit South America, Israel, Arabia, Yugoslavia and the Naga Hills of Assam.

During his depressing quest for a well-paid job he continued to write articles in order to establish himself as a serious commentator on guerrilla warfare, the problems of security from terrorism and civil unrest. In this he certainly succeeded. In April, 1973, he wrote to Ove Arup, his former employers, outlining his views on the increasing danger throughout the world of guerrilla and terrorist activity and how this should be defeated. He suggested that, while guerrillas sought to destroy the fabric and framework of society, the grievances which created support for guerrilla movements among a people should be removed by large-scale and imaginative reconstruction projects. He proposed that, on a world-wide basis, Ove Arup should become consultants on how to reconstruct insurgent areas. He stressed his contacts with heads of state in Africa, the Far East and the Middle East and suggested, naturally, that he would like a senior position in such a scheme. His proposal was not taken up.

In the years since the fall of the Berlin Wall, glasnost and the overthrow of many of the old communist régimes, Calvert's ideas may seem fanciful, but at the height of the Cold War when he was writing, the initiative always seemed to be with the left-wing insurgent forces and the threat appeared very real. He wrote from first-hand experience of the advance of communism in South-East Asia. He had visited many parts of Africa where guerrilla activity was controlled by effective leaders trained in Moscow, Peking or Prague and supported by supplies of weapons and ammunition from many communist countries. He had seen the Middle East in turmoil in the wake of the Nasser revolution and he certainly went along with the theory which argued that one country after another, like collapsing dominoes, would fall to the communist insurgents.

One of the clearest expositions of his views appeared in an address he gave to the Royal School of Military Engineering in 1973. This aroused the interest of Lord Carrington, the Defence Secretary, and Sir George Sinclair, MP, and it was widely discussed at the Ministry of Defence. He took as his theme, "The rôle of the Engineer in Counter Insurgency". He proposed that, in order to safeguard society from civil unrest or terrorist attack, the government should give high priority to the safety aspect of town planning and of all public buildings. Saboteurs and terrorists always aimed to damage society and destroy the economy by attacking vulnerable targets like electricity supplies and communication centres. New York had once suffered chaos from electricity failure. How much more damage could have been done by a well-placed bomb. He considered the grave and generally unrecognized threat to the Rhine Army that all its supplies of weapons and equipment travelled along one regular route, well known to any terrorist. The answer to guerrilla activity was to remove the socio-economic conditions which always lay at the heart of a people's support for guerrillas. This should be done by carrying out massive rebuilding programmes, by removing slum areas and by demolishing suspect blocks of flats which, like the Divis Flats in Belfast, gave succour to terrorists. His wide-ranging views also included more detailed suggestions. Bridges should be built to ensure that no ducts were available where a saboteur could place explosives. Having blown up more bridges than most western commentators, he spoke with considerable authority. He suggested that all public buildings should have alternative electricity generators and that on key road routes vegetation should be removed to a distance of 100 yards in order to prevent ambush. Roads should be built with slots so that road blocks could be quickly and easily installed. In all these schemes one man, preferably a Royal Engineers Officer, should be given widespread power, untrammelled by bureaucratic restrictions. He quoted the policy of the Portuguese in Angola where large areas were being reclaimed from guerrilla control by such methods, like land being reclaimed from flooding. (Article, Calvert Papers)

He developed a parallel theme in a paper entitled "The Answer to Penetration is Counter-Penetration". In this he elaborated the danger in many parts of the world from terrorists trained in Russia and China. They were given instruction on such subjects as "How to subvert an Army". and "How to carry out a *coup d'état*". Russia was training 500 agents every year in demolition and sabotage and despatching them to Africa, together with mines, weapons and explosives. Calvert wrote, "The communists are anaesthetising the people of the west with subtle propaganda, while they manipulate their uneducated proxies to fight their battles for them". Since Russia and China had chosen terrorism and penetration warfare, the west could not afford to stand idle. The answer was Counter-Penetration. He believed the communist states were held together by a despotism of fear and he suggested that the Western Alliance, instead of spending billions of pounds on ever more sophisticated weapons, should devote 5% of their overall expenditure on a concerted plan to subvert the peoples and the forces of the Warsaw Pact countries. If this was done, the Baltic States, some of the Balkan States and other Central Asian countries could well rise up and remove the shackles of Soviet rule. Then the West should be ready to support them. "We must penetrate communism by the concept of freedom".

Calvert remained highly critical of the military establishment and of the way money continued to be wasted on massive military expenditure. The main aim of NATO was to be able to contain a massive drive to the west by Russian tanks. The answer was not large numbers of bigger and more expensive tanks or aircraft costing millions of pounds, but a cheap basic anti-tank weapon which could be issued in thousands to any country threatened by tank attack. He illustrated this argument with the example of Giap in Vietnam who obtained Sam 7 missiles which were cheap, simple to operate and enabled a soldier with very little training to bring down American helicopters. Finally, he argued that the purpose of military forces was to train men to kill, not to act as a semi-military social service, an echo of Wingate's remark that the Indian Civil Service was a vast system of outdoor relief.

Calvert left Manchester in 1972 and moved back to the south of England in order to be closer to his main contacts in London. This period of his life shows a depressing pattern of rejected job applications, polite but firm refusals of requests for financial help, impressive articles on a range of defence matters and, generally, complete failure to complete his writing to his publisher's deadline. In 1970 he had signed a contract with Allen Lane/Penguin to write *The Pattern of Guerrilla Warfare* and they agreed to pay him £100 per month for one year. This contract was backed up by a parallel agreement with the American publisher Bobbs-Merrill for the publication of the book in the USA. Most authors would consider such contracts as a positive incentive and yet, year after year, his work was never completed. He wrote rather sad letters pointing out to the publisher that his project had grown to vast proportions and that he had had to drop his work on the book and write articles "to pay for groceries". His earlier contemptuous attitude to regular jobs, mortgages and pensions was costing him dear. Early in 1974 Bobbs-Merrill cancelled their contract for the book. He appealed to them to reconsider their decision, pointing out that originally it had been a modest project, but with the travelling made possible by the Hallsworth Fellowship it had developed into something larger and more important. Here too he explained that he occasionally had to stop his writing to produce articles to eke out his very modest disability pension. Almost at the same time he accepted a commission to write a number of articles of about 3000 words for a magazine *Secret War* at a fee of £25 per thousand words. So the pattern continued with articles and lectures taking precedence over the completion of his book.

He had been elected a member of the Conservative Monday Club and, in November, 1974, he addressed the club in the House of Commons, showing again how he enjoyed meeting important and influential people at the cost of missing his publisher's deadline. He gave an interesting and hard-hitting talk on Terrorism, pointing out that successful guerrilla leaders often ended up as prime minister, for example de Valera, Kenyatta, Makarios and others. He was critical of the English police system which had few able people at the top because the proposed Hendon Police College, designed as a staff college for training higher police ranks, had been abandoned because of the opposition of the Police Federation. Next, he fiercely criticized the run-down of the Territorial Army which was one of the main bulwarks against terrorist attacks. He deplored "the carving up and hacking to pieces of the Territorial Army and the Yeomanry by Generals Carver and Hackett". He believed that these volunteer forces had been the warp and weft of the British society since the days of the Anglo-Saxon fyrd, and because of their strength they were the main targets of the Marxist left-wing elements of the Labour party. The TA was a highly effective force throughout the country and cost £20m a year, about the cost of one aircraft. He believed that Britain was in a dangerous situation with all its forces in Germany, and had little to protect its home base from attack or subversion. This talk aroused considerable interest among MPs, but failed to obtain permanent financial support for Calvert.

Soon after his talk to the Monday Club he wrote a short article called "Drake's Drum" which supported David Stirling's call for a Technical Organization of volunteers to keep essential services running in the event of serious civil disturbance, and to prevent a take-over by power-hungry left-wing Trade Union leaders. He continued to give talks and to write articles, and was occasionally invited by the BBC to join discussion groups. In May, 1976, he took part in a discussion about urban guerrillas and the case of Ulrike Meinhof, the leader of the Bader-Meinhof group in Germany.

By the mid 1970s it became apparent that his proposed major work was never going to be completed, and in December, 1975, Allen Lane/Penguin cancelled the contract for it. At about the same time he started on another venture with Brigadier Peter Young, DSO, MC, another maverick warrior and former Reader in Military History at the Royal Military Academy, Sandhurst. They aimed to write a *Dictionary of Battles*. This project started with a fairly modest aim, but once again rapidly grew into a grandiose scheme to publish four volumes to cover the period from Roman times to the present day.

In preparing *The Pattern of Guerrilla Warfare* Calvert had built up a substantial knowledge of military history and it was quite easy for him to transfer this information to the type of writing required in the *Dictionary of Battles*. They made rapid progress on the new project and the first volume, which covered from 1816 to 1976, was published in a year. The next volume, covering the years 1715 to 1815, was published a year later, but even before the publication, the project had run into the type of difficulty which beset Calvert's previous work. In 1976, when the proofs of the first volume were almost ready, there was lengthy correspondence between him and Peter Young about financial difficulties. Calvert had organized a team of research assistants and he found that by employing them he was heavily out of pocket. He asked Young to provide a monthly salary of £250 so that he could devote himself full-time to the completion of the remaining volumes. This was not agreed, and a year later, in November, 1977, when the 1715–1815 volume was nearly ready, there was further tense correspondence with the New English Library (NEL). Calvert had virtually taken over this project as Young's health failed, but he seems to have gained very little financially. He informed the NEL that at the end of the year his researchers would be owed £1400 and he had no money. The project would have to be dropped if more money was not provided. The NEL had put up £12,000 to back the original plan for four volumes, and were not sympathetic to requests for more money. Thus, with two volumes published, the project was terminated.

While Calvert was coping with all these problems he was still actively considering other projects. He made an agreement with Orbis Publishers to write 60,000 words on guerrilla leaders since 1776, and for this he was paid £250 monthly for eight months. This book was never published. He also produced a detailed synopsis of a novel. The plot centred on Britain being taken over by Russian forces after they had occupied Iceland. The Russians invaded in the Inverness area with 150,000 troops and advanced southwards. After subduing England, they invaded the continent. After having suffered 15 million casualties, a new Britain, led by its guerrilla forces, would emerge!

By the beginning of 1978 when most of his schemes had fallen through, Calvert was relieved to have the offer of a flat in a semi-sheltered complex run by the building industry at Haywards Heath. He settled down there, and for a time he was able to augment his modest pension and allowances by working as a gardener, a task he found therapeutic both physically and mentally.

CHAPTER FOURTEEN

# FINALE – SEEKING THE TRUTH

In carrying out the research on Michael Calvert's career, it became clear that a bitter sense of injustice over the court-martial verdict had clouded the last forty years of his life. This frequently cropped up in conversation and, over the years, it appeared in his letters and papers.

He had hoarded papers from his earliest days, even an Aldershot bus time-table from 1938, but, unfortunately, there was not a single document referring to the court martial among all his voluminous correspondence. It appeared that in his mood of black despair he had destroyed everything to do with it.

While he brooded over the injustice of the court martial, he pondered whether he had been set up or framed, possibly by former Nazis, perhaps by the military establishment, perhaps by some anti-Wingate and Chindit officers, or by officers with strong homophobic feelings. His memories about these disastrous events were of course coloured by the gruesome experiences of his decade in Australia, when his alcoholism brought him close to physical and mental ruin. Inevitably this influenced his later memory of what had actually happened.

Because most of the people involved in the court martial were dead and no papers were available, my search for information started with an application to the British military authorities and continued for months. It appeared that there was usually a four-month delay in any document being made available. After waiting for more than four months, I was told that, even though I had Calvert's agreement and support, I could not actually see the documents. After further protest against a system which appeared to be obsessed with secrecy, I was at last permitted to see, not the complete file, but four pages which gave the summary of evidence from the court martial. Even to do this I was carefully scrutinized by a civil servant to ensure that I did not look at any of the other pages. The authorities did not permit photocopying, so all the detail had to be copied by hand.

After so many months of frustration, the summary of evidence was at last a step forward from all the vague anecdotes of the 1950s. The information in the summary provided the basis for Chapter 10 – The Court Martial. At last I had discovered the exact date of the court martial and the date when Calvert's appeal was dismissed.

I had met Michael Calvert in 1990 through a mutual friend, Lieutenant-Colonel Peter Cane, MC, a former Chindit Column Commander, and in the years since then I had often heard Calvert's version of the incident at Soltau which led to his court martial. He described how he was travelling in his staff car in a snowstorm and gave a lift to three youths. He took them to his house, gave them food and drink and sent them on their way. They went to the police and levied charges against him. Unfortunately this story bore no resemblance at all to the detail in the summary of evidence.

Having seen the summary of evidence and the exact date, I trawled the newspapers of July, 1952, but there were only brief paragraphs describing the verdicts of Calvert's dismissal from the army. After this disappointment, I wrote to the editor of the local paper in Hanover, the *Hannover Allgemeine Zeitung*, thinking that the court martial of a senior British officer might have aroused some local interest. The editor was helpful and sent a photocopy of their report, but this was just a brief paragraph similar to that in *The Times*.

After this setback, I considered another approach. The court martial had taken place in Hanover, but the actual incident happened in Soltau, about 60 miles to the north. Soltau is a small town on Lüneburg Heath, close to where Montgomery took the final surrender of the German forces in 1945. The town had been a major cavalry centre under the Kaisers and the Nazis, and from 1945 to 1993 was the base of the 7th Armoured Brigade, the heirs of the Deserts Rats. This was the formation to which Calvert had been attached and he lived in an army quarter opposite the barrack gates.

I then wrote to the editor of the Soltau paper, the *Böhme Zeitung*, to ask if his paper had a report of the incident, or if it was possible to inquire if there was anyone in the Soltau area who might remember Calvert's case in 1952. His reply was encouraging and I was then able to give him the names of the four men named in the court martial. He managed to contact some of them, but generally, fearing a possibly embarrassing story in the local paper, they did not appear keen to co-operate. However, the editor did suggest that I should write to the present owner of the Gruener Jaeger, the pub which was central to the court-martial incident.

After a long and fruitless search, this was the first fortunate turn. Herr Fritz Voss owns the Gruener Jaeger, now a hotel and restaurant. In 1952, as a young man of 21, he had helped his widowed mother who owned what was then a pub with a small restaurant attached. In the adjacent building was a cinema which had been taken over by the army.

Having made initial contact with Herr Voss, there was a second fortunate turn. By chance in Cambridge I had met a young German scientist who was engaged in post-doctoral research, Dr Hansjurgen Schuppe. His home is near Hanover and during 1996 he had to travel there several times from Cambridge. He kindly approached Herr Voss and discussed the matter in detail. Herr Voss was most co-operative and was able to make contact with three of the four men involved. One was seriously ill, one had died.

After Dr Schuppe's preliminary inquiries, I went to Soltau and stayed in the Gruener Jaeger, the very place involved in Calvert's downfall. With the enthusiastic support of Herr Voss and his friend Herr Fischer, I was able to meet several people who were living in Soltau in 1952. During these conversations an interesting picture of Soltau in the early fifties emerged. There was little anti-British feeling and relations between British soldiers and the local German people were good. Both German civilians and British soldiers frequented the Gruener Jaeger, partly because of the Forces cinema next door. Sometimes young Germans were allowed in to see films. The barracks were about a mile away from the pub and it was a fairly easy walk. The men who remember the incidents involving Calvert generally assumed that he might have been looking for homosexual contacts. Most British officers were considered stand-offish and aloof, but Calvert, the only British officer to visit the pub regularly, was always friendly.

Many British soldiers went to the pub because it was a good drinking place and also because a small-scale black market in cigarettes, tea, coffee, sugar and clothes flourished there. Herr Voss confirmed that it was unusual for any officer, let alone a fairly senior officer, to frequent their pub, and he thinks that it is possible that

Calvert was a bit of a joke to the local youths. In considering Calvert's situation, Herr Voss felt certain that there was no Nazi involvement in the incident. He remembers that Herr Jacob was among a group of lads who came to the Gruener Jaeger, but he was not their leader as the court martial alleged. As far as the attitude of the German community at that time towards homosexuality, Herr Voss said there was rarely any mention of it. He recollected that up to 1945, under the Nazi régime, people were shot for it. Also, he did think that some young men might have been shocked at any suggestion of homosexuality.

Herr Voss and his friends provided this important background information. Then on Monday 25 November, 1996, I had a lengthy meeting with him and Herr Jürgen Jacob, a key witness at the court martial (see Chapter 10). In Cambridge I had had a translator (German by birth) prepare the German version of the "Summary of Evidence at the Court Martial". This I gave to Herr Jacob to read before the interview. He read it, and his reaction was immediate. He said, "*Quatsch*", an expressive German word meaning "absolute rubbish".

After the interview I drew up a statement of the main points he put forward. Its relevance to the court martial is so significant that it is printed in full.

# Calvert's Court martial – A Statement

*Before this interview both Herr Jacob and Herr Voss were able to read an outline of the main details of Calvert's court martial, translated into German.*

Interviewed at the Gruener Jaeger on Monday 25 November, 1996, in the presence of the author and of Herr Voss, the present owner of the Gruener Jaeger who was also interviewed by the court-martial inquiry, Herr Jürgen Jacob made the following statement:-

1. He clearly remembers the incident at Calvert's quarter which was the main charge at the court martial, and also the inquiries for the court martial.

2. The summary of evidence which has been produced shows that the court martial completely misunderstood what actually happened.

3. At that time, 1952, there was a desperate shortage of everything, even basic food. As a result, most boys and young men stole things to help out with rations or to sell on the black market. There was a great demand for anything sweet, especially cakes baked for the NAAFI, and sugar. Cigarettes were the main currency. Many British soldiers came to the Gruener Jaeger: they always had cigarettes and often used them to get girls.

4. British officers were very aloof, and when Calvert came to the pub he was a figure of considerable interest because he was always friendly. The local youths thought that he was perhaps slightly homosexual and was possibly looking for contacts. Hence he was a vulnerable figure and could be exploited.

5. Because of this, a group of youths including Jacob and Gebien, as well as several others not mentioned in the court martial, decided one evening to go to Calvert's flat. The possibility of anything homosexual was just a pretence. They went there really for one of them to chat to Calvert, while the others went round the flat to see what there was to steal. That evening they stole some money, some cigarettes and a revolver with some ammunition. As far as any homosexual activity is concerned, *absolutely nothing happened*. They also returned to the flat on other occasions. Calvert was careless about locking his door and they found that, if they were upstairs when he returned, they could get out by the window and climb down a tree.

6. Some time later some of them were arrested by the German police and were accused of stealing from Calvert's home. They were sentenced to fourteen days in prison. During this time in prison Jacob was questioned time after time by the British Military Police. They persisted in asking about Calvert and kept on about homosexual activities. They seemed determined to find something against Calvert.

7. There were many inquiries by the British military when Jacob was in prison and after his release. All centred on the question of Calvert's possible homosexuality. This is why Herr Jacob is quoted in the summary of evidence as saying that many statements were false. In 1996 he confirmed that the description in the court-martial summary of the incident at Calvert's flat was completely wrong.

8. Herr Jacob also insisted that many of the other statements made at the court martial were inaccurate. For example, it stated that when Calvert answered the door to them at his home *he was naked*. That

was completely *untrue*. Herr Jacob remembers quite clearly that Calvert was wearing blue striped pyjamas and a brown dressing gown. *He never saw Calvert naked.* Herr Jacob says that the authorities must have put that in to make a stronger case against Calvert.

9. Several of the youths, including Jacob, Voss and Gebien, were called to the court martial, and there were more inquiries after that. They were all surprised that every inquiry centred on the homosexual issue which, to them, was completely unimportant. *Nothing serious ever took place.*

10. When, in 1996, Herr Jacob was asked why he made no complaint until after the second incident in May which involved Bartels and Fuhrop, he explained that his group never made a complaint against Calvert. It was during the inquiry about stealing that homosexuality was mentioned by the British Military Police. The boys did not put it forward.

11. The court-martial hearing and the later inquiries took a long time, and by then Calvert was no longer in Soltau, so people just forgot about him.

Herr Jacob, Herr Voss and others who were youths in Soltau at that time are appalled that what was really a boyish prank, and where no serious homosexuality took place, has caused such a complete disaster for Calvert. Also they are horrified that their later statements which tried to put right the inaccuracies of the court martial were not accepted when Calvert's appeal was heard and dismissed.

These young men are now respected and senior members of their community. Herr Bartels had died and Herr Fuhrop is critically ill with lung cancer.

When this inquiry was made in November 1996, it would have been easy for them to say that they could not remember. Instead they have co-operated willingly and openly. They are amazed and distressed to learn of the misery and damage the court martial has caused Calvert. As responsible and honourable men, they are willing to sign this statement in the hope that, even at this late stage, the injustice to Calvert can be put right.

*Signed*

Soltau 12. 12. 1996    Jürgen Jacob    Friedrich Voss

This remarkable statement reiterates much of the evidence which the German youths provided at the court martial and at the various inquiries which took place prior to Calvert's appeal. They considered it a grave injustice that their further evidence was not accepted by the British military authority (the Judge Advocate General) which dismissed Calvert's appeal.

Calvert had an absolutely outstanding wartime career: he had seven decorations for bravery and heroism, and had been recommended by his three battalion commanders for the VC; he had commanded a brigade behind the enemy lines from early March to August, 1944, and he had won the admiration of every man in his brigade. After that he had taken command of the SAS in Europe in the last six months of the war. Such achievements, linked to his academic prowess at Cambridge, and the high regard in which he was held by such distinguished wartime leaders as Earl Mountbatten and Field Marshals Slim, Montgomery and Auchinleck, should surely have brought him promotion to high command in the years after the war.

The court martial verdict and the rejection of his appeal when further significant evidence was ignored was a catastrophe. Now, forty-five years later – for him forty-five years of suffering and anguish – it has been discovered through the signed testimony of upright, honourable and respected figures in the community of Soltau where Calvert's downfall took place, that the court martial verdict was a travesty of justice, that he was convicted for something which he did not do. The new evidence strongly suggests that the British Military Police were determined to build up a case against Calvert and that they deliberately ignored the evidence of the German youths involved in the court martial. This should prompt further inquiries, but the deep and genuine concern of Herr Jacob at the damage caused to Calvert's life by the guilty verdict is the strongest argument in favour of Calvert's innocence.

Calvert deserves, not a pardon which implies guilt, but the agreement of the British Military Authorities that, in view of new evidence now before them, he was innocent of the charges brought at his court martial

# INDEX

Masters, John, 82, 83; establishes Blackpool, 91; 94; gives up Blackpool, 96; 126
Mawhood, Colonel, 25
Maymyo, 28
Mayne, Lieutenant Colonel "Paddy", 119, 166
Merrill's Marauders, 94, 95
Min Yuen, 134
Montgomery, Field Marshal Lord, 22, 126, 164
Morris Force, 75, 90, 94, 105, 164
Mountbatten, Admiral Earl, 65; to Mogaung, 107; disbands Chindits, 111
Mutaguchi, General, view of Chindits 62; 85

N

Nankan, 51–53
Nanking, 11

O

O'Leary, Trooper, 147

P

*Prisoners of Hope*, 66, 71, 108, published, 154

Q

Quebec Conference, 64

R

Rangoon, 29
Reuters, Report on Operation Longcloth, 61
Ribbentrop, 117, 160
Rome, Colonel, 76, 81
Rose, General Sir Michael, 106
Russhon, Major, Piccadilly photographs, 70

S

Scott, Brigadier, 50, 71
Sittang Bridge, 29
Slim, Field Marshal Lord, 29; launch of Operation Thursday, 68; places Chindits under Stilwell, 91; 159, helps Calvert in Australia, 167; 175